W9-CDN-805

From Stress to Success DVD from Trivium Test Prep

Dear Customer,

Thank you for purchasing from Trivium Test Prep! Whether you're a new teacher or looking to advance your career, we're honored to be a part of your journey.

To show our appreciation (and to help you relieve a little of that test-prep stress), we're offering a **FREE *TSI Essential Test Tips DVD**** by Trivium Test Prep. Our DVD includes 35 test preparation strategies that will help keep you calm and collected before and during your big exam. All we ask is that you email us your feedback and describe your experience with our product. Amazing, awful, or just so-so: we want to hear what you have to say!

To receive your **FREE *TSI Essential Test Tips DVD*,** please email us at 5star@triviumtestprep. com. Include "Free 5 Star" in the subject line and the following information in your email:

1. The title of the product you purchased.
2. Your rating from 1 – 5 (with 5 being the best).
3. Your feedback about the product, including how our materials helped you meet your goals and ways in which we can improve our products.
4. Your full name and shipping address so we can send your **FREE *TSI Essential Test Tips DVD*.**

If you have any questions or concerns please feel free to contact us directly at 5star@triviumtestprep.com.

Thank you, and good luck with your studies!

* Please note that the free DVD is not included with this book. To receive the free DVD, please follow the instructions above.

TSI Study Guide 2018-2019

2018-2019

TSI Test Prep Book and Practice Test Questions for the Texas Success Initiative Assessment

TABLE OF CONTENTS

ONLINE RESOURCES

To help you fully prepare for your TSI exam, Accepted includes online resources with the purchase of this study guide.

Practice Test

In addition to the practice test included in this book, we also offer an online exam. Since many exams today are computer based, getting to practice your test-taking skills on the computer is a great way to prepare.

Flash Cards

A convenient supplement to this study guide, Accepted flash cards enable you to review important terms easily on your computer or smartphone.

Cheat Sheets

Review the core skills you need to master the exam with easy-to-read Cheat Sheets.

From Stress to Success

Watch From Stress to Success, a brief but insightful YouTube video that offers the tips, tricks, and secrets experts use to score higher on the exam.

Reviews

Leave a review, send us helpful feedback, or sign up for Accepted promotions—including free books!

Access these materials at:

www.acceptedinc.com/tsi-online-resources

INTRODUCTION

Congratulations on choosing to take the Texas Success Initiative (TSI) Assessment! By purchasing this book, you've taken the first step toward preparing for your college and career goals. This guide will provide you with a detailed overview of the TSI, so you know exactly what to expect on test day. We'll take you through all the concepts covered on the test and give you the opportunity to test your knowledge with practice questions. Even if it's been a while since you last took a major test, don't worry; we'll make sure you're more than ready!

What is the TSI?

The TSI assesses students' abilities in reading, writing and mathematics, helping them prepare for college-level courses. These tests will help you and your academic advisors choose which classes are right for you as you get ready for academic work at the university level.

The TSI is made up of three different assessments—reading, writing, and mathematics. Each assessment is taken and scored separately, but all are mandatory parts of the entire test. All incoming college students in the state of Texas are required to take the TSI unless they have already met certain criteria, which include the following:

- The student has met the minimum college readiness standard on the ACT, SAT, or other statewide test.
- The student has already successfully completed college-level mathematics and English courses.
- The student is not seeking a degree.
- The student has been or is currently enlisted in the military.
- The student has enrolled in a Level-One certificate program (with fewer than forty-three semester credit hours).

How is the TSI Administered?

The TSI is a multiple-choice test administered by computer. Each assessment—reading, writing, and mathematics—is taken separately. The writing assessment also includes one essay of 300 – 600 words. None of the assessments are timed. You may stop, save your work, and complete the assessment at a later date; however, you must complete the assessment within fourteen days. You receive the assessment results immediately upon completion.

Students must directly contact their college counseling office to arrange to take the TSI. Your institution's test center will provide information about accommodation for disabilities, required identification or materials, and any options for taking the test remotely.

Test-takers must also complete a Pre-Assessment Activity. This mandatory activity explains the purpose and process of the TSI, provides practice questions and feedback, discusses developmental education options if you do not meet the cut-off scores for college readiness (see below), and offers other information about college resources. You must contact the college where you plan to take the TSI to arrange to take the Pre-Assessment Activity.

What's on the TSI?

The TSI assesses reading comprehension, writing, and mathematical skills. The questions are aligned with the Texas College and Career Readiness Standards, and gauge your readiness to tackle college-level coursework. Because the test is computer adaptive, you will encounter more difficult topics as you continue to correctly answer questions on the test.

What's on the TSI?

ASSESSMENT	APPROXIMATE NUMBER OF QUESTIONS	STRANDS (CONTENT AREAS)	CONCEPTS
Mathematics	20 questions	Elementary algebra and functions	Operations with algebraic expressions; linear equations, inequalities, and systems; word problems
		Intermediate algebra and functions	Quadratic and polynomial equations, expressions, and functions; working with powers, roots, and radicals; rational and exponential expressions, equations, and functions
		Geometry and measurement	Plane geometry; linear, area, and three-dimensional measurements; symmetry and transformations
		Data analysis, statistics, and probability	Data interpretation, statistics, probability
Reading	24 questions	Literary analysis	Identifying and analyzing elements and ideas in literary texts
		Main idea and supporting details	Identifying the main ideas and supporting ideas of a passage; identifying details in a passage
		Inferences in a text or texts	Appropriately connecting ideas between two passages; comparing two passages; drawing inferences about a single passage
		Author's use of language	Identifying the author's purpose, tone, use of language, organization, and rhetorical strategies; using evidence to determine the meaning of words in context

ASSESSMENT	APPROXIMATE NUMBER OF QUESTIONS	STRANDS (CONTENT AREAS)	CONCEPTS
Writing (multiple-choice questions)	20 questions	Essay revision	Improving organization, coherence, word choice, and rhetorical effectiveness; using evidence
		Agreement	Performing subject-verb agreement, pronoun agreement; determining verb tenses
		Sentence structure	Determining and resolving errors in punctuation and sentence structure
		Sentence logic	Properly placing and using transitions and modifying clauses in sentences
Writing (essay)	1 essay (300 – 600 words)		Effective, organized writing with supported and well-developed ideas, strong sentence structure, and few mechanical errors, following the conventions of Standard English

How is the TSI Scored?

The TSI is a diagnostic assessment; as such, there is no way to pass or fail it. Rather, the Texas Coordinating Board has determined cut-off scores for college readiness. As these are subject to change annually, check with the College Board and the Texas Coordinating Board for details.

The separate mathematics, writing, and reading assessments are computer adaptive. That is, they adapt to the student's skill level: a student's response to a question determines the difficulty level of the next one. If you answer a question correctly, the next one will be harder; however answering a question incorrectly yields an easier question.

The essay is scored on a scale of 8 – 0 based on clarity of purpose, organization, coherence and focus, demonstration of critical thinking, strength of argument and development, sentence variety, style, and proper use of mechanics (grammar and punctuation).

Depending on how you score, you may be asked to test further. The questions on each assessment cover four different content areas, or strands (see above). If you score below a certain threshold in one or more strands, you will be asked to answer more questions in that content area in order to best gauge your preparation for college-level coursework. These additional questions are part of the DE Diagnostic Test. Depending on your DE Diagnostic results, you may be asked to answer more questions as part of the Adult Basic Education (ABE) Tests, which also include reading, writing, and mathematics diagnostics. This process will help you and your advisors target any specific areas for improvement, ensuring you are absolutely ready for college.

About This Guide

This guide will help you master the most important test topics and develop critical test-taking skills. We have built features into our books to prepare you for your tests and increase your score. Along with a detailed summary of the test's format, content, and scoring, we offer an in-depth overview of the content knowledge required to pass the test. In the review you'll find sidebars that provide interesting information, highlight key concepts, and review content so that you can solidify your understanding of the exam's concepts. You can also test your knowledge with sample questions throughout the text and practice questions that reflect the content and format of the TSI. We're pleased you've chosen Accepted, Inc. to be a part of your journey!

PART I: MATHEMATICS

NUMBERS AND OPERATIONS

This chapter provides a review of the basic yet critical components of mathematics such as manipulating fractions, comparing numbers, and using units. These concepts will provide the foundation for more complex mathematical operations in later chapters.

Types of Numbers

Numbers are placed in categories based on their properties.

- A **NATURAL NUMBER** is greater than 0 and has no decimal or fraction attached. These are also sometimes called counting numbers {1, 2, 3, 4, ...}.

- **WHOLE NUMBERS** are natural numbers and the number 0 {0, 1, 2, 3, 4, ...}.

- **INTEGERS** include positive and negative natural numbers and 0 {..., –4, –3, –2, –1, 0, 1, 2, 3, 4, ...}.

- A **RATIONAL NUMBER** can be represented as a fraction. Any decimal part must terminate or resolve into a repeating pattern. Examples include -12, $-\frac{4}{5}$, 0.36, $7.\bar{7}$, $26\frac{1}{2}$, etc.

- An **IRRATIONAL NUMBER** cannot be represented as a fraction. An irrational decimal number never ends and never resolves into a repeating pattern. Examples include $-\sqrt{7}$, π, and $0.34567989135...$

- A **REAL NUMBER** is a number that can be represented by a point on a number line. Real numbers include all the rational and irrational numbers.

- An **IMAGINARY NUMBER** includes the imaginary unit i, where $i = \sqrt{-1}$ Because $i^2 = -1$, imaginary numbers produce a negative value when squared. Examples of imaginary numbers include $-4i$, $0.75i$, $i\sqrt{2}$ and $\frac{8}{3}i$.

◆ A **COMPLEX NUMBER** is in the form $a + bi$, where a and b are real numbers. Examples of complex numbers include $3 + 2i$, $-4 + i$, $\sqrt{3} - i\sqrt[3]{5}$ and $\frac{5}{8} - \frac{7i}{8}$. All imaginary numbers are also complex.

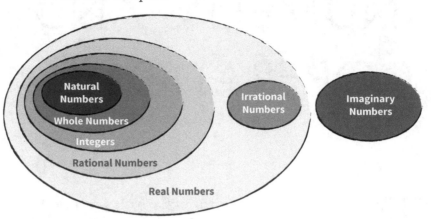

Figure 1.1. Types of Numbers

The **FACTORS** of a natural number are all the numbers that can multiply together to make the number. For example, the factors of 24 are 1, 2, 3, 4, 6, 8, 12, and 24. Every natural number is either prime or composite. A **PRIME NUMBER** is a number that is only divisible by itself and 1. (The number 1 is not considered prime.) Examples of prime numbers are 2, 3, 7, and 29. The number 2 is the only even prime number. A **COMPOSITE NUMBER** has more than two factors. For example, 6 is composite because its factors are 1, 6, 2, and 3. Every composite number can be written as a unique product of prime numbers, called the **PRIME FACTORIZATION** of the number. For example, the prime factorization of 90 is $90 = 2 \times 3^2 \times 5$. All integers are either even or odd. An even number is divisible by 2; an odd number is not.

If a real number is a natural number (e.g., 50), then it is also a whole number, an integer, and a rational number.

EXAMPLES

1) Classify the following numbers as natural, whole, integer, rational, or irrational. (The numbers may have more than one classification.)

   A. 72

   B. $-\frac{2}{3}$

   C. $\sqrt{5}$

   Answers:

   A. The number is **natural**, **whole**, an **integer**, and **rational**.

   B. The fraction is **rational**.

C. The number is **irrational**. (It cannot be written as a fraction, and written as a decimal is approximately 2.2360679...)

2) Determine the real and imaginary parts of the following complex numbers.

   A. 20

   B. $10 - i$

   C. $15i$

   Answers:

   A complex number is in the form of $a + bi$, where a is the real part and bi is the imaginary part.

   A. $20 = 20 + 0i$
   The real part is 20, and there is no imaginary part.

   B. $10 - i = 10 - 1i$
   The real part is 10, and −1i is the imaginary part.

   C. $15i = 0 + 15i$
   The real part is 0, and the imaginary part is 15i.

Scientific Notation

SCIENTIFIC NOTATION is a method of representing very large and small numbers in the form $a \times 10^n$, where a is a value between 1 and 10, and n is a nonzero integer. For example, the number 927,000,000 is written in scientific notation as 9.27×10^8. Multiplying 9.27 by 10 eight times gives 927,000,000. When performing operations with scientific notation, the final answer should be in the form $a \times 10^n$.

When adding and subtracting numbers in scientific notation, the power of 10 must be the same for all numbers. This results in like terms in which the a terms are added or subtracted and the 10^n remains unchanged. When multiplying numbers in scientific notation, multiply the a factors, and then multiply that answer by 10 to the sum of the exponents. For division, divide the a factors and subtract the exponents.

65000000.
7 6 5 4 3 2 1
↓
6.5×10^7

.0000987
-1 -2 -3 -4 -5
↓
9.87×10^{-5}

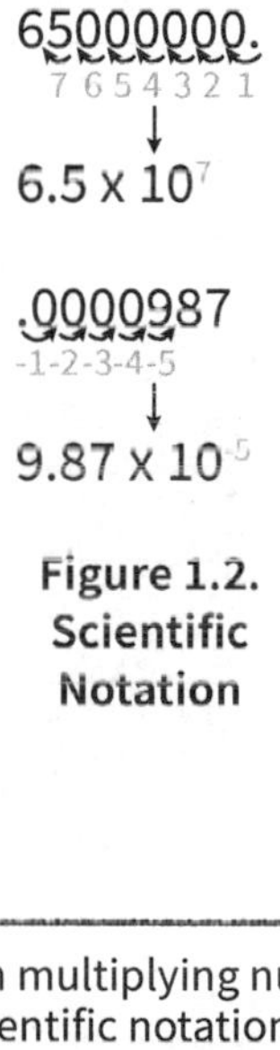

Figure 1.2. Scientific Notation

When multiplying numbers in scientific notation, add the exponents. When dividing, subtract the exponents.

EXAMPLES

1) Simplify: $(3.8 \times 10^3) + (4.7 \times 10^2)$

   Answer:

$(3.8 \times 10^3) + (4.7 \times 10^2)$	
$3.8 \times 10^3 = 3.8 \times 10 \times 10^2 = 38 \times 10^2$	To add, the exponents of 10 must be the same.
$38 \times 10^2 + 4.7 \times 10^2 = 42.7 \times 10^2$	Add the a terms together.
$= \mathbf{4.27 \times 10^3}$	Write the number in proper scientific notation.

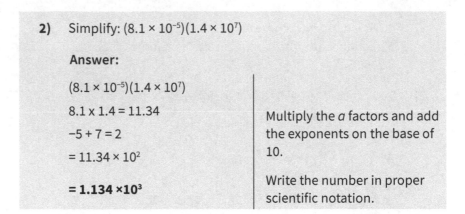

2) Simplify: $(8.1 \times 10^{-5})(1.4 \times 10^{7})$

Answer:

$(8.1 \times 10^{-5})(1.4 \times 10^{7})$	
$8.1 \times 1.4 = 11.34$	Multiply the *a* factors and add the exponents on the base of 10.
$-5 + 7 = 2$	
$= 11.34 \times 10^{2}$	
$= 1.134 \times 10^{3}$	Write the number in proper scientific notation.

Positive and Negative Numbers

POSITIVE NUMBERS are greater than 0, and NEGATIVE NUMBERS are less than 0. Both positive and negative numbers can be shown on a NUMBER LINE.

Figure 1.3. Number Line

The ABSOLUTE VALUE of a number is the distance the number is from 0. Since distance is always positive, the absolute value of a number is always positive. The absolute value of *a* is denoted $|a|$. For example, $|-2| = 2$ since -2 is two units away from 0.

Positive and negative numbers can be added, subtracted, multiplied, and divided. The sign of the resulting number is governed by a specific set of rules shown in the table below.

Table 1.1. Operations with Positive and Negative Numbers

ADDING REAL NUMBERS		SUBTRACTING REAL NUMBERS	
Positive + Positive = Positive	$7 + 8 = 15$	Negative – Positive = Negative	$-7 - 8 =$ $-7 + (-8) =$ -15
Negative + Negative = Negative	$-7 + (-8) =$ -15	Positive – Negative = Positive	$7 - (-8) =$ $7 + 8 = 15$
Negative + Positive OR Positive + Negative = Keep the sign of the number with larger absolute value	$-7 + 8 = 1$ $7 + -8 = -1$	Negative – Negative = Change the subtraction to addition and change the sign of the second number; then use addition rules.	$-7 - (-8) =$ $-7 + 8 = 1$ $-8 - (-7) =$ $-8 + 7 = -1$

Multiplying Real Numbers		Dividing Real Numbers	
Positive × Positive = Positive	8 × 4 = 32	Positive ÷ Positive = Positive	8 ÷ 4 = 2
Negative × Negative = Positive	−8 × (−4) = 32	Negative ÷ Negative = Positive	−8 ÷ (−4) = 2
Positive × Negative OR Negative × Positive = Negative	8 × (−4) = −32 −8 × 4 = −32	Positive ÷ Negative OR Negative ÷ Positive = Negative	8 ÷ (−4) = −2 −8 ÷ 4 = −2

EXAMPLES

1) Add or subtract the following real numbers:

A. $-18 + 12$

B. $-3.64 + (-2.18)$

C. $9.37 - 4.25$

D. $86 - (-20)$

Answers:

A. Since $|-18| > |12|$, the answer is negative: $|-18| - |12| = 6$. So the answer is **−6**.

B. Adding two negative numbers results in a negative number. Add the values: **−5.82**.

C. The first number is larger than the second, so the final answer is positive: **5.12**.

D. Change the subtraction to addition, change the sign of the second number, and then add: $86 - (-20) = 86 + (+20) =$ **106**.

2) Multiply or divide the following real numbers:

A. $\left(\frac{10}{3}\right)\left(\frac{9}{5}\right)$

B. $\frac{-64}{-10}$

C. $(2.2)(3.3)$

D. $-52 \div 13$

Answers:

A. Multiply the numerators, multiply the denominators, and simplify: $\frac{-90}{15} =$ **−6**.

B. A negative divided by a negative is a positive number: **6.4**.

C. Multiplying positive numbers gives a positive answer: **7.26**.

D. Dividing a negative by a positive number gives a negative answer: **−4**.

Order of Operations

The **order of operations** is simply the order in which operations are performed. **PEMDAS** is a common way to remember the order of operations:

1. **P**arentheses
2. **E**xponents
3. **M**ultiplication
4. **D**ivision
5. **A**ddition
6. **S**ubtraction

Multiplication and division, and addition and subtraction, are performed together from left to right. So, performing multiple operations on a set of numbers is a four-step process:

1. P: Calculate expressions inside parentheses, brackets, braces, etc.
2. E: Calculate exponents and square roots.
3. MD: Calculate any remaining multiplication and division in order from left to right.
4. AS: Calculate any remaining addition and subtraction in order from left to right.

Always work from left to right within each step when simplifying expressions.

EXAMPLES

1) Simplify: $2(21 - 14) + 6 \div (-2) \times 3 - 10$

   Answer:

$2(21 - 14) + 6 \div (-2) \times 3 - 10$	
$= 2(7) + 6 \div (-2) \times 3 - 10$	Calculate expressions inside parentheses.
$= 14 + 6 \div (-2) \times 3 - 10$	There are no exponents or radicals, so perform multiplication and division from left to right.
$= 14 + (-3) \times 3 - 10$	
$= 14 + (-9) - 10$	
$= 5 - 10$	Perform addition and subtraction from left to right.
$= -5$	

2) Simplify: $-(3)^2 + 4(5) + (5 - 6)^2 - 8$

   Answer:

$-(3)^2 + 4(5) + (5 - 6)^2 - 8$	
$= -(3)^2 + 4(5) + (-1)^2 - 8$	Calculate expressions inside parentheses.
$= -9 + 4(5) + 1 - 8$	Simplify exponents and radicals.

$= -9 + 20 + 1 - 8$	Perform multiplication and division from left to right.
$= 11 + 1 - 8$	
$= 12 - 8$	Perform addition and subtraction from left to right.
$= \mathbf{4}$	

3) Simplify: $\dfrac{(7-9)^3 + 8(10-12)}{4^2 - 5^2}$

Answer:

$\dfrac{(7-9)^3 + 8(10-12)}{4^2 - 5^2}$	
$= \dfrac{(-2)^3 + 8(-2)}{4^2 - 5^2}$	Calculate expressions inside parentheses.
$= \dfrac{-8 + (-16)}{16 - 25}$	Simplify exponents and radicals.
$= \dfrac{-24}{-9}$	Perform addition and subtraction from left to right.
$= \dfrac{\mathbf{8}}{\mathbf{3}}$	Simplify.

Ratios

A **RATIO** is a comparison of two numbers and can be represented as $\frac{a}{b}$, $a:b$, or a to b. The two numbers represent a constant relationship, not a specific value: for every a number of items in the first group, there will be b number of items in the second. For example, if the ratio of blue to red candies in a bag is 3:5, the bag will contain 3 blue candies for every 5 red candies. So, the bag might contain 3 blue candies and 5 red candies, or it might contain 30 blue candies and 50 red candies, or 36 blue candies and 60 red candies. All of these values are representative of the ratio 3:5 (which is the ratio in its lowest, or simplest, terms).

To find the "whole" when working with ratios, simply add the values in the ratio. For example, if the ratio of boys to girls in a class is 2:3, the "whole" is five: 2 out of every 5 students are boys, and 3 out of every 5 students are girls.

EXAMPLES

1) There are 10 boys and 12 girls in a first-grade class. What is the ratio of boys to the total number of students? What is the ratio of girls to boys?

GO ON

Answer:

number of boys: 10 number of girls: 12 number of students: 22	Identify the variables.
number of boys : number of students $= 10 : 22$ $= \frac{10}{22}$ $= \frac{5}{11}$	Write out and simplify the ratio of boys to total students.
number of girls : number of boys $= 12 : 10$ $= \frac{12}{10}$ $= \frac{6}{5}$	Write out and simplify the ratio of girls to boys.

2) A family spends $600 a month on rent, $400 on utilities, $750 on groceries, and $550 on miscellaneous expenses. What is the ratio of the family's rent to their total expenses?

Answer:

rent = 600 utilities = 400 groceries = 750 miscellaneous = 550 total expenses = 600 + 400 + 750 + 550 = 2300	Identify the variables.
rent : total expenses $= 600 : 2300$ $= \frac{600}{2300}$ $= \frac{6}{23}$	Write out and simplify the ratio of rent to total expenses.

Proportions

A **PROPORTION** is an equation which states that two ratios are equal. A proportion is given in the form $\frac{a}{b} = \frac{c}{d}$, where the a and d terms are the extremes and the b and c terms are the means. A proportion is solved using cross-multiplication ($ad = bc$) to create an equation with no fractional components. A proportion must have the same units in both numerators and both denominators.

1) Solve the proportion for x: $\frac{3x-5}{2} = \frac{x-8}{3}$.

Answer:

$$\frac{(3x-5)}{2} = \frac{(x-8)}{3}$$

$3(3x-5) = 2(x-8)$ Cross-multiply.

$9x - 15 = 2x - 16$

$7x - 15 = -16$

$7x = -1$ Solve the equation for x.

$x = -\frac{1}{7}$

2) A map is drawn such that 2.5 inches on the map equates to an actual distance of 40 miles. If the distance measured on the map between two cities is 17.25 inches, what is the actual distance between them in miles?

Answer:

$$\frac{2.5}{40} = \frac{17.25}{x}$$

Write a proportion where x equals the actual distance and each ratio is written as inches : miles.

$2.5x = 690$

$x = 276$ Cross-multiply and divide to solve for x.

The two cities are **276 miles apart**.

3) A factory knows that 4 out of 1000 parts made will be defective. If in a month there are 125,000 parts made, how many of these parts will be defective?

Answer:

$$\frac{4}{1000} = \frac{x}{125,000}$$

Write a proportion where x is the number of defective parts made and both ratios are written as defective : total.

$1000x = 500,000$

$x = 500$ Cross-multiply and divide to solve for x.

There are **500 defective parts** for the month.

Percentages

A **PERCENT** (or percentage) means per hundred and is expressed with a percent symbol (%). For example, 54% means 54 out of every 100. A percent can be converted to a decimal by removing the % symbol and moving the decimal point two places to the left, while a decimal can be converted to a percent by moving the decimal point two places to the right and attaching the % sign. A percent can be converted to a fraction by writing the percent as a fraction with 100 as the denominator and reducing. A fraction can be converted to a percent by performing the indicated division, multiplying the result by 100, and attaching the % sign.

The equation for finding percentages has three variables: the part, the whole, and the percent (which is expressed in the equation as a decimal). The equation, as shown below, can be rearranged to solve for any of these variables.

- part = whole × percent
- $percent = \dfrac{part}{whole}$
- $whole = \dfrac{part}{percent}$

This set of equations can be used to solve percent word problems. All that's needed is to identify the part, whole, and/or percent, and then to plug those values into the appropriate equation and solve.

EXAMPLES

1) Change the following values to the indicated form:

   A.   18% to a fraction

   B. $\frac{3}{5}$ to a percent

   C.   1.125 to a percent

   D.   84% to a decimal

Answers:

A.   The percent is written as a fraction over 100 and reduced: $\frac{18}{100} = \frac{9}{50}$.

B.   Dividing 5 by 3 gives the value 0.6, which is then multiplied by 100: **60%**.

C.   The decimal point is moved two places to the right: 1.125 × 100 = **112.5%**.

D.   The decimal point is moved two places to the left: 84 ÷ 100 = **0.84**.

2) In a school of 650 students, 54% of the students are boys. How many students are girls?

Answer:

Percent of students who are girls = 100% − 54% = 46%	
percent = 46% = 0.46	Identify the variables.
whole = 650 students	
part = ?	
part = whole × percent	
= 0.46 × 650 = 299	Plug the variables into the appropriate equation.
There are 299 girls.	

Percent Change

Percent change problems involve a change from an original amount. Often percent change problems appear as word problems that include discounts, growth, or markups. In order to solve percent change problems, it's necessary to identify the percent change (as a decimal), the amount of change, and the original amount. (Keep in mind that one of these will be the value being solved for.) These values can then be plugged into the equations below:

Key terms associated with percent change problems include discount, sales tax, and markup.

- amount of change = original amount × percent change

- percent change = $\dfrac{\text{amount of change}}{\text{original amount}}$

- original amount = $\dfrac{\text{amount of change}}{\text{percent change}}$

EXAMPLES

1) An HDTV that originally cost $1,500 is on sale for 45% off. What is the sale price for the item?

Answer:

original amount =$1,500	
percent change = 45% = 0.45	Identify the variables.
amount of change = ?	
amount of change = original amount × percent change	Plug the variables into the appropriate equation.
= 1500 × 0.45 = 675	
1500 − 675 = 825	To find the new price, subtract the amount of change from the original price.
The final price is $825.	

2) A house was bought in 2000 for $100,000 and sold in 2015 for $120,000. What was the percent growth in the value of the house from 2000 to 2015?

Answer:

original amount = $100,000 amount of change = 120,000 − 100,000 = 20,000 percent change = ?	Identify the variables.
percent change = $\dfrac{\text{amount of change}}{\text{original amount}}$ $= \dfrac{20,000}{100,000}$ $= 0.20$	Plug the variables into the appropriate equation.
$0.20 \times 100 =$ **20%**	To find the percent growth, multiply by 100.

Exponents and Radicals

Exponents

An expression in the form b^n is in an exponential notation where b is the **BASE** and n is an **EXPONENT**. To perform the operation, multiply the base by itself the number of times indicated by the exponent. For example, 2^3 is equal to $2 \times 2 \times 2$ or 8.

Table 1.2. Operations with Exponents

RULE	EXAMPLE	EXPLANATION
$a^0 = 1$	$5^0 = 1$	Any base (except 0) to the 0 power is 1.
$a^{-n} = \dfrac{1}{a^n}$	$5^{-3} = \dfrac{1}{5^3}$	A negative exponent becomes positive when moved from numerator to denominator (or vice versa).
$a^m a^n = a^{m+n}$	$5^3 5^4 = 5^{3+4} = 5^7$	Add the exponents to multiply two powers with the same base.
$(a^m)^n = a^{m \times n}$	$(5^3)^4 = 5^{3(4)} = 5^{12}$	Multiply the exponents to raise a power to a power.
$\dfrac{a^m}{a^n} = a^{m-n}$	$\dfrac{5^4}{5^3} = 5^{4-3} = 5^1$	Subtract the exponents to divide two powers with the same base.
$(ab)^n = a^n b^n$	$(5 \times 6)^3 = 5^3 6^3$	Apply the exponent to each base to raise a product to a power.
$\left(\dfrac{a}{b}\right)^n = \dfrac{a^n}{b^n}$	$\left(\dfrac{5}{6}\right)^3 = \dfrac{5^3}{6^3}$	Apply the exponent to each base to raise a quotient to a power.
$\left(\dfrac{a}{b}\right)^{-n} = \left(\dfrac{b}{a}\right)^n$	$\left(\dfrac{5}{6}\right)^{-3} = \left(\dfrac{6}{5}\right)^3$	Invert the fraction and change the sign of the exponent to raise a fraction to a negative power.
$\dfrac{a^m}{b^n} = \dfrac{b^{-n}}{a^{-m}}$	$\dfrac{5^3}{6^4} = \dfrac{6^{-4}}{5^{-3}}$	Change the sign of the exponent when moving a number from the numerator to denominator (or vice versa).

1) Simplify: $\dfrac{(10^2)^3}{(10^2)^2}$

Answer:

$\dfrac{(10^2)^3}{(10^2)^2}$

$= \dfrac{10^6}{10^4}$	Multiply the exponents raised to a power.
$= 10^{6-4}$	Subtract the exponent in the denominator from the one in the numerator.
$= 10^2$	Simplify.
$= \mathbf{100}$	

2) Simplify: $\dfrac{(x^{-2}y^2)^2}{x^3y}$

Answer:

$\dfrac{(x^{-2}y^2)^2}{x^3y}$

$= \dfrac{x^{-4}y^4}{x^3y}$	Multiply the exponents raised to a power.
$= x^{-4-3}y^{4-1}$	Subtract the exponent in the denominator from the one in the numerator.
$= x^{-7}y^3$	
$= \dfrac{\boldsymbol{y^3}}{\boldsymbol{x^7}}$	Move negative exponents to the denominator.

Radicals

RADICALS are expressed as $\sqrt[b]{a}$, where b is called the INDEX and a is the RADICAND. A radical is used to indicate the inverse operation of an exponent: finding the base which can be raised to b to yield a. For example, $\sqrt[3]{125}$ is equal to 5 because $5 \times 5 \times 5$ equals 125. The same operation can be expressed using a fraction exponent, so $\sqrt[b]{a} = a^{\frac{1}{b}}$. Note that when no value is indicated for b, it is assumed to be 2 (square root).

When b is even and a is positive, $\sqrt[b]{a}$ is defined to be the positive real value n such that $n^b = a$ (example: $\sqrt{16} = 4$ only, and not -4, even though $(-4)(-4) = 16$). If b is even and a is negative, $\sqrt[b]{a}$ will be a complex number (example: $\sqrt{-9} = 3i$). Finally if b is odd, $\sqrt[b]{a}$ will always be a real number regardless of the sign of a. If a is negative, $\sqrt[b]{a}$ will be negative since a number to an odd power is negative (example: $\sqrt[5]{-32} = -2$ since $(-2)^5 = -32$).

$\sqrt[n]{x}$ is referred to as the nth root of x.

- $n = 2$ is the square root

- ◆ $n = 3$ is the cube root
- ◆ $n = 4$ is the fourth root
- ◆ $n = 5$ is the fifth root

The following table of operations with radicals holds for all cases EXCEPT the case where b is even and a is negative (the complex case).

Table 1.3. Operations with Radicals

Rule	Example	Explanation
$\sqrt[b]{ac} = \sqrt[b]{a}\,\sqrt[b]{c}$	$\sqrt[3]{81} = \sqrt[3]{27}\,\sqrt[3]{3} = 3\sqrt[3]{3}$	The values under the radical sign can be separated into values that multiply to the original value.
$\sqrt[b]{\dfrac{a}{c}} = \dfrac{\sqrt[b]{a}}{\sqrt[b]{c}}$	$\sqrt{\dfrac{4}{81}} = \dfrac{\sqrt{4}}{\sqrt{81}} = \dfrac{2}{9}$	The b-root of the numerator and denominator can be calculated when there is a fraction under a radical sign.
$\sqrt[b]{a^c} = (\sqrt[b]{a})^c = a^{\frac{c}{b}}$	$\sqrt[3]{6^2} = (\sqrt[3]{6})^2 = 6^{\frac{2}{3}}$	The b-root can be written as a fractional exponent. If there is a power under the radical sign, it will be the numerator of the fraction.
$\dfrac{c}{\sqrt[b]{a}} \times \dfrac{\sqrt[b]{a}}{\sqrt[b]{a}} = \dfrac{c\sqrt[b]{a}}{a}$	$\dfrac{5}{\sqrt{2}}\,\dfrac{\sqrt{2}}{\sqrt{2}} = \dfrac{5\sqrt{2}}{2}$	To rationalize the denominator, multiply the numerator and denominator by the radical in the denominator until the radical has been canceled out.
$\dfrac{c}{b-\sqrt{a}} \times \dfrac{b+\sqrt{a}}{b+\sqrt{a}}$ $= \dfrac{c(b+\sqrt{a})}{b^2-a}$	$\dfrac{4}{3-\sqrt{2}}\,\dfrac{3+\sqrt{2}}{3+\sqrt{2}}$ $= \dfrac{4(3+\sqrt{2})}{9-2} = \dfrac{12+4\sqrt{2}}{7}$	To rationalize the denominator, the numerator and denominator are multiplied by the conjugate of the denominator.

EXAMPLES

1) Simplify: $\sqrt{48}$

   Answer:

   $\sqrt{48}$

   $= \sqrt{16 \times 3}$ Determine the largest square number that is a factor of the radicand (48) and write the radicand as a product using that square number as a factor.

   $= \sqrt{16}\,\sqrt{3}$

   $= \mathbf{4\sqrt{3}}$ Apply the rules of radicals to simplify.

2) Simplify: $\dfrac{6}{\sqrt{8}}$

Answer:

$\dfrac{6}{\sqrt{8}}$

$= \dfrac{6}{\sqrt{4}\,\sqrt{2}}$

$= \dfrac{6}{2\sqrt{2}}$

Apply the rules of radicals to simplify.

$= \dfrac{6}{2\sqrt{2}}\left(\dfrac{\sqrt{2}}{\sqrt{2}}\right)$

$= \dfrac{3\sqrt{2}}{2}$

Multiply by $\dfrac{\sqrt{2}}{\sqrt{2}}$ to rationalize the denominator.

two

ALGEBRA

Algebra, meaning "restoration" in Arabic, is the mathematical method of finding the unknown. The first algebraic book in Egypt was used to figure out complex inheritances that were to be split among many individuals. Today, algebra is just as necessary when dealing with unknown amounts.

Algebraic Expressions

The foundation of algebra is the **VARIABLE**, an unknown number represented by a symbol (usually a letter such as x or a). Variables can be preceded by a **COEFFICIENT**, which is a constant (i.e., a real number) in front of the variable, such as $4x$ or $-2a$. An **ALGEBRAIC EXPRESSION** is any sum, difference, product, or quotient of variables and numbers (for example $3x^2$, $2x + 1/y - 1$, and $\frac{5}{x}$ are algebraic expressions). **TERMS** are any quantities that are added or subtracted (for example, the terms of the expression $x^2 - 3x + 5$ are x^2, $3x$, and 5). A **POLYNOMIAL EXPRESSION** is an algebraic expression where all the exponents on the variables are whole numbers. A polynomial with only two terms is known as a **BINOMIAL**, and one with three terms is a **TRINOMIAL**. A **MONOMIAL** has only one term.

EVALUATING EXPRESSIONS is another way of saying "find the numeric value of an expression if the variable is equal to a certain number." To evaluate the expression, simply plug the given value(s) for the variable(s) into the equation and simplify. Remember to use the order of operations when simplifying:

1. Parentheses
2. Exponents
3. Multiplication
4. Division
5. Addition
6. Subtraction

Simplified expressions are ordered by variable terms alphabetically with highest exponent first then down to constants.

Operations with Expressions

Adding and Subtracting

Expressions can be added or subtracted by simply adding and subtracting LIKE TERMS, which are terms with the same variable part (the variables must be the same, with the same exponents on each variable). For example, in the expressions $2x + 3xy - 2z$ and $6y + 2xy$, the like terms are $3xy$ and $2xy$. Adding the two expressions yields the new expression $2x + 6xy - 2z + 6y$. Note that the other terms did not change; they cannot be combined because they have different variables.

Operations with polynomials can always be checked by evaluating equivalent expressions for the same value.

Distributing and Factoring

Distributing and factoring can be seen as two sides of the same coin. DISTRIBUTION multiplies each term in the first factor by each term in the second factor to get rid of parentheses. FACTORING reverses this process, taking a polynomial in standard form and writing it as a product of two or more factors.

When distributing a monomial through a polynomial, the expression outside the parentheses is multiplied by each term inside the parentheses. Using the rules of exponents, coefficients are multiplied and exponents are added.

When simplifying two polynomials, each term in the first polynomial must multiply each term in the second polynomial. A binomial (two terms) multiplied by a binomial, will require 2 × 2 or 4 multiplications. For the binomial × binomial case, this process is sometimes called **FOIL**, which stands for first, outside, inside, and last. These terms refer to the placement of each term of the expression: multiply the first term in each expression, then the outside terms, then the inside terms, and finally the last terms. A binomial (two terms) multiplied by a trinomial (three terms), will require 2 × 3 or 6 products to simplify. The first term in the first polynomial multiplies each of the three terms in the second polynomial, then the second term in the first polynomial multiplies each of the three terms in the second polynomial. A trinomial (three terms) by a trinomial will require 3 × 3 or 9 products, and so on.

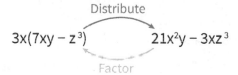

Figure 2.1. Distribution and Factoring

Factoring is the reverse of distributing: the first step is always to remove ("undistribute") the GCF of all the terms, if there is a GCF (besides 1). The GCF is the product of any constants and/or variables that <u>every</u> term shares. (For example, the GCF of $12x^3$, $15x^2$ and $6xy^2$ is $3x$ because $3x$ evenly divides all three terms.) This shared factor can be taken out of each term and moved to the outside of the parentheses, leaving behind a polynomial where each term is the original term divided by the GCF. (The remaining terms for the terms in the example would be $4x^2$, $5x$, and $2xy$.) It may be possible to factor the polynomial in the parentheses further, depending on the problem.

EXAMPLES

1) Expand the following expression: $5x(x^2 - 2c + 10)$

   Answer:

   $5x(x^2 - 2c + 10)$

   $(5x)(x^2) = 5x^3$

   $(5x)(-2c) = -10xc$ Distribute and multiply the term outside the parentheses to all three terms inside the parentheses.

   $(5x)(10) = 50x$

   $= \mathbf{5x^3 - 10xc + 50x}$

2) Expand the following expression: $(x^2 - 5)(2x - x^3)$

Answer:

$(x^2 - 5)(2x - x^3)$	
$(x^2)(2x) = 2x^3$	
$(x^2)(-x^3) = -x^5$	Apply FOIL: first, outside, inside, and last.
$(-5)(2x) = -10x$	
$(-5)(-x^3) = 5x^3$	
$= 2x^3 - x^5 - 10x + 5x^3$	Combine like terms and put them in order.
$\mathbf{= -x^5 + 7x^3 - 10x}$	

3) Factor the expression $16z^2 + 48z$

Answer:

$16z^2 + 48z$	Both terms have a z, and 16 is a common factor of both 16 and 48. So the greatest common factor is $16z$. Factor out the GCF.
$\mathbf{= 16z(z + 3)}$	

4) Factor the expression $6m^3 + 12m^3n - 9m^2$

Answer:

$6m^3 + 12m^3n - 9m^2$	All the terms share the factor m^2, and 3 is the greatest common factor of 6, 12, and 9. So, the GCF is $3m^2$.
$\mathbf{= 3m^2(2m + 4mn - 3)}$	

Factoring Trinomials

If the leading coefficient is $a = 1$, the trinomial is in the form $x^2 + bx + c$ and can often be rewritten in the factored form, as a product of two binomials: $(x + m)(x + n)$. Recall that the product of two binomials can be written in expanded form $x^2 + mx + nx + mn$. Equating this expression with $x^2 + bx + c$, the constant term c would have to equal the product mn. Thus, to work backward from the trinomial to the factored form, consider all the numbers m and n that multiply to make c. For example, to factor $x^2 + 8x + 12$, consider all the pairs that multiply to be 12 ($12 = 1 \times 12$ or 2×6 or 3×4). Choose the pair that will make the coefficient of the middle term (8) when added. In this example 2 and 6 add to 8, so making $m = 2$ and $n = 6$ in the expanded form gives:

$x^2 + 8x + 12 = x^2 + 2x + 6x + 12$	
$= (x^2 + 2x) + (6x + 12)$	Group the first two terms and the last two terms.
$= x(x + 6) + 2(x + 6)$	Factor the GCF out of each set of parentheses.

$= (x + 6)(x + 2)$	The two terms now have the common factor $(x + 6)$, which can be removed, leaving $(x + 2)$ and the original polynomial is factored.

In general:

$$x^2 + bx + c = x^2 + mx + nx + mn, \text{ where } c = mn \text{ and } b = m + n$$

$= (x^2 + mx) + (nx + mn)$	Group.
$= x(x + m) + n(x + m)$	Factor each group.
$= (x + m)(x + n)$	Factor out the common binomial.

Note that if none of the factors of c add to the value b, then the trinomial cannot be factored, and is called PRIME.

If the leading coefficient is not 1 ($a \neq 1$), first make sure that any common factors among the three terms are factored out. If the a-value is negative, factor out –1 first as well. If the a-value of the new polynomial in the parentheses is still not 1, follow this rule: Identify two values r and s that multiply to be ac and add to be b. Then write the polynomial in this form: $ax^2 + bx + c = ax^2 + rx + sx + c$, and proceed by grouping, factoring, and removing the common binomial as above.

There are a few special factoring cases worth memorizing: difference of squares, binomial squared, and the sum and difference of cubes.

- **Difference of squares** (each term is a square and they are subtracted):
  - $a^2 - b^2 = (a + b)(a - b)$
  - Note that a SUM of squares is never factorable.
- **Binomial squared**:
  - $a^2 + 2ab + b^2 = (a + b)(a + b) = (a + b)^2$
- **Sum and difference of cubes**:
  - $a^3 + b^3 = (a + b)(a^2 - ab + b^2)$
  - $a^3 - b^3 = (a - b)(a^2 + ab + b^2)$
  - Note that the second factor in these factorizations will never be able to be factored further.

EXAMPLES

1) Factor: $16x^2 + 52x + 30$

   Answer:

$16x^2 + 52x + 30$	
$= 2(8x^2 + 26x + 15)$	Remove the GCF of 2.

$= 2(8x^2 + 6x + 20x + 15)$	To factor the polynomial in the parentheses, calculate $ac = (8)(15) = 120$, and consider all the pairs of numbers that multiply to be 120: 1×120, 2×60, 3×40, 4×30, 5×24, 6×20, 8×15, and 10×12. Of these pairs, choose the pair that adds to be the b-value 26 (6 and 20).
$= 2[(8x^2 + 6x) + (20x + 15)]$	Group.
$= 2[2x(4x + 3) + 5(4x + 3)]$	Factor out the GCF of each group.
$= 2[(4x + 3)(2x + 5)]$	Factor out the common binomial.
$2(4x + 3)(2x + 5)$	

If there are no values r and s that multiply to be ac and add to be b, then the polynomial is prime and cannot be factored.

2) Factor $-21x^2 - x + 10$

Answer:

$-21x^2 - x + 10$	
$= -(21x^2 + x - 10)$	Factor out the negative.
$= -(21x^2 - 14x + 15x - 10)$	Factor the polynomial in the parentheses. $ac = 210$ and $b = 1$ The numbers 15 and -14 can be multiplied to get 210 and subtracted to get 1.
$= -[(21x^2 - 14x) + (15x - 10)]$	Group.
$= -[7x(3x - 2) + 5(3x - 2)]$	Factor out the GCF of each group.
$= -(3x - 2)(7x + 5)$	Factor out the common binomial.

Linear Equations

An **EQUATION** states that two expressions are equal to each other. Polynomial equations are categorized by the highest power of the variables they contain: the highest power of any exponent of a linear equation is 1, a quadratic equation has a variable raised to the second power, a cubic equation has a variable raised to the third power, and so on.

Solving Linear Equations

Solving an equation means finding the value or values of the variable that make the equation true. To solve a linear equation, it is necessary to manipulate the terms so that the variable being solved for appears alone on one side of the equal sign while everything else in the equation is on the other side.

The way to solve linear equations is to "undo" all the operations that connect numbers to the variable of interest. Follow these steps:

1. Eliminate fractions by multiplying each side by the least common multiple of any denominators.

2. Distribute to eliminate parentheses, braces, and brackets.

3. Combine like terms.

4. Use addition or subtraction to collect all terms containing the variable of interest to one side, and all terms not containing the variable to the other side.

5. Use multiplication or division to remove coefficients from the variable of interest.

Sometimes there are no numeric values in the equation or there are a mix of numerous variables and constants. The goal is to solve the equation for one of the variables in terms of the other variables. In this case, the answer will be an expression involving numbers and letters instead of a numeric value.

On multiple choice tests, it is often easier to plug the possible values into the equation and determine which solution makes the equation true than to solve the equation.

EXAMPLES

1) Solve for x: $\dfrac{100(x+5)}{20} = 1$

Answer:

$\dfrac{100(x+5)}{20} = 1$	
$(20)(\dfrac{100(x+5)}{20}) = (1)(20)$ $100(x+5) = 20$	Multiply both sides by 20 to cancel out the denominator.
$100x + 500 = 20$	Distribute 100 through the parentheses.
$100x = -480$	"Undo" the +500 by subtracting 500 on both sides of the equation to isolate the variable term.
$x = \dfrac{-480}{100}$	"Undo" the multiplication by 100 by dividing by 100 on both sides to solve for x.
$x = \mathbf{-4.8}$	

2) Solve for x: $2(x+2)^2 - 2x^2 + 10 = 42$

Answer:

$2(x+2)^2 - 2x^2 + 10 = 42$	
$2(x+2)(x+2) - 2x^2 + 10 = 42$	Eliminate the exponents on the left side.

$2(x^2 + 4x + 4) - 2x^2 + 10 = 42$	Apply FOIL.
$2x^2 + 8x + 8 - 2x^2 + 10 = 42$	Distribute the 2.
$8x + 18 = 42$	Combine like terms on the left-hand side.
$8x = 24$	Isolate the variable. "Undo" +18 by subtracting 18 on both sides.
$x = 3$	"Undo" multiplication by 8 by dividing both sides by 8.

3) Solve the equation for D: $\dfrac{A(3B + 2D)}{2N} = 5M - 6$

Answer:

$\dfrac{A(3B + 2D)}{2N} = 5M - 6$	
$3AB + 2AD = 10MN - 12N$	Multiply both sides by $2N$ to clear the fraction, and distribute the A through the parentheses.
$2AD = 10MN - 12N - 3AB$	Isolate the term with the D in it by moving $3AB$ to the other side of the equation.
$D = \dfrac{(10MN - 12N - 3AB)}{2A}$	Divide both sides by $2A$ to get D alone on the right-hand side.

Graphs of Linear Equations

The most common way to write a linear equation is SLOPE-INTERCEPT FORM, $y = mx + b$. In this equation, m is the slope, which describes how steep the line is, and b is the y-intercept. Slope is often described as "rise over run" because it is calculated as the difference in y-values (rise) over the difference in x-values (run). The slope of the line is also the rate of change of the dependent variable y with respect to the independent variable x. The y-intercept is the point where the line crosses the y-axis, or where x equals zero.

To graph a linear equation, identify the y-intercept and place that point on the y-axis. If the slope is not written as a fraction, make it a fraction by writing it over 1 $\left(\frac{m}{1}\right)$. Then use the slope to count up (or down, if negative) the "rise" part of the slope and over the "run" part of the slope to find a second point. These points can then be connected to draw the line.

To find the equation of a line, identify the y-intercept, if possible, on the graph and use two easily identifiable points to find the slope. If the y-intercept is not easily identified, identify the slope by choosing easily identifiable points; then choose one point on the graph, plug the point and the slope values into the equation, and solve for the missing value b.

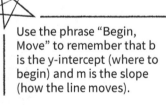

Use the phrase "Begin, Move" to remember that b is the y-intercept (where to begin) and m is the slope (how the line moves).

slope-intercept form:
$y = mx + b$
slope:
$m = \dfrac{y_2 - y_1}{x_2 - x_1}$

- standard form: $Ax + By = C$
- $m = -\dfrac{A}{B}$
- x-intercept $= \dfrac{C}{A}$
- y-intercept $= \dfrac{C}{B}$

Another way to express a linear equation is standard form: $Ax + By = C$. In order to graph equations in this form, it is often easiest to convert them to point-slope form. Alternately, it is easy to find the x- or y-intercept from this form, and once these two points are known, a line can be drawn through them. To find the x-intercept, simply make $y = 0$ and solve for x. Similarly, to find the y-intercept, make $x = 0$ and solve for y.

EXAMPLES

1) What is the slope of the line whose equation is $6x - 2y - 8 = 0$?

Answer:

$6x - 2y - 8 = 0$	
$-2y = -6x + 8$ $y = \dfrac{-6x + 8}{-2}$ $y = 3x - 4$	Rearrange the equation into slope-intercept form by solving the equation for y.
$m = 3$	The slope is 3, the value attached to x.

2) What is the equation of the following line?

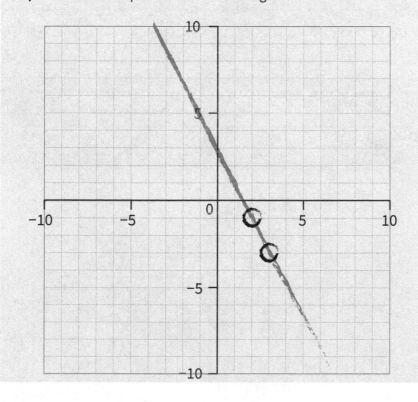

Answer:

$b = 3$	The y-intercept can be identified on the graph as $(0, 3)$.
$m = \dfrac{(-3) - (-1)}{3 - 2} = \dfrac{-2}{1} = -2$	To find the slope, choose any two points and plug the values into the slope equation. The two points chosen here are $(2, -1)$ and $(3, -3)$.
$y = -2x + 3$	Replace m with -2 and b with 3 in $y = mx + b$.

3) Write the equation of the line which passes through the points $(-2, 5)$ and $(-5, 3)$.

Answer:

$(-2, 5)$ and $(-5, 3)$	
$m = \dfrac{3 - 5}{(-5) - (-2)}$ $= \dfrac{-2}{-3}$ $= \dfrac{2}{3}$	Calculate the slope.
$5 = \dfrac{2}{3}(-2) + b$ $5 = \dfrac{-4}{3} + b$ $b = \dfrac{19}{3}$	To find b, plug into the equation $y = mx + b$ the slope for m and a set of points for x and y.
$y = \dfrac{2}{3}x + \dfrac{19}{3}$	Replace m and b to find the equation of the line.

4) What is the equation of the following graph?

Answer:

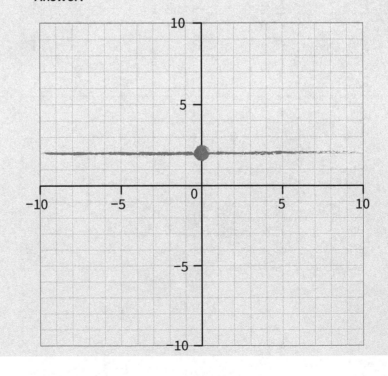

$y = 0x + 2$, or $y = 2$	The line has a rise of 0 and a run of 1, so the slope is $\frac{0}{1} = 0$. There is no x-intercept. The y-intercept is $(0, 2)$, meaning that the b-value in the slope-intercept form is 2.

Systems of Linear Equations

Systems of equations are sets of equations that include two or more variables. These systems can only be solved when there are at least as many equations as there are variables. Systems involve working with more than one equation to solve for more than one variable. For a system of linear equations, the solution to the system is the set of values for the variables that satisfies every equation in the system. Graphically, this will be the point where every line meets. If the lines are parallel (and hence do not intersect), the system will have no solution. If the lines are multiples of each other, meaning they share all coordinates, then the system has infinitely many solutions (because every point on the line is a solution).

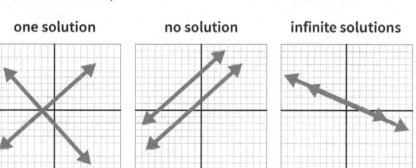

one solution   **no solution**   **infinite solutions**

Figure 2.2. Systems of Equations

Plug answers back into both equations to ensure the system has been solved properly.

There are three common methods for solving systems of equations. To perform SUBSTITUTION, solve one equation for one variable, and then plug in the resulting expression for that variable in the second equation. This process works best for systems of two equations with two variables where the coefficient of one or more of the variables is 1.

To solve using ELIMINATION, add or subtract two equations so that one or more variables are eliminated. It's often necessary to multiply one or both of the equations by a scalar (constant) in order to make the variables cancel. Equations can be added or subtracted as many times as necessary to find each variable.

Yet another way to solve a system of linear equations is to use a MATRIX EQUATION. In the matrix equation $AX = B$, A contains the system's coefficients, X contains the variables, and B contains the constants (as shown below). The matrix equation can then be solved by multiplying B by the inverse of A: $X = A^{-1}B$

$$ax + by = e$$
$$cx + dy = f$$
$\boxtimes A = \begin{bmatrix} a & b \\ c & d \end{bmatrix}$ $X = \begin{bmatrix} x \\ y \end{bmatrix}$ $B = \begin{bmatrix} e \\ f \end{bmatrix}$ $\boxtimes AX = B$

This method can be extended to equations with three or more variables. Technology (such as a graphing calculator) is often employed when solving using this method if more than two variables are involved.

EXAMPLES

1) Solve for x and y:

$2x - 4y = 28$

$4x - 12y = 36$

Answer:

$2x - 4y = 28$ $x = 2y + 14$	Solve the system with substitution. Solve one equation for one variable.
$4x - 12y = 36$ $4(2y + 14) - 12y = 36$ $8y + 56 - 12y = 36$ $-4y = -20$ $y = 5$	Plug in the resulting expression for x in the second equation and simplify.
$2x - 4y = 28$ $2x - 4(5) = 28$ $2x - 20 = 28$ $2x = 48$ $x = 24$ The answer is $y = 5$ and $x = 24$ or **(24, 5)**.	Plug the solved variable into either equation to find the second variable.

2) Solve for the system for x and y:

$3 = -4x + y$

$16x = 4y + 2$

Answer:

$3 = -4x + y$ $y = 4x + 3$	Isolate the variable in one equation.
$16x = 4y + 2$ $16x = 4(4x + 3) + 2$ $16x = 16x + 12 + 2$ $0 = 14$ **No solution exists.**	Plug the expression into the second equation. Both equations have slope 4. This means the graphs of the equations are parallel lines, so no intersection (solution) exists.

3) Solve the system of equations:

$6x + 10y = 18$

$4x + 15y = 37$

Answer:

Because solving for x or y in either equation will result in messy fractions, this problem is best solved using elimination. The goal is to eliminate one of the variables by making the coefficients in front of one set of variables the same, but with different signs, and then adding both equations.

$6x + 10y = 18 \xrightarrow{(-2)} -12x - 20y = -36$ $4x + 15y = 37 \xrightarrow{(3)} 12x + 45y = \underline{111}$	To eliminate the x's in this problem, find the least common multiple of coefficients 6 and 4. The smallest number that both 6 and 4 divide into evenly is 12. Multiply the top equation by −2, and the bottom equation by 3.
$25y = 75$	Add the two equations to eliminate the x's.
$y = 3$	Solve for y.
$6x + 10(3) = 18$ $6x + 30 = 18$ $x = -2$	Replace y with 3 in either of the original equations.
The solution is **(−2, 3).**	

4) Solve the following systems of equations using matrix arithmetic:

$2x - 3y = -5$

$3x - 4y = -8$

Answer:

$\begin{bmatrix} 2 & -3 \\ 3 & -4 \end{bmatrix} \begin{bmatrix} x \\ y \end{bmatrix} = \begin{bmatrix} -5 \\ -8 \end{bmatrix}$	Write the system in matrix form, **AX = B**.
$\begin{bmatrix} 2 & -3 \\ 3 & -4 \end{bmatrix}^{-1}$ $= \frac{1}{(2)(-4)-(-3)(3)} \begin{bmatrix} -4 & 3 \\ -3 & 2 \end{bmatrix} =$ $\begin{bmatrix} -4 & 3 \\ -3 & 2 \end{bmatrix}$	Calculate the inverse of Matrix **A**.
$\begin{bmatrix} x \\ y \end{bmatrix} = \begin{bmatrix} -4 & 3 \\ -3 & 2 \end{bmatrix} \begin{bmatrix} -5 \\ -8 \end{bmatrix} = \begin{bmatrix} -4 \\ -1 \end{bmatrix}$	Multiply **B** by the inverse of **A**.
$x = -4$ $y = -1$	Match up the 2 × 1 matrices to identify x and y.

Building Equations

In word problems, it is often necessary to translate a verbal description of a relationship into a mathematical equation. No matter the problem, this process can be done using the same steps:

1. Read the problem carefully and identify what value needs to be solved for.
2. Identify the known and unknown quantities in the problem, and assign the unknown quantities a variable.
3. Create equations using the variables and known quantities.
4. Solve the equations.
5. Check the solution: Does it answer the question asked in the problem? Does it make sense?

Use the acronym STAR to remember word-problem strategies: Search the problem, Translate into an expression or equation, Answer, and Review.

EXAMPLES

1) A school is holding a raffle to raise money. There is a $3 entry fee, and each ticket costs $5. If a student paid $28, how many tickets did he buy?

   Answer:

Number of tickets = x Cost per ticket = 5 Cost for x tickets = $5x$ Total cost = 28 Entry fee = 3	Identify the quantities.
$5x + 3 = 28$	Set up equations. The total cost for x tickets will be equal to the cost for x tickets plus the $3 flat fee.
$5x + 3 = 28$ $5x = 25$ $x = 5$ The student bought **5 tickets**.	Solve the equation for x.

2) Kelly is selling shirts for her school swim team. There are two prices: a student price and a nonstudent price. During the first week of the sale, Kelly raised $84 by selling 10 shirts to students and 4 shirts to nonstudents. She earned $185 in the second week by selling 20 shirts to students and 10 shirts to nonstudents. What is the student price for a shirt?

   Answer:

Student price = s Nonstudent price = n	Assign variables.

$10s + 4n = 84$ $20s + 10n = 185$	Create two equations using the number of shirts Kelly sold and the money she earned.
$10s + 4n = 84$ $10n = -20s + 185$ $n = -2s + 18.5$ $10s + 4(-2s + 18.5) = 84$ $10s - 8s + 74 = 84$ $2s + 74 = 84$ $2s = 10$ $s = 5$	Solve the system of equations using substitution.
The student cost for shirts is **$5**.	

Linear Inequalities

An inequality shows the relationship between two expressions, much like an equation. However, the equal sign is replaced with an inequality symbol that expresses the following relationships:

- $<$ less than
- $\leq$ less than or equal to
- $>$ greater than
- $\geq$ greater than or equal to

Inequalities are read from left to right. For example, the inequality $x \leq 8$ would be read as "x is less than or equal to 8," meaning x has a value smaller than or equal to 8. The set of solutions of an inequality can be expressed using a number line. The shaded region on the number line represents the set of all the numbers that make an inequality true. One major difference between equations and inequalities is that equations generally have a finite number of solutions, while inequalities generally have infinitely many solutions (an entire interval on the number line containing infinitely many values).

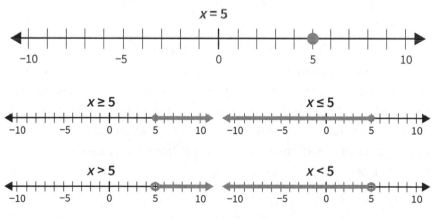

Figure 2.3. Inequalities on a Number Line

Linear inequalities can be solved in the same way as linear equations, with one exception. When multiplying or dividing both sides of an inequality by a negative number, the direction of the inequality sign must reverse—"greater than" becomes "less than" and "less than" becomes "greater than."

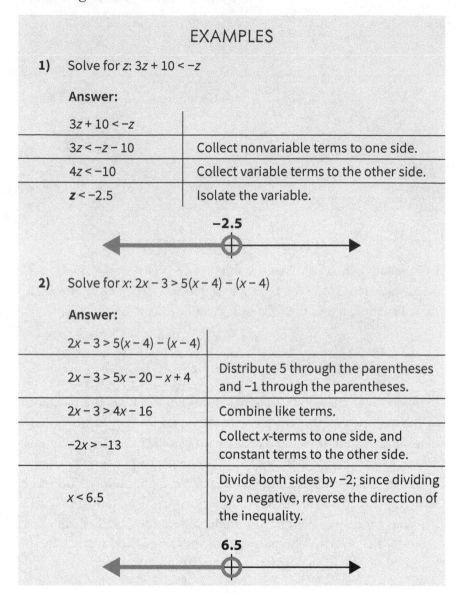

EXAMPLES

1) Solve for z: $3z + 10 < -z$

   Answer:

$3z + 10 < -z$	
$3z < -z - 10$	Collect nonvariable terms to one side.
$4z < -10$	Collect variable terms to the other side.
$z < -2.5$	Isolate the variable.

2) Solve for x: $2x - 3 > 5(x - 4) - (x - 4)$

   Answer:

$2x - 3 > 5(x - 4) - (x - 4)$	
$2x - 3 > 5x - 20 - x + 4$	Distribute 5 through the parentheses and −1 through the parentheses.
$2x - 3 > 4x - 16$	Combine like terms.
$-2x > -13$	Collect x-terms to one side, and constant terms to the other side.
$x < 6.5$	Divide both sides by −2; since dividing by a negative, reverse the direction of the inequality.

Compound Inequalities

Compound inequalities have more than one inequality expression. Solutions of compound inequalities are the sets of all numbers that make *all* the inequalities true. Some compound inequalities may not have any solutions, some will have solutions that contain some part of the number line, and some will have solutions that include the entire number line.

Table 2.1. Unions and Intersections

INEQUALITY	MEANING IN WORDS	NUMBER LINE
$a < x < b$	All values x that are greater than a and less than b	
$a \leq x \leq b$	All values x that are greater than or equal to a and less than or equal to b	
$x < a$ or $x > b$	All values of x that are less than a or greater than b	
$x \leq a$ or $x \geq b$	All values of x that are less than or equal to a or greater than or equal to b	

Compound inequalities can be written, solved, and graphed as two separate inequalities. For compound inequalities in which the word *and* is used, the solution to the compound inequality will be the set of numbers on the number line where both inequalities have solutions (where both are shaded). For compound inequalities where *or* is used, the solution to the compound inequality will be *all* the shaded regions for *either* inequality.

EXAMPLES

1) Solve the compound inequalities: $2x + 4 < -18$ *or* $4(x + 2) > 18$

Answer:

$2x + 4 < -10$ *or* $4(x + 2) > 18$

$2x < -14$	$4x + 8 > 18$	
$x < -7$	$4x > 10$	Solve each inequality independently.
	$x > 2.5$	

The solution to the original compound inequality is **the set of all x for which $x < -7$ or $x > 2.5$.**

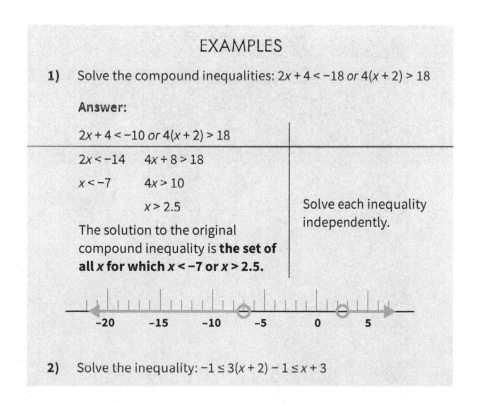

2) Solve the inequality: $-1 \leq 3(x + 2) - 1 \leq x + 3$

Answer:

$-1 \le 3(x+2) - 1 \le x + 3$	
$-1 \le 3(x+2) - 1$ *and* $3(x+2) - 1 \le x + 3$	Break up the compound inequality into two inequalities.
$-1 \le 3x + 6 - 1 \qquad 3x + 6 - 1 \le x + 3$ $-6 \le 3x \qquad\qquad 2x \le -2$ $-2 \le x \qquad$ and $\quad x \le -1$	Solve separately.
$-2 \le x \le -1$	The only values of x that satisfy *both* inequalities are the values between -2 and -1 (inclusive).

Graphing Linear Inequalities in Two Variables

Linear inequalities in two variables can be graphed in much the same way as linear equations. Start by graphing the corresponding equation of a line (temporarily replace the inequality with an equal sign, and then graph). This line creates a boundary line of two half-planes. If the inequality is a "greater/less than," the boundary should not be included and a dotted line is used. A solid line is used to indicate that the boundary should be included in the solution when the inequality is "greater/less than or equal to."

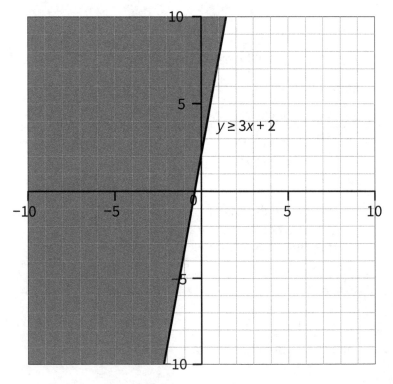

Figure 2.4. Graphing Inequalities

One side of the boundary is the set of all points (x, y) that make the inequality true. This side is shaded to indicate that all these values are solutions. If y is greater than the expression containing x, shade above the line; if it is less than, shade below. A point can also be used to check which side of the line to shade.

A set of two or more linear inequalities is a **SYSTEM OF INEQUALITIES**. Solutions to the system are all the values of the variables that make every inequality in the system true. Systems of inequalities are solved graphically by graphing all the inequalities in the same plane. The region where all the shaded solutions overlap is the solution to the system.

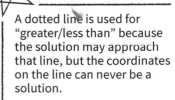

A dotted line is used for "greater/less than" because the solution may approach that line, but the coordinates on the line can never be a solution.

EXAMPLES

1) What is the inequality represented on the graph below?

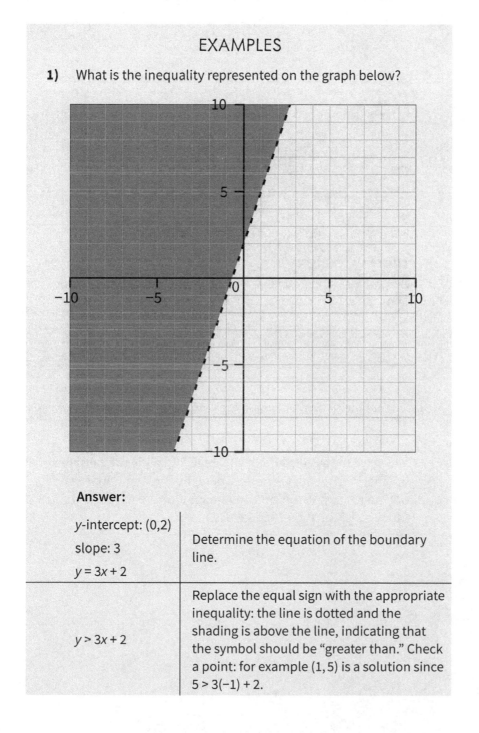

Answer:

y-intercept: $(0,2)$ slope: 3 $y = 3x + 2$	Determine the equation of the boundary line.
$y > 3x + 2$	Replace the equal sign with the appropriate inequality: the line is dotted and the shading is above the line, indicating that the symbol should be "greater than." Check a point: for example $(1, 5)$ is a solution since $5 > 3(-1) + 2$.

2) Graph the following inequality: $3x + 6y \leq 12$.

Answer:

$3x + 6y \leq 12$	
$3(0) + 6y = 12$	
$y = 2$	
y-intercept: $(0, 2)$	Find the x- and y-intercepts.
$3x + 6(0) \leq 12$	
$x = 4$	
x-intercept: $(4, 0)$	

Graph the line using the intercepts, and shade below the line.

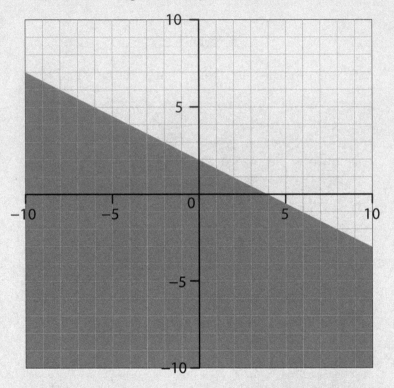

3) Graph the system of inequalities: $-x + y \leq 1, x \geq -1, y > 2x - 4$

Answer:

To solve the system, graph all three inequalities in the same plane; then identify the area where the three solutions overlap. All points (x, y) in this area will be solutions to the system since they satisfy all three inequalities.

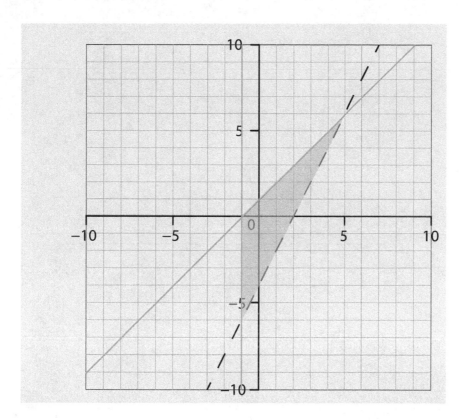

Quadratic Equations and Inequalities

Quadratic equations are degree 2 polynomials; the highest power on the dependent variable is two. While linear functions are represented graphically as lines, the graph of a quadratic function is a **PARABOLA**. The graph of a parabola has three important components. The **VERTEX** is where the graph changes direction. In the parent graph $y = x^2$, the origin $(0,0)$ is the vertex. The **AXIS OF SYMMETRY** is the vertical line that cuts the graph into two equal halves. The line of symmetry always passes through the vertex. On the parent graph, the y-axis is the axis of symmetry. The **ZEROS** or **ROOTS** of the quadratic are the x-intercepts of the graph.

Forms of Quadratic Equations

Quadratic equations can be expressed in two forms:

- **STANDARD FORM:** $y = ax^2 + bx + c$
  Axis of symmetry: $x = -\dfrac{b}{2a}$ Vertex: $\left(-\dfrac{b}{2a}, f\left(-\dfrac{b}{2a}\right)\right)$

- **VERTEX FORM:** $y = a(x - h)^2 + k$
  Vertex: (h, k) Axis of symmetry: $x = h$

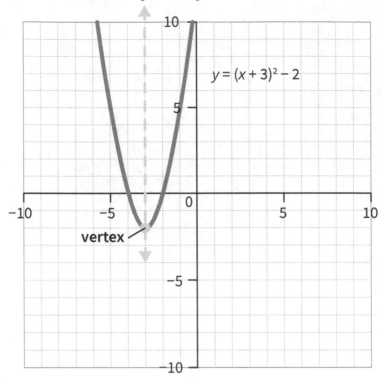

axis of symmetry

$$y = (x + 3)^2 - 2$$

vertex

Figure 2.5. Parabola

In both equations, the sign of a determines which direction the parabola opens: if a is positive, then it opens upward; if a is negative, then it opens downward. The wideness or narrowness is also determined by a. If the absolute value of a is less than one (a proper fraction), then the parabola will get wider the closer $|a|$ is to zero. If the absolute value of a is greater than one, then the larger $|a|$ becomes, the narrower the parabola will be.

Equations in vertex form can be converted to standard form by squaring out the $(x - h)^2$ part (using FOIL), distributing the a, adding k, and simplifying the result.

Equations can be converted from standard form to vertex form by **COMPLETING THE SQUARE.** Take an equation in standard form, $y = ax^2 + bc + c$.

1. Move c to the left side of the equation.
2. Divide the entire equation through by a (to make the coefficient of x^2 be 1).
3. Take half of the coefficient of x, square that number, and then add the result to both sides of the equation.
4. Convert the right side of the equation to a perfect binomial squared, $(x + m)^2$.
5. Isolate y to put the equation in proper vertex form.

EXAMPLES

1) What is the line of symmetry for $y = -2(x + 3)^2 + 2$?

Answer:

This quadratic is given in vertex form, with $h = -3$ and $k = 2$. The vertex of this equation is $(-3, 2)$. The line of symmetry is the vertical line that passes through this point. Since the x-value of the point is -3, the line of symmetry is $x = -3$.

2) What is the vertex of the parabola $y = -3x^2 + 24x - 27$?

Answer:

$y = -3x^2 + 24x - 27$	
$x = -\dfrac{b}{2a}$ where $a = -3$, $b = 24$ $x = -\dfrac{24}{2(-3)} = 4$	This quadratic equation is in standard form. Use the formula for finding the x-value of the vertex.
$y = -3(4)^2 + 24(4) - 27 = 21$ The vertex is at **(4, 21)**.	Plug $x = 4$ into the original equation to find the corresponding y-value.

3) Write $y = -3x^2 + 24x - 27$ in vertex form by completing the square.

Answer:

$y = -3x^2 + 24x - 27$	
$y + 27 = -3x^2 + 24x$	Move c to the other side of the equation.
$\dfrac{y}{-3} - 9 = x^2 - 8x$	Divide through by a (-3 in this example).
$\dfrac{y}{-3} - 9 + 16 = x^2 - 8x + 16$	Take half of the new b, square it, and add that quantity to both sides: $\frac{1}{2}(-8) = -4$. Squaring it gives $(-4)^2 = 16$.
$\dfrac{y}{-3} + 7 = (x - 4)^2$	Simplify the left side, and write the right side as a binomial squared.
$y = -3(x - 4)^2 + 21$	Subtract 7, and then multiply through by -3 to isolate y.

Solving Quadratic Equations

Solving the quadratic equation $ax^2 + bx + c = 0$ finds x-intercepts of the parabola (by making $y = 0$). These are also called the **ROOTS** or **ZEROS** of the quadratic function. A quadratic equation may have zero, one, or two real solutions. There are several ways of finding the zeros. One way is to factor the quadratic into a product of two binomials, and then use the zero product property. (If $m \times n = 0$, then either $m = 0$ or $n = 0$.) Another way is to complete the square and square root both sides.

One way that works every time is to memorize and use the QUADRATIC FORMULA:

$$x = \frac{-b \pm \sqrt{b^2 - 4ac}}{2a}$$

The *a*, *b*, and *c* come from the standard form of quadratic equations above. (Note that to use the quadratic equation, the right-hand side of the equation must be equal to zero.)

The part of the formula under the square root radical ($b^2 - 4ac$) is known as the DISCRIMINANT. The discriminant tells how many and what type of roots will result without actually calculating the roots.

Table 2.2. Discriminants

IF $b^2 - 4ac$ IS	THERE WILL BE	AND THE PARABOLA
zero	only 1 real root	has its vertex on the *x*-axis
positive	2 real roots	has **two** *x*-intercepts
negative	0 real roots 2 complex roots	has **no** *x*-intercepts

EXAMPLES

1) Find the zeros of the quadratic equation: $y = -(x + 3)^2 + 1$.

Answer:

Method 1: Make $y = 0$; isolate *x* by square rooting both sides:

$0 = -(x + 3)^2 + 1$	Make $y = 0$.
$-1 = -(x + 3)^2$	Subtract 1 from both sides.
$1 = (x + 3)^2$	Divide by −1 on both sides.
$(x + 3) = \pm 1$	Square root both sides. Don't forget to write plus OR minus 1.
$(x + 3) = 1 \ or \ (x + 3) = -1$	Write two equations using +1 and −1.
$x = -2 \ or \ x = -4$	Solve both equations. These are the zeros.

Method 2: Convert vertex form to standard form, and then use the quadratic formula.

$y = -(x + 3)^2 + 1$ $y = -(x^2 + 6x + 9) + 1$ $y = -x^2 - 6x - 8$	Put the equation in standard form by distributing and combining like terms.

$$x = \frac{-b \pm \sqrt{(b^2 - 4ac)}}{2a}$$

$$x = \frac{-(-6) \pm \sqrt{(-6)^2 - 4(-1)(-8)}}{2(-1)}$$

$$x = \frac{6 \pm \sqrt{36 - 32}}{-2}$$

Find the zeros using the quadratic formula.

$$x = \frac{6 \pm \sqrt{4}}{-2}$$

$$x = -4, -2$$

33) Find the root(s) for: $z^2 - 4z + 4 = 0$

Answer:

This polynomial can be factored in the form $(z - 2)(z - 2) = 0$, so the only root is $z = 2$. There is only one x-intercept, and the vertex of the graph is *on* the x-axis.

34) Write a quadratic function that has zeros at $x = -3$ and $x = 2$ that passes through the point $(-2, 8)$.

Answer:

If the quadratic has zeros at $x = -3$ and $x = 2$, then it has factors of $(x + 3)$ and $(x - 2)$. The quadratic function can be written in the factored form $y = a(x + 3)(x - 2)$. To find the a-value, plug in the point $(-2, 8)$ for x and y:

$$8 = a(-2 + 3)(-2 - 2)$$

$$8 = a(-4)$$

$$a = -2$$

The quadratic function is $y = -2(x + 3)(x - 2)$.

Graphing Quadratic Equations

The final expected quadratic skills are graphing a quadratic function given its equation and determining the equation of a quadratic function from its graph. The equation's form determines which quantities are easiest to obtain:

Table 2.3 Obtaining Quantities from Quadratic Functions

Name of Form	Equation of Quadratic	Easiest Quantity to Find	How to Find Other Quantities
vertex form	$y = a(x - h)^2 + k$	vertex at (h, k) and axis of symmetry $x = h$	Find zeros by making $y = 0$ and solving for x.
factored form	$y = a(x - m)(x - n)$	x – intercepts at $x = m$ and $x = n$	Find axis of symmetry by averaging m and n: $x = \frac{m+n}{2}$. This is also the x-value of the vertex.

Table 2.3 Obtaining Quantities from Quadratic Functions (continued)

NAME OF FORM	EQUATION OF QUADRATIC	EASIEST QUANTITY TO FIND	HOW TO FIND OTHER QUANTITIES
standard form	$y = ax^2 + bx + c$	y – intercept at $(0, c)$	Find axis of symmetry and x-value of the vertex using $x = \frac{-b}{2a}$. Find zeros using quadratic formula.

To graph a quadratic function, first determine if the graph opens up or down by examining the a-value. Then determine the quantity that is easiest to find based on the form given, and find the vertex. Then other values can be found, if necessary, by choosing x-values and finding the corresponding y-values. Using symmetry instantly doubles the number of points that are known.

Given the graph of a parabola, the easiest way to write a quadratic equation is to identify the vertex and insert the h- and k-values into the vertex form of the equation. The a-value can be determined by finding another point the graph goes through, plugging these values in for x and y, and solving for a.

EXAMPLES

1) Graph the quadratic $y = 2(x - 3)^2 + 4$.

Answer:

Start by marking the vertex at (3, 4) and recognizing this parabola opens upward. The line of symmetry is $x = 3$. Now, plug in an easy value for x to get one point on the curve; then use symmetry to find another point. In this case, choose $x = 2$ (one unit to the left of the line of symmetry) and solve for y:

$y = 2(2 - 3)^2 + 4$

$y = 2(1) + 4$

$y = 6$

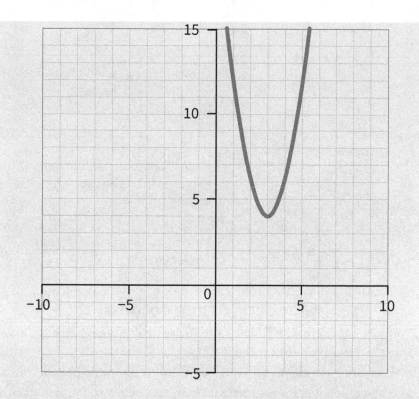

Thus the point $(2, 6)$ is on the curve. Then use symmetry to find the corresponding point one unit to the right of the line of symmetry, which must also have a *y* value of 6. This point is $(4, 6)$. Draw a parabola through the points.

2) What Is the vertex form of the equation shown on the following graph?

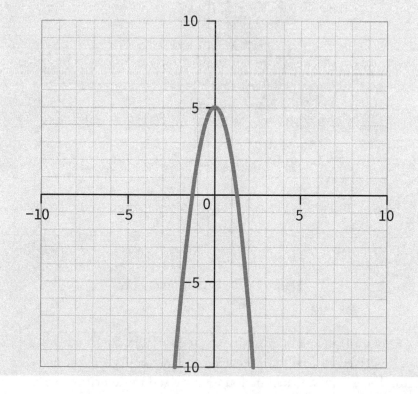

Answer:	
$(h, k) = (0, 5)$ $y = a(x - h)^2 + k$ $y = a(x - 0)^2 + 5$ $y = ax^2 + 5$	Locate the vertex and plug values for h and k into the vertex form of the quadratic equation.
$(x, y) = (1, 2)$ $y = ax^2 + 5$ $2 = a(1)^2 + 5$ $a = -3$	Choose another point on the graph to plug into this equation to solve for a.
$y = -3x^2 + 5$	Plug a into the vertex form of the equation.

Quadratic Inequalities

Quadratic inequalities with two variables, such as $y < (x + 3)^2 - 2$ can be graphed much like linear inequalities: graph the equation by treating the inequality symbol as an equal sign, then shade the graph. Shade above the graph when y is greater is than, and below the graph when y is less than.

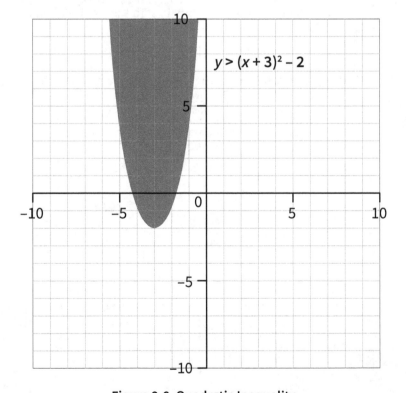

$y > (x + 3)^2 - 2$

Figure 2.6. Quadratic Inequality

Quadratic inequalities with only one variable, such as $x^2 - 4x > 12$, can be solved by first manipulating the inequality so that one side is zero. The zeros can then be found and used to determine where the inequality is greater than zero (positive) or less than zero (negative).

Often it helps to set up intervals on a number line and test a value within each range created by the zeros to identify the values that create positive or negative values.

EXAMPLE

Find the values of x such that $x^2 - 4x > 12$.

Answer:

$x^2 - 4x = 12$		
$x^2 - 4x - 12 = 0$		Find the zeros of the
$(x + 2)(x - 6) = 0$		inequality.
$x = -2, 6$		

x	$(x + 2)(x - 6)$	Create a table or number line with the intervals created by the zeros. Use a test value to determine whether the expression is positive or negative.
$-\infty < x < -2$	$+$	
$-2 < x < 6$	$-$	
$6 < x < \infty$	$+$	

$x < -2$ or $x > 6$	Identify the values of x which make the expression positive.

Absolute Value Equations and Inequalities

The **ABSOLUTE VALUE** of a number means the distance between that number and zero. The absolute value of any number is positive since distance is always positive. The notation for absolute value of a number is two vertical bars:

$|-27| = 27$ The distance from −27 to 0 is 27.

$|27| = 27$ The distance from 27 to 0 is 27.

Solving equations and simplifying inequalities with absolute values usually requires writing two equations or inequalities, which are then solved separately using the usual methods of solving equations. To write the two equations, set one equation equal to the positive value of the expression inside the absolute value and the other equal to the negative value. Two inequalities can be written in the same manner. However, the inequality symbol should be flipped for the negative value.

The formal definition of the absolute value is

$$|x| = \begin{cases} -x, & x < 0 \\ x, & x \geq 0 \end{cases}$$

This is true because whenever x is negative, the opposite of x is the answer (for example, $|-5| = -(-5) = 5$, but when x is positive, the answer is just x. This type of function is called a **PIECE-WISE FUNCTION**. It is defined in two (or more) distinct pieces. To graph the absolute value function, graph each piece separately. When $x < 0$ (that is, when it is negative), graph the line $y = -x$. When $x > 0$ (that is, when x is positive), graph the line $y = x$. This creates a V-shaped graph that is the parent function for absolute value functions.

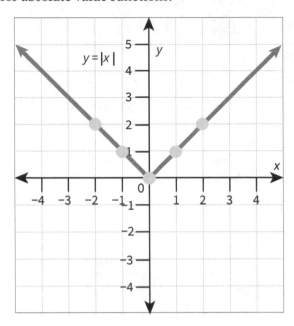

Figure 2.7. Absolute Value Parent Function

EXAMPLES

1) Solve for x: $|x - 3| = 27$

    Answer:

    Set the quantity inside the parentheses equal to 27 or –27, and solve:

    $x - 3 = 27$ $\qquad\qquad$ $x - 3 = -27$

    $\boldsymbol{x = 30}$ $\qquad\qquad\quad$ $\boldsymbol{x = -24}$

2) Solve for r: $\frac{|r - 7|}{5} = 27$

    Answer:

    The first step is to isolate the absolute value part of the equation. Multiplying both sides by 5 gives:

    $|r - 7| = 135$

    If the quantity in the absolute value bars is 135 or –135, then the absolute value would be 135:

    $r - 7 = 135$ $\qquad\qquad$ $r - 7 = -135$

    $\boldsymbol{r = 142}$ $\qquad\qquad\quad$ $\boldsymbol{r = -128}$

3) Find the solution set for the following inequality: $\left|\frac{3x}{7}\right| \geq 4 - x$.

Answer:	
$\left|\frac{3x}{7}\right| \geq 4 - x$	
$\frac{\|3x\|}{7} \geq 4 - x$ $\|3x\| \geq 28 - 7x$	Simplify the equation.
$3x \geq 28 - 7x$ $10x \geq 28$ $x \geq \frac{28}{10}$ $-(3x) \leq 28 - 7x$ $-3x \leq 28 - 7x$ $4x \leq 28$ $x \leq 7$	Create and solve two inequalities. When including the negative answer, flip the inequality.
$\frac{28}{10} \leq x \leq 7$	Combine the two answers to find the solution set.

Functions

Working with Functions

Functions can be thought of as a process: when something is put in, an action (or operation) is performed, and something different comes out. A **FUNCTION** is a relationship between two quantities (for example x and y) in which, for every value of the independent variable (usually x), there is exactly one value of the dependent variable (usually y). Briefly, each input has *exactly one* output. Graphically this means the graph passes the **VERTICAL LINE TEST**: anywhere a vertical line is drawn on the graph, the line hits the curve at exactly one point.

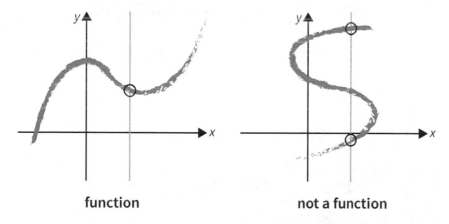

function   not a function

Figure 2.8. Vertical Line Test

The notation $f(x)$ or $g(t)$, etc., is often used when a function is being considered. This is **FUNCTION NOTATION**. The input value is x and the output value y is written as $y = f(x)$. Thus, $f(2)$ represents the output value (or y value) when $x = 2$, and $f(2) = 5$ means that when $x = 2$ is plugged into the $f(x)$ function, the output (y value) is 5. In other words, $f(2) = 5$ represents the point $(2, 5)$ on the graph of $f(x)$.

Every function has an **INPUT DOMAIN** and **OUTPUT RANGE**. The domain is the set of all the possible x values that can be used as input values (these are found along the horizontal axis on the graph), and the range includes all the y values or output values that result from applying $f(x)$ (these are found along the vertical axis on the graph). Domain and range are usually intervals of numbers and are often expressed as inequalities, such as $x < 2$ (the domain is all values less than 2) or $3 < x < 15$ (all values between 3 and 15).

Interval notation can also be used to show domain and range. Round brackets indicate that an end value is not included, and square brackets show that it is. The symbol ⊠ means *or*, and the symbol ⊠ means *and*. For example, the statement (–infinity, 4) ⊠ (4, infinity) describes the set of all real numbers except 4.

A function $f(x)$ is **EVEN** if $f(-x) = f(x)$. Even functions have symmetry across the y-axis. An example of an even function is the parent quadratic $y = x^2$, because any value of x (for example, 3) and its opposite $-x$ (for example, –3) have the same y value (for example, $3^2 = 9$ and $(-3)^2 = 9$). A function is **ODD** if $f(-x) = -f(x)$. Odd functions have symmetry about the origin. For example, $f(x) = x^3$ is an odd function because $f(3) = 27$, and $f(-3) = -27$. A function may be even, odd, or neither.

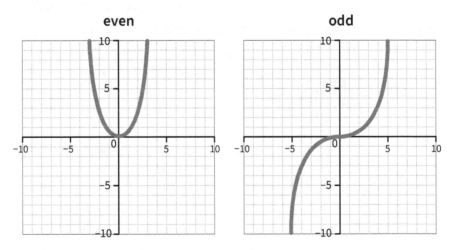

Figure 2.9. Even and Odd Functions

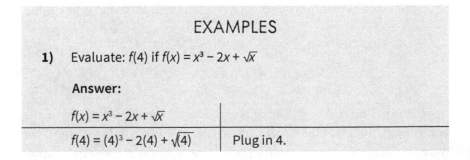

EXAMPLES

1) Evaluate: $f(4)$ if $f(x) = x^3 - 2x + \sqrt{x}$

    Answer:

$f(x) = x^3 - 2x + \sqrt{x}$	
$f(4) = (4)^3 - 2(4) + \sqrt{(4)}$	Plug in 4.

$= 64 - 8 + 2$

$= \mathbf{58}$

Follow the PEMDAS order of operations.

2) What are the domain and range of the following function?

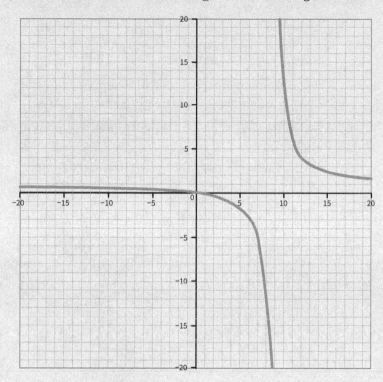

Answer:

This function has an asymptote at $x = 9$, so is not defined there. Otherwise, the function is defined for all other values of x.

D: $-\infty < x < \mathbf{9}$ or $\mathbf{9} < x < \infty$

Since the function has a horizontal asymptote at $y = 1$ that it never crosses, the function never takes the value 1, so the range is all real numbers except 1: **R:** $-\infty < y < 1 \ or \ 1 < y < \infty$.

3) Which of the following represents a function?

A.

X	G(X)
0	0
1	1
2	2
1	3

B.

X	F(X)
0	1
0	2
0	3
0	4

C.

T	F(T)
1	1
2	2
3	3
4	4

D.

X	F(X)
0	0
5	1
0	2
5	3

Put any function into the $y =$ part of a calculator and look at the table to get domain and range values. Looking at −100, −10, 0, 10, and 100 give a sense about any function's limitations.

Answer:

For a set of numbers to represent a function, every input must generate a unique output. Therefore, if the same input (x) appears more than once in the table, determine if that input has two different outputs. If so, then the table does not represent a function.

A. This table is not a function because input value 1 has two different outputs (1 and 3).

B. Table B is not function because 0 is the only input and results in four different values.

C. This table shows a function because each input has one output.

D. This table also has one input going to two different values, so it is not a function.

4)   What is the domain and the range of the following graph?

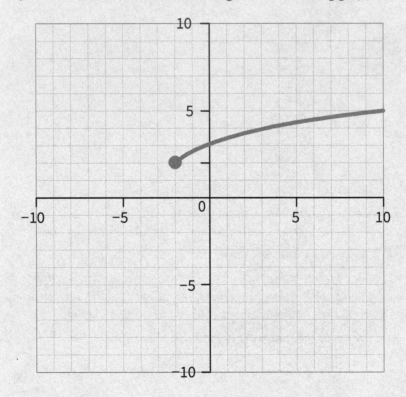

Answer:

For the domain, this graph goes on to the right to positive infinity. Its leftmost point, however, is $x = -2$. Therefore, its domain is all real numbers equal to or greater than −2, **D: − 2 ≤ x < ∞**, or **[−2, ∞)**.

The lowest range value is $y = 2$. Although it has a decreasing slope, this function continues to rise. Therefore, the domain is all real numbers greater than 2, **R: 2 ≤ y < ∞ or [2, ∞)**.

Inverse Functions

INVERSE FUNCTIONS switch the inputs and the outputs of a function. If $f(x) = k$ then the inverse of that function would read $f^{-1}(k) = x$. The domain of $f^{-1}(x)$ is the range of $f(x)$, and the range of $f^{-1}(x)$ is the domain of $f(x)$. If point (a, b) is on the graph of $f(x)$, then point (b, a) will be on the graph of $f^{-1}(x)$. Because of this fact, the graph of $f^{-1}(x)$ is a reflection of the graph of $f(x)$ across the line $y = x$. Inverse functions "undo" all the operations of the original function.

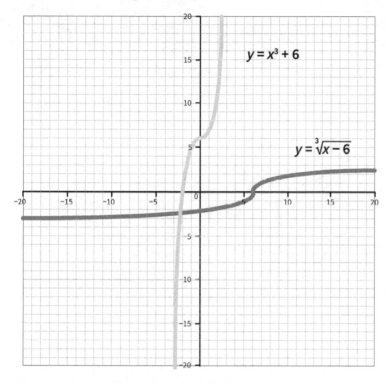

Figure 2.10. Inverse Functions

The steps for finding an inverse function are:

1. Replace $f(x)$ with y to make it easier manipulate the equation.
2. Switch the x and y.
3. Solve for y.
4. Label the inverse function as $f^{-1}(x) =$.

EXAMPLESS

1) What is the inverse of function of $f(x) = 5x + 5$?

Answer:

$y = 5x + 5$	Replace $f(x)$ with y
$x = 5y + 5$	Switch the places of y and x.

$$x = 5y + 5$$
$$x - 5 = 5y \qquad \text{Solve for } y.$$
$$y = \frac{x}{5} - 1$$
$$\mathbf{f^{-1}(x) = \frac{x}{5} - 1}$$

2) Find the inverse of the graph of $f(x) = -1 - \frac{1}{5}x$

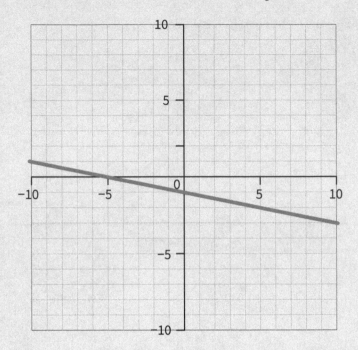

Answer:

This is a linear graph with some clear coordinates: $(-5, 0)$, $(0, -1)$, $(5, -2)$, and $(10, -3)$. This means the inverse function will have coordinate $(0, -5)$, $(-1, 0)$, $(-2, 5)$, and $(-3, 10)$. The inverse function is reflected over the line $y = x$ and is the line $f^{-1}(x) = -5(x + 1)$ below.

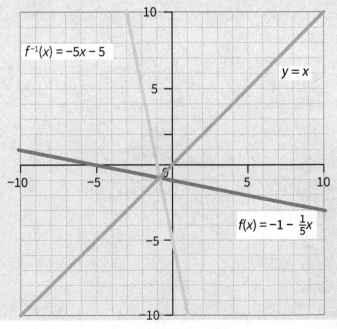

Compound Functions

COMPOUND FUNCTIONS take two or more functions and combine them using operations or composition. Functions can be combined using addition, subtraction, multiplication, or division:

$$\text{addition: } (f + g)(x) = f(x) + g(x)$$

$$\text{subtraction: } (f - g)(x) = f(x) - g(x)$$

$$\text{multiplication: } (fg)(x) = f(x)g(x)$$

$$\text{division: } \left(\frac{f}{g}\right)(x) = \frac{f(x)}{g(x)} \ \text{ (note that } g(x) \neq 0)$$

Functions can also be combined using **COMPOSITION**. Composition of functions is indicated by the notation $(f \circ g)(x)$. Note that the $\circ$ symbol does NOT mean multiply. It means take the output of $g(x)$ and make it the input of $f(x)$:

$$(f \circ g)(x) = f(g(x))$$

This equation is read f of g of x, and will be a new function of x. Note that order is important. In general, $f(g(x)) \neq g(f(x))$. They *will* be equal when $f(x)$ and $g(x)$ are inverses of each other, however, as both will simplify to the original input x. This is because performing a function on a value and then using that output as the input to the inverse function should bring you back to the original value.

The domain of a composition function is the set of x values that are in the domain of the "inside" function $g(x)$ such that $g(x)$ is in the domain of the outside function $f(x)$. For example, if $f(x) = \frac{1}{x}$ and $g(x) = \sqrt{x}$, $f(g(x))$ has a domain of $x > 0$ because $g(x)$ has a domain of $x \geq 0$. But when $f(x)$ is applied to the $\sqrt{x}$ function, the composition function becomes $\frac{1}{\sqrt{x}}$ and the value $x = 0$ is no longer allowed because it would result in 0 in the denominator, so the domain must be further restricted.

EXAMPLES

1) If $z(x) = 3x - 3$ and $y(x) = 2x - 1$, find $(y \circ z)(-4)$.

Answer:

$(y \circ z)(-4) = y(z(-4))$	
$z(-4)$ $= 3(-4) - 3$ $= -12 - 3$ $= -15$	Starting on the inside, evaluate z.
$y(z(-4))$ $= y(-15)$ $= 2(-15) - 1$ $= -30 - 1$ $= \mathbf{-31}$	Replace $z(-4)$ with -15, and simplify.

2) Find $(k \circ t)(x)$ if $k(x) = \frac{1}{x} - 3$ and $t(x) = \frac{1}{x} - 2$.

Answer:

$(k \circ t)(x) = k(t(x))$	
$= k(\frac{1}{2}x - 2)$	Replace x in the $k(x)$ function with $\frac{1}{2}x - 2$
$= \frac{11}{22}x - 2) - 3$	
$= \frac{1}{4}x - 1 - 3$	Simplify.
$= \frac{1}{4}x - 4$	
$(k \circ t)(x) = \frac{1}{4}x - 4$	

3) The wait (W) in minutes to get on a ride at an amusement park depends on the number of people (N) in the park. The number of people in the park depends on the number of hours, t, that the park has been open. Suppose $N(t) = 400t$ and $W(N) = 5(1.2)\frac{N}{100}$. What is the value and the meaning in context of $N(4)$ and $W(N(4))$?

Answer:

$N(4) = 400(4) = 1600$ and means that 4 hours after the park opens there are 1600 people in the park. $W(N(4)) = W(1600) = 96$ and means that 4 hours after the park opens the wait time is about **96 minutes** for the ride.

Transforming Functions

Many functions can be graphed using simple transformation of parent functions. Transformations include reflections across axes, vertical and horizontal translations (or shifts), and vertical or horizontal stretches or compressions. The table gives the effect of each transformation to the graph of any function $y = f(x)$.

Table 2.4. Effects of Transformations

EQUATION	EFFECT ON GRAPH
$y = -f(x)$	reflection across the x-axis (vertical reflection)
$y = f(x) + k$	vertical shift up k units ($k > 0$) or down k units ($k < 0$)
$y = kf(x)$	vertical stretch (if $k > 1$) or compression (if $k < 1$)
$y = f(-x)$	reflection across the y-axis (horizontal reflection)
$y = f(x + k)$	horizontal shift right k units ($k < 0$) or left k units ($k > 0$)
$y = f(kx)$	horizontal stretch ($k < 1$) or compression ($k > 1$)

Note that the first three equations have an operation applied to the *outside* of the function $f(x)$ and these all cause *vertical changes* to the graph of the function that are *intuitive* (for example, adding a value moves it up). The last three equations have an operation applied to the *inside* of the function $f(x)$ and these all cause *horizontal changes* to the graph of the function that are *counterintuitive* (for example, multiplying the x's by a fraction results in stretch, not compression, which would seem more intuitive). It is helpful to group these patterns together to remember how each transformation affects the graph.

EXAMPLES

1) Graph: $y = |x+1| + 4$

Answer:

This function is the absolute value function with a vertical shift up of 4 units (since the 4 is outside the absolute value bars), and a horizontal shift left of 1 unit (since it is inside the bars). The vertex of the graph is at $(-1, 4)$ and the line $x = -1$ is an axis of symmetry.

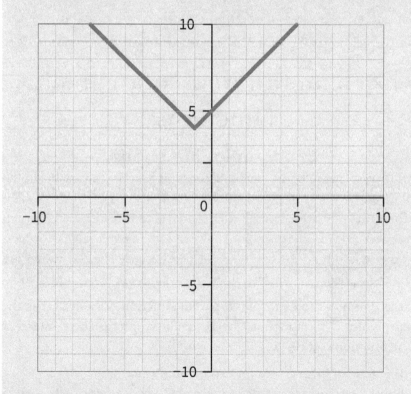

2) Graph: $y = -3|x-2| + 2$

Answer:

The negative sign in front of the absolute value means the graph will be reflected across the x-axis, so it will open down. The 3 causes a vertical stretch of the function, which results in a narrower graph. The basic curve is shifted 2 units right (since the

−2 is an inside change) and 2 units up (since the +2 is an outside change), so the vertex is at (2, 2).

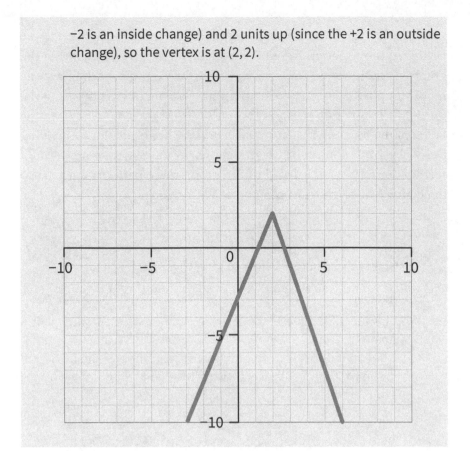

Exponential and Logarithmic Functions

Exponential Functions

An **EXPONENTIAL FUNCTION** has a constant base and a variable in the exponent: $f(x) = b^x$ is an exponential function with base b and exponent x. The value b is the quantity that the y value is multiplied by each time the x value is increased by 1. When looking at a table of values, an exponential function can be identified because the $f(x)$ values are being multiplied. (In contrast, linear $f(x)$ values are being added to.)

The graph of the exponential parent function does not cross the x-axis, which is the function's horizontal asymptote. The y-intercept of the function is at $(0, 1)$.

The general formula for an exponential function, $f(x) = ab^{(x-h)} + k$, allows for transformations to be made to the function. The value h moves the function left or right (moving the y-intercept) while the value k moves the function up or down (moving both the y-intercept and the horizontal asymptote). The value a stretches or compresses the function (moving the y-intercept).

Exponential equations have at least one variable in an exponent position. One way to solve these equations is to make the bases on both side of the equation equivalent, and then equate the exponents. Many

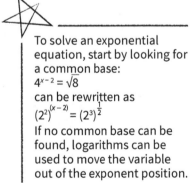

To solve an exponential equation, start by looking for a common base:
$4^{x-2} = \sqrt{8}$
can be rewritten as
$(2^2)^{(x-2)} = (2^3)^{\frac{1}{2}}$
If no common base can be found, logarithms can be used to move the variable out of the exponent position.

exponential equations do not have a solution. Negative numbers often lead to no solutions: for example, $2^x = -8$. The domain of exponential functions is only positive numbers, as seen above, so there is no x value that will result in a negative output.

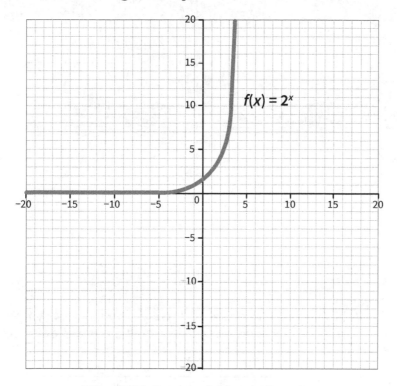

Figure 2.11. Exponential Parent Function

EXAMPLES

1) Graph the exponential function $f(x) = 5^x - 2$.

Answer:

One way to do this is to use a table:

x	$5^x - 2$
−2	$\frac{1}{25} - 2 = -\frac{49}{25}$
−1	$\frac{1}{5} - 2 = -\frac{9}{5}$
0	$1 - 2 = -1$
1	$5 - 2 = 3$
2	$25 - 2 = 23$

Another way to graph this is simply to see this function as the parent function $y = b^x$ (with $b = 5$), shifted down by a vertical shift of 2 units. Thus the new horizontal asymptote will be at $y = 2$, and the new y-intercept will be $y = -1$.

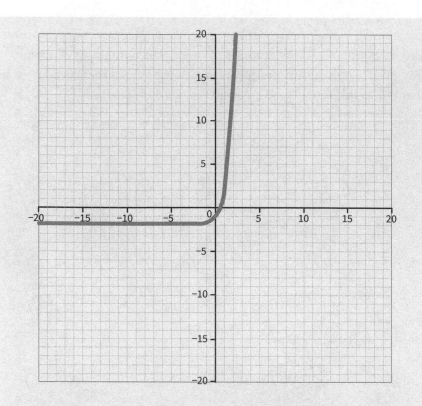

2) If the height of grass in a yard in a humid summer week grows by 5% every day, how much taller would the grass be after six days?

Answer:

Any time a question concerns growth or decay, an exponential function must be created to solve it. In this case, create a table with initial value a, and a daily growth rate of $(1+0.05) = 1.05$ per day.

Days (x)	Height (h)
0	a
1	$1.05a$
2	$1.05(1.05a) = (1.05)^2a$
3	$(1.05)^2(1.05a) = (1.05)^3a$
x	$(1.05)^xa$

After six days the height of the grass is $(1.05)^6 = $ **1.34 times as tall**. The grass would grow 34% in one week.

3) Solve for x: $4^{x+1} = \frac{1}{256}$

Answer:

$$4^{x+1} = \frac{1}{256}$$

$4^{x+1} = 4^{-4}$	Find a common base and rewrite the equation.
$x + 1 = -4$ **$x = -5$**	Set the exponents equal and solve for x.

Logarithmic Functions

The **LOGARITHMIC FUNCTION (LOG)** is the inverse of the exponential function.

$$y = \log_3 x \boxtimes 3^y = x$$

x	y
$\frac{1}{9}$	-2
$\frac{1}{3}$	-1

$y = \log_3 x \boxtimes 3^y = x$ (continued)

1	0
3	1
9	2
27	3

A log is used to find out to what power an input is raised to get a desired output. In the table, the base is 3. The log function determines to what power 3 must be raised so that $\frac{1}{9}$ is the result in the table (the answer is –2). As with all inverse functions, these exponential and logarithmic functions are reflections of each other across the line $y = x$.

A **NATURAL LOGARITHM (LN)** has the number e as its base. Like n, e is an irrational number that is a nonterminating decimal. It is usually shortened to 2.71 when doing calculations. Although the proof of e is beyond the scope of this book, e is to be understood as the upper limit of the range of this rational function: $(1 + \frac{1}{n})^n$.

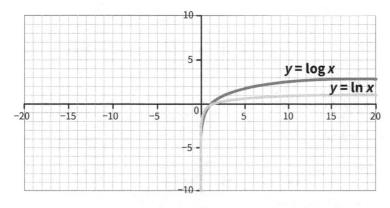

Figure 2.12. Logarithmic Parent Functions

In order to make use of and solve logarithmic functions, log rules are often employed that allow simplification:

Table 2.5. Properties of Logarithms

Change of base	$\log_b(m) = \dfrac{\log(m)}{\log(b)}$
Logs of products	$\log_b(mn) = \log_b(m) + \log_b(n)$
Logs of quotients	$\log_b(\frac{m}{n}) = \log_b(m) - \log_b(n)$
Log of a power	$\log_b(m^n) = n \times \log_b(m)$
Equal logs/equal arguments	$\log_b M = \log_b N \boxtimes M = N$

Note that when the base is not written out, such as in $\log(m)$, it is understood that the base is 10. Just like a 1 is not put in front of a variable because its presence is implicitly understood, 10 is the implicit base whenever a base is not written out.

EXAMPLES

1) Expand $\log_5(\frac{25}{x})$

   Answer:

   Since division of a term can be written as a subtraction problem, this simplifies to:

   $\log_5(25) - \log_5(x)$

   The first term asks "what power of 5 gives 25?" The power is 2. Therefore, the most expanded form is:

   $2 - \log_5(x)$

2) Solve for x: $\ln x + \ln 4 = 2\ln 4 - \ln 2$

   Answer:

$\ln x + \ln 4 = 2\ln 4 - \ln 2$	
$\ln(4x) = \ln 4^2 - \ln 2$ $\ln(4x) = \ln 16 - \ln 2$	Apply the log of product and log of exponent rules.
$\ln(4x) = \ln 8$	Follow log of quotient rule.
$4x = 8$ **$x = 2$**	Set the arguments equal to each other.

3) Solve for x: $2^x = 40$

   Answer:

$\log_2 2^x = \log_2 40$	Take the $\log_2$ of both sides.
$x\log_2 2 = \log_2 40$	Drop the x down using properties of logs.
$x = \log_2 40$	$\log_2 2$ simplifies to 1.

≈ **5.32**	Use the change of base rule or a calculator to calculate the value of $\log_2(40)$.

Special Equations

There are three exponential function formulas that frequently show up in word problems:

The **Growth Formula:**

$y = a(1 + r)^t$ Initial amount a increases at a rate of r per time period

The **Decay Formula:**

$y = a(1 - r)^t$ Initial amount a decreases at a rate of r per time period

In these formulas, a is the initial amount (at time $t = 0$), r is the rate of growth or decay (written as a decimal in the formula), and t is the number of growth or decay cycles that have passed.

A special case of the growth function is known as the **Compound-Interest Formula:**

$$A = P(1 + \tfrac{r}{n})^{nt}$$

In this formula, A is the future value of an investment, P is the initial deposit (or principal), r is the interest rate as a percentage, n is the number of times interest is compounded within a time period, or how often interest is applied to the account in a year (once per year, $n = 1$; monthly, $n = 12$; etc.), and t is the number of compounding cycles (usually years).

EXAMPLES

1) In the year 2000, the number of text messages sent in a small town was 120. If the number of text messages grew every year afterward by 124%, how many years would it take for the number of text messages to surpass 36,000?

Answer:

$y = a(1 + r)^t$	Plug the given values into the
$36{,}000 = 120(1 + 1.24)^t$	growth equation.
$300 = (2.24)^t$	
$\log_{2.24} 300 = \log_{2.24}(2.24)^t$	
$7.07 \approx t$	Use the properties of logarithms to solve the equation.
The number of text messages will pass 36,000 in **7.07 years**.	

2) The half-life of a certain isotope is 5.5 years. If there were 20 grams of one such isotope left after 22 years, what was its original weight?

Answer:

$t = \frac{22}{5.5} = 4$ $r = 0.5$ $a = ?$	Identify the variables.
$20 = a(1 - 0.50)^4$ $20 = a(0.5)^4$ $20 = a(\frac{1}{2})^4$ $20 = a(\frac{1}{16})$ $320 = a$ The original weight is **320 grams**.	Plug these values into the decay formula and solve.

3) If there were a glitch at a bank and a savings account accrued 5% interest five times per week, what would be the amount earned on a $50 deposit after twelve weeks?

Answer:

$r = 0.05$ $n = 5$ $t = 12$ $P = 50$	Identify the variables.
$A = 50(1 + \frac{0.05}{5})^{5(12)}$ $A = 50(1.01)^{60}$ $A = 50(1.82) = 90.83$	Use the compound-interest formula, since this problem has many steps of growth within a time period.
$90.83 - 50$ **= \$40.83**	Subtract the original deposit to find the amount of interest earned.

Polynomial Functions

A polynomial is any equation or expression with two or more terms with whole number exponents. All polynomials with only one variable are functions. The zeros, or roots, of a polynomial function are where the function equals zero and crosses the x-axis.

A linear function is a degree 1 polynomial and always has one zero. A quadratic function is a degree 2 polynomial and always has exactly two roots (including complex roots and counting repeated roots separately). This pattern is extended in the FUNDAMENTAL THEOREM OF ALGEBRA:

A polynomial function with degree $n > 0$ such as $f(x) = ax^n + bx^{n-1} + cx^{n-2} + \ldots + k$, has exactly n (real or complex) roots (some roots may be repeated). Simply stated, whatever the degree of the polynomial is, that is how many roots it will have.

Table 2.6. Zeros of Polynomial Functions

POLYNOMIAL DEGREE, N	NUMBER AND POSSIBLE TYPES OF ZEROS
1	1 real zero (guaranteed)
2	0, 1, or 2 real zeros possible 2 real **or** complex zeros (guaranteed)
3	1, 2, or 3 real zeros possible (there must be at least one real zero) Or 1 real zero (guaranteed) and 2 complex zeros (guaranteed)
4	0, 1, 2, 3, or 4 real zeros (possible) Or 2 real zeros and 2 complex zeros or 4 complex zeros
…	…

All the zeros of a polynomial satisfy the equation $f(x) = 0$. That is, if k is a zero of a polynomial, then plugging in $x = k$ into the polynomial results in 0. This also means that the polynomial is evenly divisible by the factor $(x - k)$.

All polynomials where n is an odd number will have at least one real zero or root. Complex zeros always come in pairs (specifically, complex conjugate pairs).

EXAMPLE

Find the roots of the polynomial: $y = 3t^4 - 48$

Answer:

$y = 3t^4 - 48$	
$3(t^4 - 16) = 0$	Factor the polynomial. Remove the common factor of 3 from each term and make $y = 0$.
$3(t^2 - 4)(t^2 + 4) = 0$ $3(t + 2)(t - 2)(t^2 + 2) = 0$	Factor the difference of squares. $t^2 - 4$ is also a difference of squares.
$t + 2 = 0 \quad t - 2 = 0 \quad t^2 + 2 = 0$ $t = -2 \quad\quad t = 2 \quad t^2 = -2$ $t = \pm\sqrt{-2} = \pm 2i$	Set each factor equal to zero. Solve each equation.

This degree 4 polynomial has four roots, two real roots: **2 or −2**, and two complex roots: **2i or −2i**. The graph will have two *x*-intercepts at (−2, 0) and (2, 0).

Rational Functions

Operations with Rational Functions

Rational functions are ratios of polynomial functions in the form $f(x) = \frac{g(x)}{h(x)}$. Just like rational numbers, rational functions form a closed system under addition, subtraction, multiplication, and division by a nonzero rational expression. This means adding two rational functions, for example, results in another rational function.

To add or subtract rational expressions, the least common denominator of the factors in the denominator must be found. Then, numerators are added, just like adding rational numbers. To multiply rational expressions, factors can be multiplied straight across, canceling factors that appear in the numerator and denominator. To divide rational functions, use the "invert and multiply" rule.

Rational equations are solved by multiplying through the equation by the least common denominator of factors in the denominator. Just like with radical equations, this process can result in extraneous solutions, so all answers need to be checked by plugging them into the original equation.

EXAMPLES

1) If $f(x) = \frac{2}{3x^2y}$ and $g(x) = \frac{5}{21y}$, find the difference between the functions, $f(x) - g(x)$.

Answer:

$f(x) - g(x) = \frac{2}{3x^2y} - \frac{5}{21y}$	Write the difference.
$= \frac{2}{3x^2y}(\frac{7}{7}) - \frac{5}{21y}(\frac{x^2}{x^2})$ $= \frac{14}{21x^2y} - \frac{5x^2}{21x^2y}$	Figure out the least common denominator. Every factor must be represented to the highest power it appears in either denominator. So, the LCD $= 3(7)x^2y$.
$f(x) - g(x) = \frac{14 - 5x^2}{21x^2y}$	Subtract the numerators the find the answer.

2) If $f(x) = \frac{(x-1)(x+2)^2}{5x^2 + 10x}$ and $g(x) = \frac{x^2 + x - 2}{x + 5}$, find the quotient $\frac{f(x)}{g(x)}$.

Answer:

$$\frac{f(x)}{g(x)} = \frac{\frac{(x-1)(x+2)^2}{5x^2+10x}}{\frac{x^2+x-2}{x+5}}$$ $$= \frac{(x-1)(x+2)^2}{5x^2+10x} \times \frac{x+5}{x^2+x-2}$$	Write the quotient; then invert and multiply.
$$= \frac{(x-1)(x+2)^2}{5x(x+2)} \times \frac{x+5}{(x+2)(x-1)}$$	Factor all expressions, and then cancel any factors that appear in both the numerator and the denominator.
$$= \frac{x+5}{5x}$$	

3) Solve the rational equation $\frac{x}{x+2} + \frac{2}{x^2+5x+6} = \frac{5}{x+3}$.

Answer:

$$\frac{x}{x+2} + \frac{2}{x^2+5x+6} = \frac{5}{x+3}$$	
$$\frac{x}{x+2} + \frac{2}{(x+3)(x+2)} = \frac{5}{x+3}$$	Factor any denominators that need factoring.
$$x(x+3) + 2 = 5(x+2)$$	Multiply through by the LCM of the denominators, which is $(x+2)(x+3)$.
$$x^2 + 3x + 2 - 5x - 10 = 0$$ $$x^2 - 2x - 8 = 0$$	Simplify the expression.
$$(x-4)(x+2) = 0$$	Factor the quadratic.

Plugging $x = -2$ into the original equation results in a 0 in the denominator. So this solution is an extraneous solution and must be thrown out.

Plugging in $x = 4$ gives $\frac{4}{6} + \frac{2}{16+20+6} = \frac{5}{7}$.

So **$x = 4$** is a solution to the equation.

Graphing Rational Functions

Rations functions are graphed by examining the function to find key features of the graph, including asymptotes, intercepts, and holes.

A **VERTICAL ASYMPTOTE** exists at any value that makes the denominator of a (simplified) rational function equal zero. A vertical asymptote is a vertical line through an x value that is not in the domain of the rational function (the function is undefined at this value because division by 0 is not allowed). The function approaches, but never crosses, this line, and the y values increase (or decrease) without bound (or "go to infinity") as this x value is approached.

To find x-intercepts and vertical asymptotes, factor the numerator and denominator of the function. Cancel any terms that appear in the numerator and denominator (if there are any). These values will appear as **HOLES** on the final graph. Since a fraction only equals 0 when its numerator is 0, set the simplified numerator equal to 0 and solve to find the *x*-intercepts. Next, set the denominator equal to 0 and solve to find the vertical asymptotes.

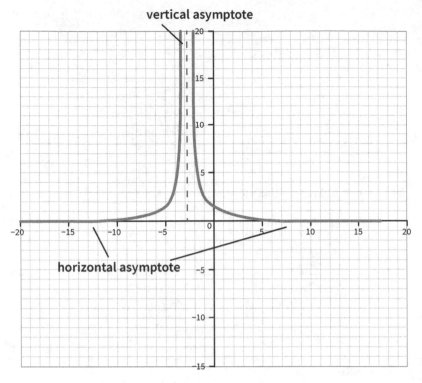

Figure 2.13. Graphing Rational Functions

HORIZONTAL ASYMPTOTES are horizontal lines that describe the "end behavior" of a rational function. In other words, the horizontal asymptote describes what happens to the *y*-values of the function as the *x*-values get very large ($x \to \infty$) or very small ($x \to -\infty$). A horizontal asymptote occurs if the degree of the numerator of a rational function is less than or equal to the degree in the denominator. The table summarizes the conditions for horizontal asymptotes:

Table 2.7. Conditions for Horizontal Asymptotes

For polynomials with first terms $\frac{ax^n}{bx^d}$ ...

$n < d$	as $x \to \infty$, $y \to 0$ as $x \to -\infty$, $y \to 0$	The *x*-axis ($y = 0$) is a horizontal asymptote.
$n = d$	as $x \to \pm\infty$, $y \to \frac{a}{b}$	There is a horizontal asymptote at $y = \frac{a}{b}$.
$n > d$	as $x \to \infty$, $y \to \infty$ or $-\infty$ as $x \to -\infty$, $y \to \infty$ or $-\infty$	There is no horizontal asymptote.

EXAMPLES

1) Graph the function: $f(x) = \dfrac{3x^2 - 12x}{x^2 - 2x - 3}$.

Answer:

$y = \dfrac{3x^2 - 12x}{x^2 - 2x - 3}$ $= \dfrac{3x(x-4)}{(x-3)(x+1)}$	Factor the equation.
$3x(x-4) = 0$ $x = 0, 4$	Find the roots by setting the numerator equal to zero.
$(x-3)(x+1) = 0$ $x = -1, 3$	Find the vertical asymptotes by setting the denominator equal to zero.
The degree of the numerator and denominator are equal, so the asymptote is the ratio of the coefficients: $y = \dfrac{3}{1} = 3$	Find the horizontal asymptote by looking at the degree of the numerator and the denominator.

Use the roots and asymptotes to graph the function.

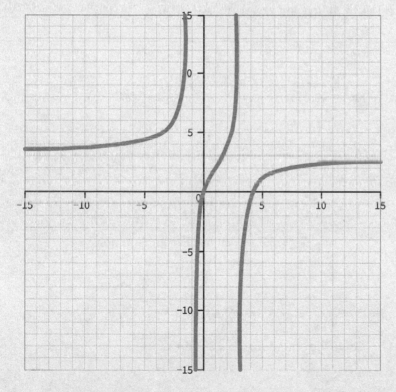

2) Create a function that has an x-intercept at $(5, 0)$ and vertical asymptotes at $x = 1$ and $x = -1$.

Answer:

The numerator will have a factor of $(x - 5)$ in order to have a zero at $x = 5$. The denominator will need factors of $(x - 1)$ and $(x + 1)$

Radical Functions

Radical functions have rational (fractional) exponents, or include the radical symbol. For example, $f(x) = 2(x - 5)^{\frac{1}{3}}$ and $g(t) = \sqrt[4]{5 - x}$ are radical functions. The domain of even root parent functions is $0 \le x \le \infty$ and the range is $y \ge 0$. For odd root parent functions, the domain is all real numbers (because you can take cube roots, etc., of negative numbers). The range is also all real numbers.

To solve equations involving radical functions, first isolate the radical part of the expression. Then "undo" the fractional exponent by raising both sides to the reciprocal of the fractional exponent (for example, undo square roots by squaring both sides). Then solve the equation using inverse operations, as always. All answers should be checked by plugging them back into the original equation, as **EXTRANEOUS SOLUTIONS** result when an equation is raised to powers on both sides. This means there may be some answers that are not actually solutions, and should be eliminated.

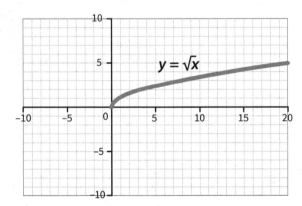

Figure 2.14. Radical Parent Function

EXAMPLES

1) Solve the equation: $\sqrt{2x-5} + 4 = x$

    Answer:

$\sqrt{2x-5} + 4 = x$	
$\sqrt{2x-5} = x - 4$	Isolate the $\sqrt{2x-5}$ by subtracting 4.
$2x - 5 = x^2 - 8x + 16$	Square both sides to clear the $\sqrt{\ }$.
$x^2 - 10x + 21 = 0$	Collect all variables to one side.

$(x-7)(x-3) = 0$ $x = 7$ or $x = 3$	Factor and solve.
$\sqrt{2(7)-5} + 4 = 7$ $\sqrt{2(3)-5} + 4 = 3$ $\sqrt{9} + 4 = 7$ $\sqrt{1} + 4 = 3$ **$x = 7$**	Check solutions by plugging into the original, as squaring both sides can cause extraneous solutions. True, $x = 7$ is a solution. False, $x = 3$ is NOT a solution (extraneous solution).

2) Solve the equation: $2(x^2 - 7x)^{\frac{2}{3}} = 8$

Answer:

$2(x^2 - 7x)^{\frac{2}{3}} = 8$	
$(x^2 - 7x)^{\frac{2}{3}} = 4$	Divide by 2 to isolate the radical.
$x^2 - 7x = 4^{\frac{3}{2}}$ $x^2 - 7x = 8$	Raise both sides to the $\frac{3}{2}$ power to clear the $\frac{2}{3}$ exponent.
$x^2 - 7x - 8 = 0$	This is a quadratic, so collect all terms to one side.
$(x \quad 8)(x \mid 1) = 0$ **$x = 8$ or $x = -1$**	Factor and solve for x.

Plugging both solutions into the original equation confirms that both are solutions.

Modeling Relationships

Modeling relationships requires use of one of four of the function types examined above with an appropriate equation for a word problem or scenario.

GO ON

Table 2.8. Function Types

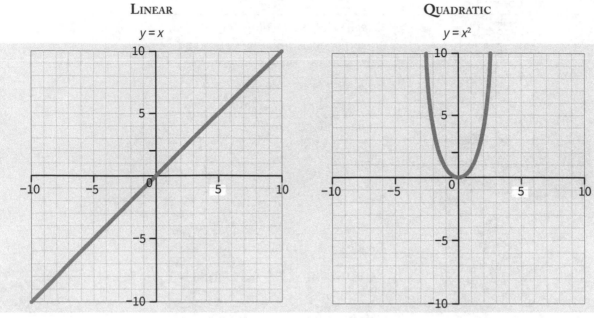

LINEAR

$y = x$

Key words: constant change, slope, equal

QUADRATIC

$y = x^2$

Key words: area, squared, parabola

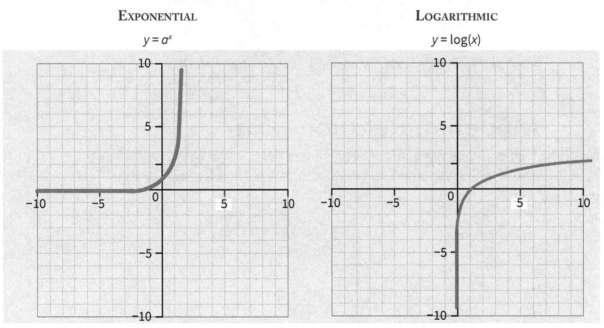

EXPONENTIAL

$y = a^x$

Key words: growth, decay, interest, double, triple, half-life

LOGARITHMIC

$y = \log(x)$

Key words: log-scale, base, log equations

Since exponential functions and log functions are inverses of each other, it will often be the case that exponential or log problems can be solved by either type of equation.

EXAMPLES

1) Consider the following sets of coordinate pairs of a function: {(-1, 0.4), (0, 1), (2, 6.25), and (3, 15.625)}. What kind of function does this represent?

Answer:

Graphing on the coordiante plane shows what looks like an exponential function.

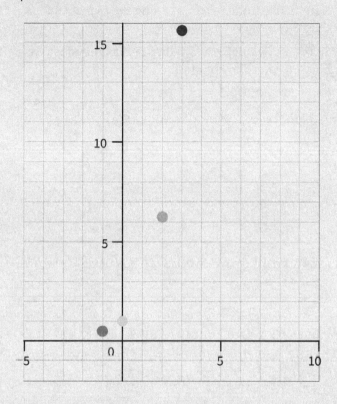

If it is exponential, then its equation is $y = ab^x$, where a is the y intercept, so $a = 1$ in this case. The b is the growth or decay value. Plug in another point, such as (2, 6.25) to solve for b:

$y = ab^x$

$6.25 = (1)b^2$

$b = \sqrt{6.25} = 2.5$

The equation, then, is $y = 2.5^x$.

Check another point to confirm: Is $0.4 = 2.5^{-1}$? Since $2.5 = \frac{5}{2}$, and $\left(\frac{5}{2}\right)^{-1} = \frac{2}{5} = 0.4$, the equation works. The function is **exponential**.

2) At a recent sporting event, there were 20,000 people in attendance. When it ended, people left the building at a rate of 1,000 people in the first minute, 1,000 more in the second minute, 1,000 in the third minute, and so on. What equation describes the behavior of attendees leaving the event for every minute after the event finished?

Answer:

The dependent variable is the number of attendees leaving the event (y). There is a constant change of 1,000 people per minute. Note that this is an additive pattern in the table: every increase of 1 in time results in a subtraction of the same value (1,000) in y. Because it is a constant rate of change, a linear model is required:

$y = 20,000 - 1,000x$

Here 20,000 is the y-intercept, and the rate of change, −1,000, is the slope.

To test this model, confirm that 18,000 attendees were left in the building after two minutes:

$y = 20,000 - 1,000(2) = 18,000$

The model is correct.

three

GEOMETRY

eometry is the study of shapes, angles, volumes, areas, lines, points, and the relationships among them. It is normally approached as an axiomatic system; that is, a small number of entities are taken for granted as true, and everything else is derived logically from them.

Equality, Congruence, and Similarity

When discussing shapes in geometry, the term **CONGRUENT** is used to mean that two shapes have the same shape and size (but not necessarily the same orientation or location). This concept is slightly different from equality, which is used in geometry to describe numerical values. For example, if the length of two lines are equal, the two lines themselves are called congruent. Congruence is written using the symbol ⊠. On figures, congruent parts are denoted with hash marks.

Shapes which are **SIMILAR** have the same shape but the not the same size, meaning their corresponding angles are the same but their lengths are not. For two shapes to be similar, the ratio of their corresponding sides must be a constant (usually written as k). Similarity is described using the symbol ~.

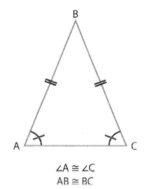

$\angle A \cong \angle C$
$AB \cong BC$

Figure 3.1. Congruent Parts of a Triangle

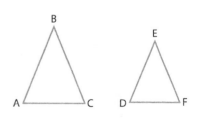

$ABC \sim DEF$

$$\frac{AB}{DE} = \frac{BC}{EF} = \frac{AC}{DF}$$

Figure 3.2. Similar Triangles

Properties of Shapes

Basic Definitions

The basic figures from which many other geometric shapes are built are points, lines, and planes. A **POINT** is a location in a plane. It has no size or shape, but is represented by a dot. It is labeled using a capital letter.

A **LINE** is a one-dimensional collection of points that extends infinitely in both directions. At least two points are needed to define a line, and any points that lie on the same line are **COLINEAR**. Lines are represented by two points, such as **A** and **B**, and the line symbol: ($\overleftrightarrow{AB}$). Two lines on the same plane will intersect unless they are **PARALLEL**, meaning they have the same slope. Lines that intersect at a 90 degree angle are **PERPENDICULAR**.

A **LINE SEGMENT** has two endpoints and a finite length. The length of a segment, called the measure of the segment, is the distance from **A** to **B**. A line segment is a subset of a line, and is also denoted with two points, but with a segment symbol: ($\overline{AB}$). The **MIDPOINT** of a line segment is the point at which the segment is divided into two equal parts. A line, segment, or plane that passes through the midpoint of a segment is called a **BISECTOR** of the segment, since it cuts the segment into two equal segments.

A **RAY** has one endpoint and extends indefinitely in one direction. It is defined by its endpoint, followed by any other point on the ray: $\overrightarrow{AB}$. It is important that the first letter represents the endpoint. A ray is sometimes called a half line.

Table 3.1. Basic Geometric Figures

Term	Dimensions	Graphic	Symbol
point	zero	●	·A
line segment	one	A ——— B	$\overline{AB}$
ray	one	A ———→ B	$\overrightarrow{AB}$
line	one	←———→	$\overleftrightarrow{AB}$
plane	two	▱	Plane M

A **PLANE** is a flat sheet that extends indefinitely in two directions (like an infinite sheet of paper). A plane is a two-dimensional (2D) figure. A plane can always be defined through any three noncollinear points in three-dimensional (3D) space. A plane is named using any three points that are in the plane (for example, plane **ABC**). Any points lying in the same plane are said to be **COPLANAR**. When two planes intersect, the intersection is a line.

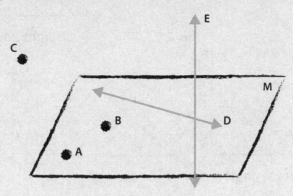
Angles

ANGLES are formed when two rays share a common endpoint. They are named using three letters, with the vertex point in the middle (for example ∠*ABC*, where *B* is the vertex). They can also be labeled with a number or named by their vertex alone (if it is clear to do so). Angles are also classified based on their angle measure. A RIGHT ANGLE has a measure of exactly 90°. ACUTE ANGLES have measures that are less than 90°, and OBTUSE ANGLES have measures that are greater than 90°.

Any two angles that add to make 90° are called COMPLEMENTARY ANGLES. A 30° angle would be complementary to a 60° angle. SUPPLEMENTARY ANGLES add up to 180°. A supplementary angle to a 60° angle would be a 120° angle; likewise, 60° is the SUPPLEMENT of 120°. The complement and supplement of any angle must always be positive. For example, a 140 degree has no complement. Angles that are next to each other and share a common ray are called ADJACENT ANGLES. Angles that are adjacent and supplementary are called a LINEAR PAIR of angles. Their nonshared rays form a line (thus the *linear* pair). Note that angles that are supplementary do not need to be adjacent; their measures simply need to add to 180°.

VERTICAL ANGLES are formed when two lines intersect. Four angles will be formed; the vertex of each angle is at the intersection point of the lines. The vertical angles across from each other will be equal in measure. The angles adjacent to each other will be linear pairs and therefore supplementary.

> Angles can be measured in degrees or radian. Use the conversion factor
> 1 rad = 57.3 degrees
> to convert between them.

A ray, line, or segment that divides an angle into two equal angles is called an **ANGLE BISECTOR**.

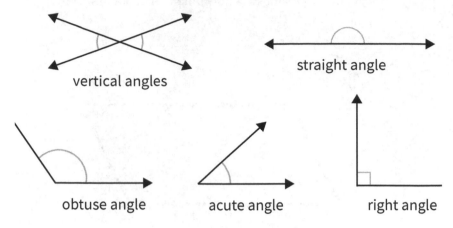

Figure 3.3. Types of Angles

EXAMPLES

1) How many linear pairs of angles are there in the following figure?

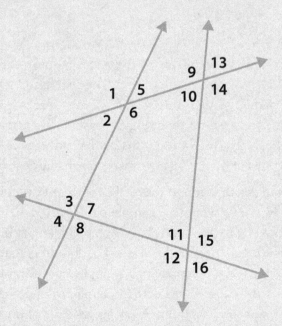

Answers:

Any two adjacent angles that are supplementary are linear pairs, so there are 16 linear pairs in the figure (∠1 and ∠5, ∠2 and ∠6, ∠5 and ∠6, ∠2 and ∠1, and so on).

2) If angles M and N are supplementary and ∠M is 30° less than twice ∠N, what is the degree measurement of each angle?

Answer:

$\angle M + \angle N = 180°$	Set up a system of equations.
$\angle M = 2\angle N - 30°$	
$\angle M + \angle N = 180°$	
$(2\angle N - 30°) + \angle N = 180°$	
$3\angle N - 30° = 180°$	Use substitution to solve for $\angle N$.
$3\angle N = 210°$	
$\angle N = 70°$	
$\angle M + \angle N = 180°$	Solve for $\angle M$ using the original equation.
$\angle M + 70° = 180°$	
$\angle M = 110°$	

Circles

A **CIRCLE** is the set of all the points in a plane that are the same distance from a fixed point called the **CENTER**. The distance from the center to any point on the circle is the **RADIUS** of the circle. The distance around the circle (the perimeter) is called the **CIRCUMFERENCE**.

The ratio of a circle's circumference to its diameter is a constant value called pi (π), an irrational number which is commonly rounded to 3.14. The formula to find a circle's circumference is $C = 2\pi r$. The formula to find the enclosed area of a circle is $A = \pi r^2$.

Circles have a number of unique parts and properties:

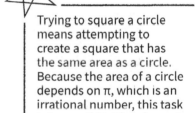

Trying to square a circle means attempting to create a square that has the same area as a circle. Because the area of a circle depends on π, which is an irrational number, this task is impossible. The phrase is often used to describe trying to do something that can't be done.

- The **DIAMETER** is the largest measurement across a circle. It passes through the circle's center, extending from one side of the circle to the other. The measure of the diameter is twice the measure of the radius.

- A line that cuts across a circle and touches it twice is called a **SECANT** line. The part of a secant line that lies within a circle is called a **CHORD**. Two chords within a circle are of equal length if they are are the same distance from the center.

- A line that touches a circle or any curve at one point is **TANGENT** to the circle or the curve. These lines are always exterior to the circle. A line tangent to a circle and a radius drawn to the point of tangency meet at a right angle (90°).

- An **ARC** is any portion of a circle between two points on the circle. The **MEASURE** of an arc is in degrees, whereas the **LENGTH OF THE ARC** will be in linear measurement (such as centimeters or inches). A **MINOR ARC** is the small arc between the two points (it measures less than 180°), whereas a **MAJOR ARC** is the large arc between the two points (it measures greater than 180°).

- An angle with its vertex at the center of a circle is called a **CENTRAL ANGLE**. For a central angle, the measure of the arc intercepted by the sides of the angle (in degrees) is the same as the measure of the angle.

- A **SECTOR** is the part of a circle *and* its interior that is inside the rays of a central angle (its shape is like a slice of pie).

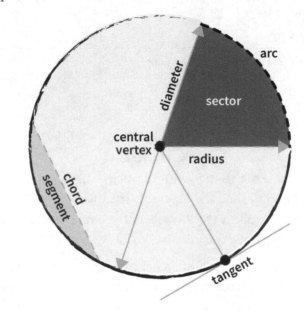

Figure 3.4. Parts of a Circle

	Area of Sector	Length of an Arc
Degrees	$A = \dfrac{\theta}{360°} \times \pi r^2$	$s = \dfrac{\theta}{360°} \times 2\pi r$
Radians	$A = \dfrac{1}{2} \pi^2 \theta$	$s = r\theta$

- An **INSCRIBED ANGLE** has a vertex on the circle and is formed by two chords that share that vertex point. The angle measure of an inscribed angle is one-half the angle measure of the central angle with the same endpoints on the circle.

- A **CIRCUMSCRIBED ANGLE** has rays tangent to the circle. The angle lies outside of the circle.

- Any angle outside the circle, whether formed by two tangent lines, two secant lines, or a tangent line and a

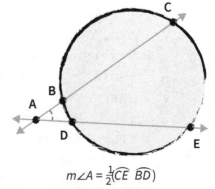

$m\angle A = \frac{1}{2}(\overset{\frown}{CE} - \overset{\frown}{BD})$

Figure 3.5. Angles Outside a Circle

secant line, is equal to half the difference of the intercepted arcs.

- ◆ Angles are formed within a circle when two chords intersect in the circle. The measure of the smaller angle formed is half the sum of the two smaller arc measures (in degrees). Likewise, the larger angle is half the sum of the two larger arc measures.

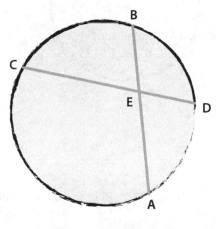

$$m\angle E = \tfrac{1}{2}(\overset{\frown}{AC} + \overset{\frown}{BD})$$

Figure 3.6. Intersecting Chords

- ◆ If a chord intersects a line tangent to the circle, the angle formed by this intersection measures one half the measurement of the intercepted arc (in degrees).

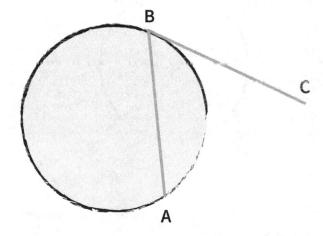

$$m\angle ABC = \tfrac{1}{2}m\overset{\frown}{AB}$$

Figure 3.7. Intersecting Chord and Tangent

GO ON

EXAMPLES

1) Find the area of the sector *NHS* of the circle below with center at *H*:

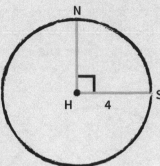

Answer:

$r = 4$ $\angle NHS = 90°$	Identify the important parts of the circle.
$A = \frac{\theta}{360°} \times \pi r^2$ $= \frac{90}{360} \times \pi(4)^2$	Plug these values into the formula for the area of a sector.
$= \frac{1}{4} \times 16\pi$ $\mathbf{= 4\pi}$	Plug these values into the formula for the area of a sector (continued).

2) In the circle below with center *O*, the minor arc *ACB* measures 5 feet. What is the measurement of *m⊠AOB*?

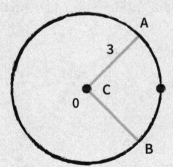

Answer:

$r = 3$ length of $\overline{ACB} = 5$	Identify the important parts of the circle.
$s = \frac{\theta}{360°} \times 2\pi r$ $5 = \frac{\theta}{360°} \times 2\pi(3)$ $\frac{5}{6\pi} = \frac{\theta}{360°}$ $\theta = 95.5°$ $\mathbf{\mathit{m}\angle AOB = 95.5°}$	Plug these values into the formula for the length of an arc and solve for θ.

Triangles

Much of geometry is concerned with triangles as they are commonly used shapes. A good understanding of triangles allows decomposition of other shapes (specifically polygons) into triangles for study.

Triangles have three sides, and the three interior angles always sum to 180°. The formula for the area of a triangle is $A = \frac{1}{2}bh$ or one-half the product of the base and height (or altitude) of the triangle.

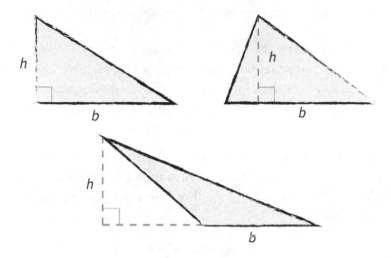

Figure 3.8. Finding the Base and Height of Triangles

Some important segments in a triangle include the angle bisector, the altitude, and the median. The ANGLE BISECTOR extends from the side opposite an angle to bisect that angle. The ALTITUDE is the shortest distance from a vertex of the triangle to the line containing the base side opposite that vertex. It is perpendicular to that line and can occur on the outside of the triangle. The MEDIAN extends from an angle to bisect the opposite side.

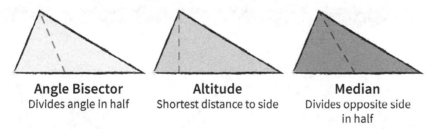

| **Angle Bisector** | **Altitude** | **Median** |
| Divides angle in half | Shortest distance to side | Divides opposite side in half |

Figure 3.9. Important Segments in a Triangle

Triangles have two "centers." The ORTHOCENTER is formed by the intersection of a triangle's three altitudes. The CENTROID is where a triangle's three medians meet.

Triangles can be classified in two ways: by sides and by angles.

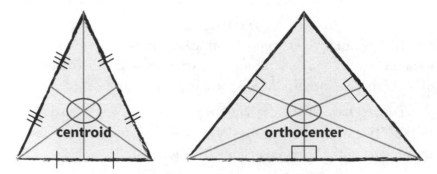

Figure 3.10. Centroid and Orthocenter of a Triangle

A **SCALENE TRIANGLE** has no equal sides or angles. An **ISOSCELES TRIANGLE** has two equal sides and two equal angles, often called **BASE ANGLES**. In an **EQUILATERAL TRIANGLE**, all three sides are equal as are all three angles. Moreover, because the sum of the angles of a triangle is always 180°, each angle of an equilateral triangle must be 60°.

A **RIGHT TRIANGLE** has one right angle (90°) and two acute angles. An **ACUTE TRIANGLE** has three acute angles (all angles are less than 90°). An **OBTUSE TRIANGLE** has one obtuse angle (more than 90°) and two acute angles.

Triangles Based on Sides

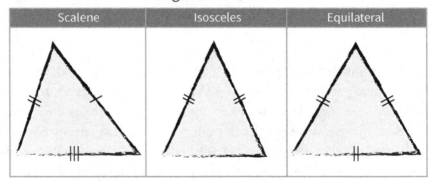

Scalene	Isosceles	Equilateral

Triangles Based on Angles

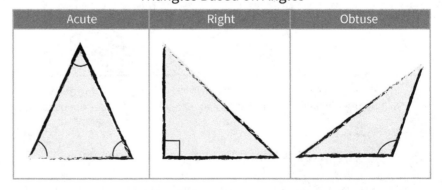

Acute	Right	Obtuse

Figure 3.11. Types of Triangles

Trigonometric functions can be employed to find missing sides and angles of a triangle.

For any triangle, the side opposite the largest angle will have the longest length, while the side opposite the smallest angle will have the shortest length. The **TRIANGLE INEQUALITY THEOREM** states that the sum of any two sides of a triangle must be greater than the third side. If this inequality does not hold, then a triangle cannot be formed. A consequence of this theorem is the **THIRD-SIDE RULE**: if b and c are two sides of a triangle, then the measure of the third side a must be between the sum of the other two sides and the difference of the other two sides: $c - b < a < c + b$.

Solving for missing angles or sides of a triangle is a common type of triangle problem. Often a right triangle will come up on its own or within another triangle. The relationship among a right triangle's sides is known as the **PYTHAGOREAN THEOREM**: $a^2 + b^2 = c^2$, where c is the hypotenuse and is across from the 90° angle. Right triangles with angle measurements of 90° – 45° – 45° and 90° – 60° – 30° are known as "special" right triangles and have specific relationships between their sides and angles.

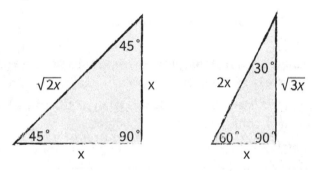

Figure 3.12. Special Right Triangles

EXAMPLES

1) What are the minimum and maximum values of x to the nearest hundredth?

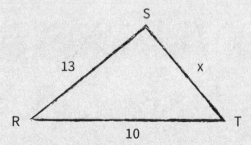

Answers:

The sum of two sides is 23 and their difference is 3. To connect the two other sides and enclose a space, x must be less than the sum and greater than the difference (that is, $3 < x < 23$). Therefore, **x's minimum value to the nearest hundredth is 3.01 and its maximum value is 22.99.**

2) Examine and classify each of the following triangles:

1.

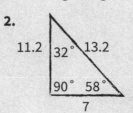

2.

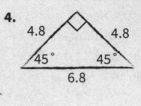

3.

4.

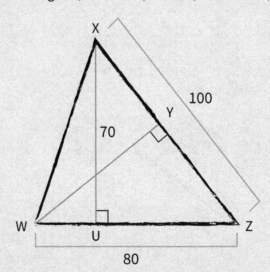

Answers:

Triangle 1 is an equilateral triangle (all 3 sides are equal, and all 3 angles are equal)

Triangle 2 is a scalene, right triangle (all 3 sides are different, and there is a 90° angle)

Triangle 3 is an obtuse isosceles triangle (there are 2 equal sides and, consequently, 2 equal angles)

Triangle 4 is a right, isosceles triangle (there are 2 equal sides and a 90° angle)

3) Given the diagram, if $XZ = 100$, $WZ = 80$, and $XU = 70$, then $WY = ?$

Answer:

$WZ = b_1 = 80$

$XU = h_1 = 70$

$XZ = b_2 = 100$

$WY = h_2 = ?$

$A = \frac{1}{2}bh$

$A_1 = \frac{1}{2}(80)(70) = 2800$

$A_2 = \frac{1}{2}(100)(h_2)$

$2800 = \frac{1}{2}(100)(h_2)$

$h_2 = 56$

WY = 56

The given values can be used to write two equation for the area of $\triangle WXZ$ with two sets of bases and heights.

Set the two equations equal to each other and solve for WY.

Quadrilaterals

All closed, four-sided shapes are QUADRILATERALS. The sum of all internal angles in a quadrilateral is always 360°. (Think of drawing a diagonal to create two triangles. Since each triangle contains 180°, two triangles, and therefore the quadrilateral, must contain 360°.) The AREA OF ANY QUADRILATERAL is $A = bh$, where b is the base and h is the height (or altitude).

A PARALLELOGRAM is a quadrilateral with two pairs of parallel sides. A rectangle is a parallelogram with two pairs of equal sides and four right angles. A KITE also has two pairs of equal sides, but its equal sides are consecutive. Both a SQUARE and a RHOMBUS have four equal sides. A square has four right angles, while a rhombus has a pair of acute opposite angles and a pair of obtuse opposite angles. A TRAPEZOID has exactly one pair of parallel sides.

All squares are rectangles and all rectangles are parallelograms; however, not all parallelograms are rectangles and not all rectangles are squares.

Table 3.2 Properties of Parallelograms

Term	Shape	Properties
Parallelogram		Opposite sides are parallel. Consecutive angles are supplementary. Opposite angles are equal. Opposite sides are equal. Diagonals bisect each other.
Rectangle		All parallelogram properties hold. Diagonals are congruent *and* bisect each other. All angles are right angles.
Square		All rectangle properties hold. All four sides are equal. Diagonals bisect angles. Diagonals intersect at right angles and bisect each other.

Table 3.2 Properties of Parallelograms (continued)

Term	Shape	Properties
Kite	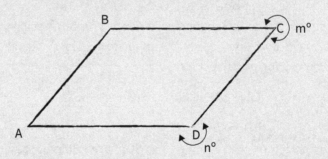	One pair of opposite angles is equal. Two pairs of consecutive sides are equal. Diagonals meet at right angles.
Rhombus		All four sides are equal. Diagonals bisect angles. Diagonals intersect at right angles and bisect each other.
Trapezoid		One pair of sides is parallel. Bases have different lengths. Isosceles trapezoids have a pair of equal sides (and base angles).

EXAMPLES

1) In parallelogram *ABCD*, the measure of angle *m* is is $m° = 260°$. What is the measure of $n°$?

Answers:

$260° + m\angle C = 360°$ $m\angle C = 100°$	Find $\angle C$ using the fact that the sum of $\angle C$ and *m* is 360°.
$m\angle C + m\angle D = 180°$ $100° + m\angle D = 180°$ $m\angle D = 80°$	Solve for $\angle D$ using the fact that consecutive interior angles in a quadrilateral are supplementary.
$m\angle D + n = 360°$ **$n = 280°$**	Solve for *n* by subtracting $m\angle D$ from 360°.

2) A rectangular section of a football field has dimensions of *x* and *y* and an area of 1000 square feet. Three additional lines drawn vertically divide the section into four smaller rectangular areas as seen in the diagram below. If all the lines

shown need to be painted, calculate the total number of linear feet, in terms of x, to be painted.

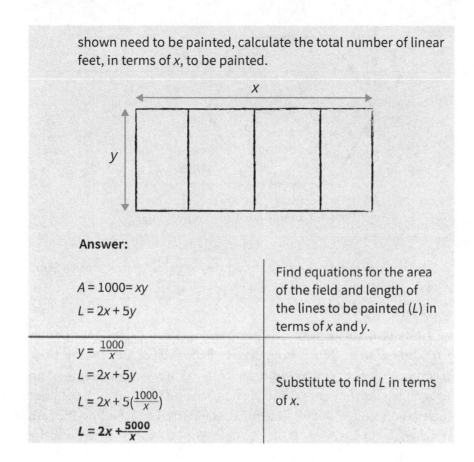

Answer:

$A = 1000 = xy$ $L = 2x + 5y$	Find equations for the area of the field and length of the lines to be painted (L) in terms of x and y.
$y = \frac{1000}{x}$ $L = 2x + 5y$ $L = 2x + 5(\frac{1000}{x})$ $L = 2x + \frac{5000}{x}$	Substitute to find L in terms of x.

Polygons

Any closed shape made up of three or more line segments is a polygon. In addition to triangles and quadrilaterals, HEXAGONS and OCTAGONS are two common polygons.

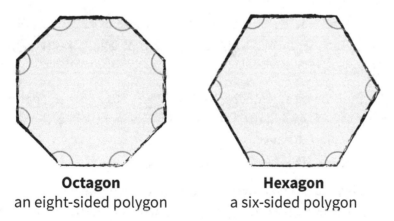

Octagon
an eight-sided polygon

Hexagon
a six-sided polygon

Figure 3.13. Common Polygons

The two polygons depicted above are REGULAR POLYGONS, meaning that they are equilateral (all sides having equal lengths) and equiangular (all angles having equal measurements). Angles inside a polygon are INTERIOR ANGLES, whereas those formed by one side of the polygon and a line extending outside the polygon are EXTERIOR ANGLES:

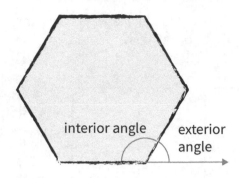

Figure 3.14 Interior and Exterior Angles

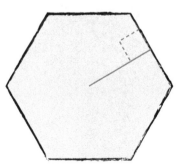

Breaking an irregular polygon down into triangles and quadrilaterals helps in finding its area.

The sum of the all the exterior angles of a polygon is always 360°. Dividing 360° by the number of a polygon's sides finds the measure of the polygon's exterior angles.

To determine the sum of a polygon's interior angles, choose one vertex and draw diagonals from that vertex to each of the other vertices, decomposing the polygon into multiple triangles. For example, an octagon has six triangles within it, and therefore the sum of the interior angles is 6 × 180° = 1080°. In general, the formula for finding the sum of the angles in a polygon is *sum of angles* = (*n* – 2) × 180°, where *n* is the number of sides of the polygon.

To find the measure of a single interior angle in a regular polygon, simply divide the sum of the interior angles by the number of angles (which is the same as the number of sides). So, in the octagon example, each angle is $\frac{1080}{8}$ = 135°.

In general, the formula to find the measure of a regular polygon's interior angles is: *interior angle* = $\frac{(n-2)}{n}$ × 180° where *n* is the number of sides of the polygon.

To find the area of a polygon, it is helpful to know the perimeter of the polygon (*p*), and the **APOTHEM** (*a*). The apothem is the shortest (perpendicular) distance from the polygon's center to one of the sides of the polygon. The formula for the area is: *area* = $\frac{ap}{2}$.

Finally, there is no universal way to find the perimeter of a polygon (when the side length is not given). Often, breaking the polygon down into triangles and adding the base of each triangle all the way around the polygon is the easiest way to calculate the perimeter.

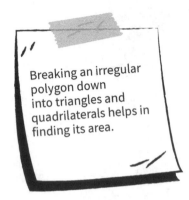

Figure 3.15. Apothem in a Hexagon

EXAMPLES

1) What is the measure of an exterior angle and an interior angle of a regular 400-gon?

   Answer:

The sum of the exterior angles is 360°. Dividing this sum by 400 gives $\frac{360°}{400} = \textbf{0.9°}$. Since an interior angle is supplementary to an exterior angle, all the interior angles have measure $180 - 0.9 = \textbf{179.1°}$. Alternately, using the formula for calculating the interior angle gives the same result:

$interior\ angle = \frac{400 - 2}{400} \times 180° = 179.1°$

2) The circle and hexagon below both share center point *T*. The hexagon is entirely inscribed in the circle. The circle's radius is 5. What is the area of the shaded area?

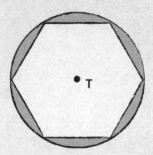

Answer:

$A_c = \pi r^2$ $= \pi(5)^2$ $= 25\pi$	The area of the shaded region will be the area of the circle minus the area of the hexagon. Use the radius to find the area of the circle.
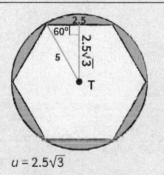 $a = 2.5\sqrt{3}$ $A_H = \frac{ap}{2}$ $= \frac{(2.5\sqrt{3})(30)}{2}$ $= 64.95$	To find the area of the hexagon, draw a right triangle from the vertex, and use special right triangles to find the hexagon's apothem. Then, use the apothem to calculate the area.
$= A_c - A_H$ $= 25\pi - 2.5\sqrt{3}$ $\approx \textbf{13.59}$	Subtract the area of the hexagon from the circle to find the area of the shaded region.

Three-Dimensional Shapes

Properties of Three-Dimensional Shapes

THREE-DIMENSIONAL SHAPES have depth in addition to width and length. VOLUME is expressed as the number of cubic units any solid can hold—that is, what it takes to fill it up. SURFACE AREA is the sum of the areas of the two-dimensional figures that are found on its surface. Some three-dimensional shapes also have a unique property called a slant height (ℓ), which is the distance from the base to the apex along a lateral face.

Table 3.3 Three-Dimensional Shapes and Formulas

TERM	SHAPE	FORMULA	
Prism		$V = Bh$ $SA = 2lw + 2wh + 2lh$ $d^2 = a^2 + b^2 + c^2$	B = area of base h = height l = length w = width d = longest diagonal
Cube	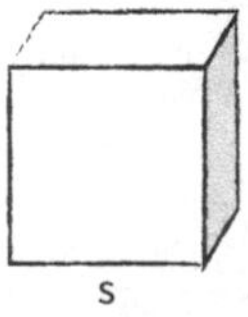	$V = s^3$ $SA = 6s^2$	s = cube edge
Sphere	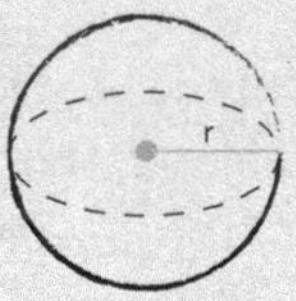	$V = \frac{4}{3}\pi r^3$ $SA = 4\pi r^2$	r = radius
Cylinder	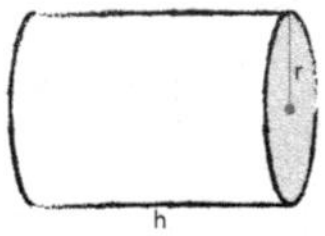	$V = Bh = \pi r^2 h$ $SA = 2\pi r^2 + 2\pi rh$	B = area of base h = height r = radius
Cone	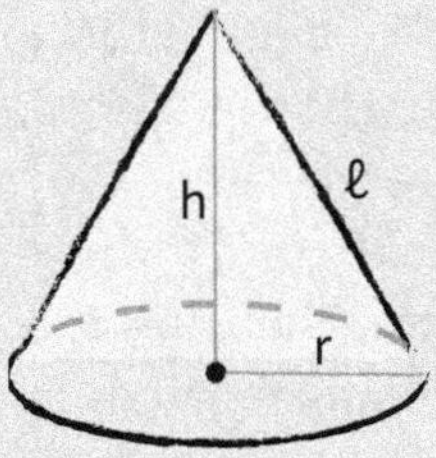	$V = \frac{1}{3}\pi r^2 h$ $SA = \pi r^2 + \pi rl$	r = radius h = height l = slant height
Pyramid	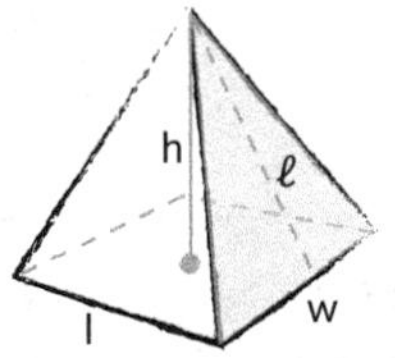	$V = \frac{1}{3}Bh$ $SA = B + \frac{1}{2}(p)l$	B = area of base h = height p = perimeter l = slant height

Finding the surface area of a three-dimensional solid can be made easier by using a NET. This two-dimensional "flattened" version of a three-dimensional shape shows the component parts that comprise the surface of the solid.

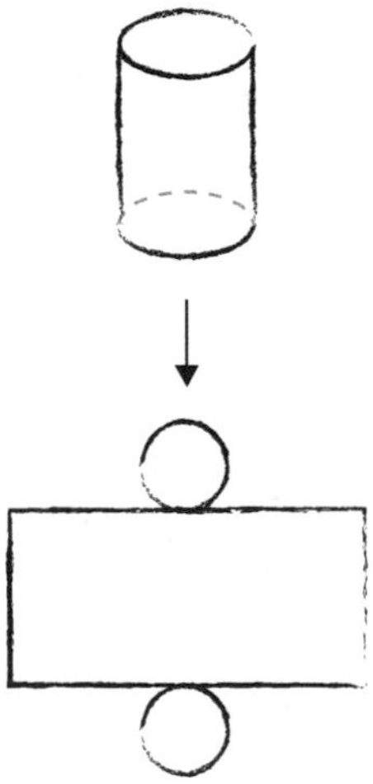

Figure 3.16. Net of a Cylinder

EXAMPLES

1) A sphere has a radius z. If that radius is increased by t, by how much is the surface area increased? Write the answer in terms of z and t.

Answer:

$SA_1 = 4\pi z^2$	Write the equation for the area of the original sphere.
$SA_2 = 4\pi(z + t)^2$ $= 4\pi(z^2 + 2zt + t^2)$ $= 4\pi z^2 + 8\pi zt + 4\pi t^2$	Write the equation for the area of the new sphere.
$A_2 - A_1 = 4\pi z^2 + 8\pi zt + 4\pi t^2$ $- 4\pi z^2$ $= \mathbf{4\pi t^2 + 8\pi zt}$	To find the difference between the two, subtract the original from the increased surface area:

2) A cube with volume 27 cubic meters is inscribed within a sphere such that all of the cube's vertices touch the sphere. What is the length of the sphere's radius?

Answer:

Since the cube's volume is 27, each side length is equal to $\sqrt[3]{27} = 3$. The long diagonal distance from one of the cube's vertices to its opposite vertex will provide the sphere's diameter:

$$d = \sqrt{3^2 + 3^2 + 3^2} = \sqrt{27} = 5.2$$

Half of this length is the radius, which is **2.6 meters**.

Congruence and Similarity in Three-Dimensional Shapes

Three-dimensional shapes may also be congruent if they are the same size and shape, or similar if their corresponding parts are proportional. For example, a pair of cones is similar if the ratios of the cones' radii and heights are proportional. For rectangular prisms, all three dimensions must be proportional for the prisms to be similar. If two shapes are similar, their corresponding areas and volumes will also be proportional. If the constant of proportionality of the linear measurements of a 3D shape is k, the constant of proportionality between the areas will be k^2, and the constant of proportionality between the volumes will be k^3.

All spheres are similar as a dilation of the radius of a sphere will make it equivalent to any other sphere.

GO ON

EXAMPLES

1) A square-based pyramid has a height of 10 cm. If the length of the side of the square is 6 cm, what is the surface area of the pyramid?

   Answer:

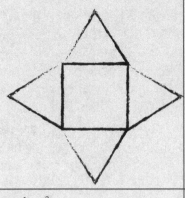

	The surface area will be the area of the square base plus the area of the four triangles.
$A = s^2$ $= 6^2 = 36$	Find the area of the square.
$c^2 = a^2 + b^2$ $\ell^2 = 100 + 9$ $\ell = \sqrt{109}$	To find the area of the triangles, first find the pyramid's slant height.
$A = \frac{1}{2} bh$ $A = \frac{1}{2}(6)(\sqrt{109})$ $A = 3\sqrt{109}$	Find the area of the triangle face using the slant height as the height of the triangle face.
$SA = 36 + 4(3\sqrt{109})$ **≈ 161.3 cm²**	Add the area of the square base and the four triangles to find the total surface area.

2) Given that two cones are similar and one cone's radius is three times longer than the other's radius, what is the volume of the smaller cone if the larger cone has a volume of 81 π cubic inches and a height of 3 inches?

   Answer:

$V_1 = 81\pi$ $h_1 = 3$	Identify the given variables.
$V_1 = \frac{1}{3}\pi r_1^2 h_1$ $81\pi = \frac{1}{3}\pi(r_1)(3)$ $r_1 = 9$	Find the radius of the larger cone with the given information.

$$r_2 = \tfrac{1}{3} r_1$$

$$r_2 = \tfrac{1}{3}(9)$$

$$r_2 = 3$$

$$h_2 = \tfrac{1}{3} h_1$$

$$h_2 = \tfrac{1}{3}(3)$$

$$h_2 = 1$$

$$V_2 = \tfrac{1}{3}\pi r_2^2 h_2$$

$$V_2 = \tfrac{1}{3}\pi(3)^2(1)$$

$$\mathbf{V_2 = 3\pi}$$

Use the given scale factor to find the second cone's radius and height.

Find the area of the smaller cone.

Transformations of Geometric Figures

Basic Transformations

Geometric figures are often drawn in the coordinate xy-plane, with the vertices or centers of the figures indicated by ordered pairs. These shapes can then be manipulated by performing TRANSFORMATIONS, which alter the size or shape of the figure using mathematical operations. The original shape is called the PRE-IMAGE, and the shape after a transformation is applied is called the IMAGE.

A TRANSLATION transforms a shape by moving it right or left, or up or down. Translations are sometimes called slides. After this transformation, the image is identical in size and shape to the pre-image. In other words, the image is CONGRUENT, or identical in size, to the pre-image. All corresponding pairs of angles are congruent, and all corresponding side lengths are congruent.

Translations are often in brackets: (x, y). The first number represents the change in the x direction (left/right), while the second number shows the change in the y direction (up/down).

Transformation follow the order of operations. For example, to transform the function $y = a[f(x - h)] + k$:
1. Translate the function right/left h units.
2. Dilate the function by the scale factor a.
3. Reflect the graph if $a < 0$.
4. Translate the function up/down k units.

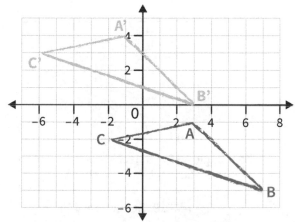

The translation moved triangle ABC left 4 units and up 6 units to produce triangle A'B'C'.

Figure 3.17. Translation

Similarly, rotations and reflections preserve the size and shape of the figure, so congruency is preserved. A ROTATION takes a pre-image and rotates it about a fixed point (often the origin) in the plane. Although the position or orientation of the shape changes, the angles and side lengths remain the same.

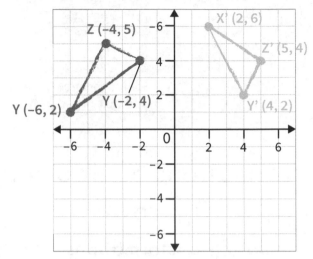

The triangle XYZ is rotated 90 in the clockwise direction about the origin (0, 0).

Figure 3.18. Rotation

A REFLECTION takes each point in the pre-image and flips it over a point or line in the plane (often the *x*- or *y*-axis, but not necessarily). The image is congruent to the pre-image. When a figure is flipped across the *y*-axis, the signs of all *x*-coordinates will change. The *y*-coordinates change sign when a figure is reflected across the *x*-axis.

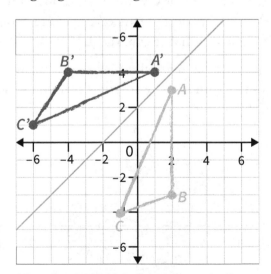

The triangle ABC is reflected over the line to produce the triangle A'B'C'.

Figure 3.19. Reflection

Dilations and Similarity

A **DILATION** increases (or decreases) the size of a figure by some **SCALE FACTOR**. Each coordinate of the points that make up the figure is multiplied by the same factor. If the factor is greater than 1, multiplying all the factors enlarges the shape; if the factor is less than 1 (but greater than 0), the shape is reduced in size.

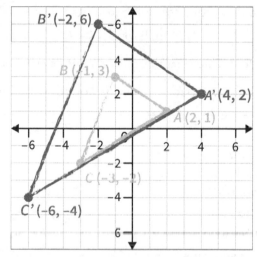

The triangle ABC is dilated by the scale factor 2 to produce triangle A'B'C'.

Figure 3.20. Dilation

In addition to the scale factor, a dilation needs a **CENTER OF DILATION**, which is a fixed point in the plane about which the points are multiplied. Usually, but not always, the center of dilation is the origin (0, 0). For dilations about the origin, the image coordinates are calculated by multiplying each coordinate by the scale factor k. Thus, point $(x, y) \rightarrow (kx, ky)$. Although dilations do not result in congruent figures, the orientation of the figure is preserved; consequently, corresponding line segments will be parallel.

Importantly, dilations do NOT create images that are congruent to the original because the size of each dimension is increased or decreased (the only exception being if the scale factor is exactly 1).

If two shapes are similar, their angle measurements will be equal and the ratio of equivalent sides will be the value k.

However, the shape of the figure is maintained. The corresponding angle measures will be congruent, but the corresponding side lengths will be *proportional*. In other words, the image and pre-image will be SIMILAR shapes (described with the symbol ~).

EXAMPLE

If quadrilateral *ABCD* has vertices *A* (–6, 4), *B* (–6, 8), *C* (2, 8), and *D* (4, –4), what are the new vertices if *ABCD* is increased by a factor of 5 about the origin?

Answer:

Multiply each point by the scale factor of 5 to find the new vertices: **A (–30, 20), B (–30, 40), C (10, 40), and D (20, –20)**.

Transforming Coordinates

Transformations in a plane can actually be thought of as functions. An input pair of coordinates, when acted upon by a transformation, results in a pair of output coordinates. Each point is moved to a unique new point (a one-to-one correspondence).

Table 3.4. How Coordinates Change for Transformations in a Plane

TYPE OF TRANSFORMATION	COORDINATE CHANGES
Translation right *m* units and up *n* units	$(x, y) \rightarrow (x + m, y + n)$
Rotations about the origin in positive (counterclockwise) direction	
Rotation 90°	$(x, y) \rightarrow (-y, x)$
Rotation 180°	$(x, y) \rightarrow (-x, -y)$
Rotation 270°	$(x, y) \rightarrow (y, -x)$
Reflections about the	
***x*-axis**	$(x, y) \rightarrow (x, -y)$
***y*-axis**	$(x, y) \rightarrow (-x, y)$
line ***y* = *x***	$(x, y) \rightarrow (y, x)$
Dilations about the origin by a factor of *k* **0 < *k* < 1 → size reduced** **k > 1 → size enlarged**	$(x, y) \rightarrow (kx, ky)$

EXAMPLES

1) If quadrilateral *ABCD* has vertices *A* (–6, 4), *B* (–6, 8), *C* (2, 8), and *D* (4, –4), what are the new vertices if *ABCD* is rotated 270° and then reflected across the *x*-axis?

Answer:

When a figure is rotated 270°, the coordinates change: $(a, b) \rightarrow (b, -a)$. After the rotation, the new coordinates are (4, 6), (8, 6),

(8, −2), and (−4, −4). Reflecting across the *x*-axis requires that every *y*-value is multiplied by −1 to arrive at the completely transformed quadrilateral with vertices of (4, −6), (8, −6), (8, 2), and (−4, 4).

2) Triangle *ABC* with coordinates (2, 8), (10, 2), and (6, 8) is transformed in the plane as shown in the diagram. What transformations result in the image triangle *A'B'C'*?

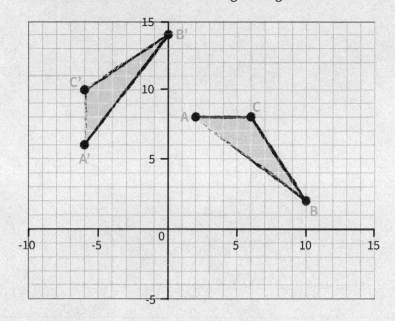

Answer:

Since the orientation of the triangle is different from the original, it must have been rotated. A counterclockwise rotation of 90° about the point *A* (2, 8) results in a triangle with the same orientation. Then the triangle must be translated to move it to the image location. Pick one point, say *A*, and determine the translation necessary to move it to point *A'*. In this case, each point on the pre-image must be translated 8 units left and 2 units down, or (−8, −2) (note that this is one of many possible answers).

four

STATISTICS

S tatistics is the study of DATA, which are simply sets of qualitative and quantitative values. These values are often the result of observations or measurements collected as part of experiments or surveys. The sections below discuss how to organize, analyze, and present data in a variety of ways.

Describing Sets of Data

Measures of Central Tendency

Measures of central tendency help identify the center, or most typical, value within a data set. There are three such central tendencies that describe the "center" of the data in different ways. The MEAN is the arithmetic average and is found by dividing the sum of all measurements by the number of measurements. The mean of a population is written as μ and the mean of a sample is written as $\overline{x}$.

$$\text{population mean} = \mu = \frac{x_1 + x_2 + ...x_N}{N} = \frac{\Sigma x}{N}$$

$$\text{sample mean} = \overline{x} = \frac{x_1 + x_2 + ...x_n}{n} = \frac{\Sigma x}{n}$$

The data points are represented by x's with subscripts; the sum is denoted using the Greek letter sigma (Σ); N is the number of data points in the entire population; and n is the number of data points in a sample set.

The MEDIAN divides the measurements into two equal halves. The median is the measurement right in the middle of an odd set of measurements or the average of the two middle numbers in an even data set. When calculating the median, it is important to order the data values from least to greatest before attempting to locate the middle value. The MODE is simply the measurement that occurs most often. There can

When the same value is added to each term in a set, the mean increases by that value and the standard deviation is unchanged. When each term in a set is multiplied by the same value, both the mean and standard deviation will also be multiplied by that value.

be many modes in a data set, or no mode. Since measures of central tendency describe a *center* of the data, all three of these measures will be between the lowest and highest data values (inclusive).

Unusually large or small values, called OUTLIERS, will affect the mean of a sample more than the mode. If there is a high outlier, the mean will be greater than the median; if there is a low outlier, the mean will be lower than the median. When outliers are present, the median is a better measure of the data's center than the mean because the median will be closer to the terms in the data set.

EXAMPLES

1) What is the mean of the following data set? {1000, 0.1, 10, 1}

   Answer:

   Use the equation to find the mean of a sample:

   $\frac{1000 + 0.1 + 10 + 1}{4} = \textbf{252.78}$

2) What is the median of the following data set? {1000, 10, 1, 0.1}

   Answer:

   Since there are an even number of data points in the set, the median will be the mean of the two middle numbers. Order the numbers from least to greatest: 0.1, 1, 10, and 1000. The two middle numbers are 1 and 10, and their mean is:

   $\frac{1 + 10}{2} = \textbf{5.5}$

3) Josey has an average of 81 on four equally weighted tests she has taken in her statistics class. She wants to determine what grade she must receive on her fifth test so that her mean is 83, which will give her a B in the course, but she does not remember her other scores. What grade must she receive on her fifth test?

   Answer:

   Even though Josey does not know her test scores, she knows her average. Therefore it can be assumed that each test score was 81, since four scores of 81 would average to 81. To find the score, x, that she needs use the equation for the mean of a sample:

   $\frac{4(81) + x}{5} = 83$

   $324 + x = 415$

   $x = \textbf{91}$

Measures of Variation

The values in a data set can be very close together (close to the mean), or very spread out. This is called the SPREAD or DISPERSION of the data. There are a few MEASURES OF VARIATION (or MEASURES OF DISPERSION) that quantify the spread within a data set. RANGE is the difference between the largest and smallest data points in a set:

$$R = \textit{largest data point} - \textit{smallest data point}$$

Notice range depends on only two data points (the two extremes). Sometimes these data points are outliers; regardless, for a large data set, relying on only two data points is not an exact tool.

The understanding of the data set can be improved by calculating QUARTILES. To calculate quartiles, first arrange the data in ascending order and find the set's median (also called quartile 2 or Q2). Then find the median of the lower half of the data, called quartile 1 (Q1), and the median of the upper half of the data, called quartile 3 (Q3). These three points divide the data into four equal groups of data (thus the word *quartile*). Each quartile contains 25% of the data.

INTERQUARTILE RANGE **(IQR)** provides a more reliable range that is not as affected by extremes. IQR is the difference between the third quartile data point and the first quartile data point and gives the spread of the middle 50% of the data:

$$IQR = Q_3 - Q_1$$

A measure of variation that depends on the mean is STANDARD DEVIATION, which uses every data point in a set and calculates the average distance of each data point from the mean of the data. Standard deviation can be computed for an entire population (written σ) or for a sample of a population (written s):

$$\sigma = \sqrt{\frac{\Sigma(x_i - \mu)^2}{N}} \qquad s = \sqrt{\frac{\Sigma(x_i - \bar{x})^2}{n - 1}}$$

Thus, to calculate standard deviation, the difference between the mean and each data point is calculated. Each of these differences is squared (so that each is positive). The average of the squared values is computed by summing the squares and dividing by N or $(n - 1)$. Then the square root is taken, to "undo" the previous squaring.

The VARIANCE of a data set is simply the square of the standard variation:

$$V = \sigma^2 = \frac{1}{N} \sum_{i=1}^{N} (x_i - \mu)^2$$

Variance measures how narrowly or widely the data points are distributed. A variance of zero means every data point is the same; a large variance means the data is widely spread out.

> Standard deviation and variance are also affected by extreme values. Though much simpler to calculate, interquartile range is the more accurate depiction of how the data is scattered when there are outlier values.

EXAMPLES

1) What are the range and interquartile range of the following set? {3, 9, 49, 64, 81, 100, 121, 144, 169}

Answer:

R = largest point – smallest point = 169 – 3 = **166**	Use the equation for range.
3 9 → Q1 = $\frac{49 + 9}{2}$ = 29 49 64 81 → Q2 100 121 → Q3 = $\frac{121 + 144}{2}$ = 132.5 144 169	Place the terms in numerical order and identify Q1, Q2, and Q3.
IQR = Q3 – Q1 = 132.5 – 29 = **103.5**	Find the IQR by subtracting Q1 from Q3.

2) In a group of 7 people, 1 person has no children, 2 people have 1 child, 2 people have 2 children, 1 person has 5 children, and 1 person has 17 children. To the nearest hundredth of a child, what is the standard deviation in this group?

Answer:

{0, 1, 1, 2, 2, 5, 17}	Create a data set out of this scenario.
$\mu = \frac{x_1 + x_2 + \ldots x_N}{N} = \frac{\Sigma x}{N}$ $\mu = \frac{0 + 1 + 1 + 2 + 2 + 5 + 17}{7} = 4$	Calculate the population mean.
$(0 - 4)^2 = (-4)^2 = 16$ $(1 - 4)^2 = (-3)^2 = 9$ $(1 - 4)^2 = (-3)^2 = 9$ $(2 - 4)^2 = (-2)^2 = 4$ $(2 - 4)^2 = (-2)^2 = 4$ $(5 - 4)^2 = (1)^2 = 1$ $(17 - 4)^2 = (13)^2 = 169$	Find the square of the difference of each term and the mean $(x_i - \mu)^2$.
$\sigma = \sqrt{\frac{\Sigma(x_i - \mu)^2}{N}}$ $\sigma = \sqrt{\frac{212}{7}} = \sqrt{30.28} = $ **5.50**	Plug the sum (Σ) of these squares, 212, into the standard deviation formula.

Box Plots

A box plot depicts the median and quartiles along a scaled number line. It is meant to summarize the data in a visual manner and emphasize central trends while decreasing the pull of outlier data. To construct a box plot:

1. Create a number line that begins at the lowest data point and terminates at the highest data point.

2. Find the quartiles of the data. Create a horizontal rectangle (the "box") whose left border is Q_1 and right border is Q_3.

3. Draw a vertical line within the box to mark the median.

4. Draw a horizontal line going from the left edge of the box to the smallest data value.

5. Draw a horizontal line going from the right edge of the box to the largest data value.

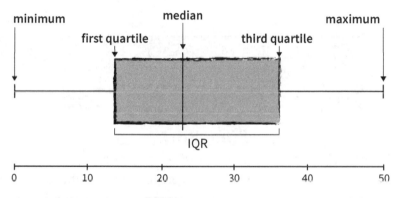

Figure 4.1. Box Plot

When reading a box plot, the following stands out:

♦ Reading from left to right: the horizontal line (whisker) shows the spread of the first quarter; the box's left compartment shows the spread of the second quarter; the box's right compartment shows the spread of the third quarter; and the right horizontal line shows the spread of the fourth quarter.

♦ The length of the box is the IQR, or the middle 50% of the data.

♦ Each of the four pieces (the whiskers and two pieces in the box) represent 25% of the data.

♦ The horizontal lines show by their length whether the data higher or lower than the middle 50% is prominent.

Box plots are also known as box-and-whisker plots, because if they are drawn correctly the two horizontal lines look like whiskers.

A recent survey asked 8 people how many pairs of shoes they wear per week. Their answers are in the following data set: {1, 3, 5, 5, 7, 8, 12}. Construct a box plot from this data.

Answer:

Create a number line that begins at 1 and ends at 12. Q_1 is 3, the median (Q_2) is 5, and Q_3 is 8. A rectangle must be drawn whose length is 5 and that borders on Q_1 and Q_3. Mark the median of 5 within the rectangle. Draw a horizontal line going left to 1. Draw a horizontal line going right to 12.

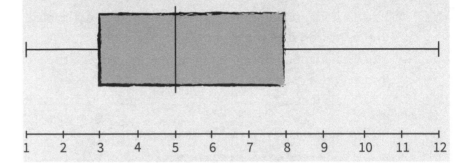

Graphs, Charts, and Tables

Pie Charts

A pie chart simply states the proportion of each category within the whole. To construct a pie chart, the categories of a data set must be determined. The frequency of each category must be found and that frequency converted to a percent of the total. To draw the pie chart, determine the angle of each slice by multiplying the percentage by 360°.

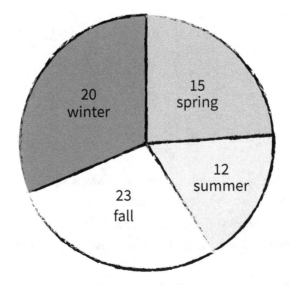

Figure 4.2. Pie Chart

EXAMPLE

A firm is screening applicants for a job by education-level attainment. There are 125 individuals in the pool: 5 have a doctorate, 20 have a master's degree, 40 have a bachelor's degree, 30 have an associate degree, and 30 have a high school degree. Construct a pie chart showing the highest level of education attained by the applicants.

Answer:

Create a frequency table to find the percentages and angle measurement for each category.

Category	Frequency	Percent	Angle Measure
High School	30	24%	86.4
Associate	30	24%	86.4
Bachelor's	40	32%	115.2
Master's	20	16%	57.6
Doctorate	5	4%	14.4

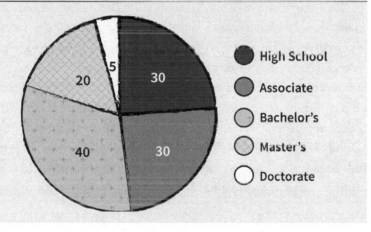

Scatter Plots

A scatter plot is displayed in the first quadrant of the *xy*-plane where all numbers are positive. Data points are plotted as ordered pairs, with one variable along the horizontal axis and the other along the vertical axis. Scatter plots can show if there is a correlation between two variables. There is a **POSITIVE CORRELATION** (expressed as a positive slope) if increasing one variable appears to result in an increase in the other variable. A **NEGATIVE CORRELATION** (expressed as a negative slope) occurs when an increase in one variable causes a decrease in the other. If the scatter plot shows no discernible pattern, then there is no correlation (a zero, mixed, or indiscernible slope).

Calculators or other software can be used to find the linear regression equation, which describes the general shape of the data. Graphing this equation produces the regression line, or line of best fit. The equation's **correlation coefficient** (*r*) can be used to determine how closely the equation fits the data. The value of r is between –1 and 1. The closer r is to 1 (if the line has a positive slope) or –1 (if the line has a negative slope), the better the regression line fits the data. The closer the r value is to 0, the weaker the correlation between the line and the data. Generally, if the absolute value of the correlation coefficient is 0.8 or higher, then it is considered to be a strong correlation, while an |r| value of less than 0.5 is considered a weak correlation.

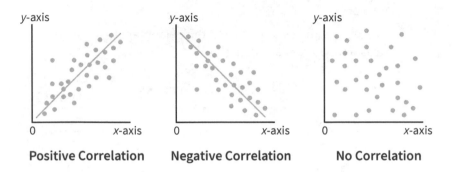

Figure 4.3. Scatter Plots and Correlation

To determine which curve is the "best fit" for a set of data, RESIDUALS are calculated. The calculator automatically calculates and saves these values to a list called RESID. These values are all the differences between the actual y-value of data points and the y-value calculated by the best-fit line or curve for that x-value. These values can be plotted on an xy-plane to produce a RESIDUAL PLOT. The residual plot helps determine if a line is the best model for the data. Residual points that are randomly dispersed above and below the horizontal indicate that a linear model is appropriate, while a u shape or upside-down u shape indicate a nonlinear model would be more appropriate.

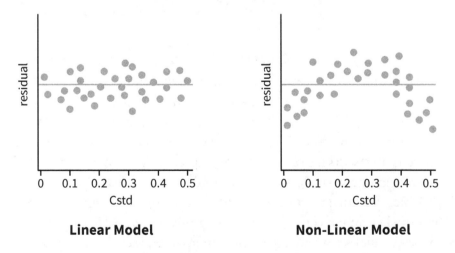

Figure 4.4. Residual Plots

Once a best-fit line is established, it can be used to estimate output values given an input value within the domain of the data. For a short extension outside that domain, reasonable predictions may be possible.

However, the further from the domain of the data the line is extended, the greater the reduction in the accuracy of the prediction.

It is important to note here that just because two variables have a strong positive or negative correlation, it cannot necessarily be inferred that those two quantities have a *causal* relationship—that is, that one variable changing *causes* the other quantity to change. There are often other factors that play into their relationship. For example, a positive correlation can be found between the number of ice cream sales and the number of shark attacks at a beach. It would be incorrect to say that selling more ice cream *causes* an increase in shark attacks. It is much more likely that on hot days more ice cream is sold, and many more people are swimming, so one of them is more likely to get attacked by a shark. Confusing correlation and causation is one of the most common statistical errors people make.

A graphing calculator can provide the regression line, r value, and residuals list.

EXAMPLE

Based on the scatter plot below, where the *x*-axis represents hours spent studying per week and the *y*-axis represents the average percent grade on exams during the school year, is there a correlation between the amount of studying for a test and test results?

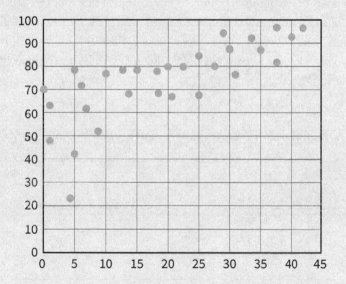

Answer:

There is a somewhat weak positive correlation. As the number of hours spent studying increases, the average percent grade also generally increases.

Line Graphs

Line graphs are used to display a relationship between two variables, such as change over time. Like scatter plots, line graphs exist in quadrant 1 of the *xy*-plane. Line graphs are constructed by graphing each point and connecting each point to the next consecutive point by a line. To create a line graph, it may be necessary to consolidate data into single bivariate data points. Thus, a line graph is a function, with each *x*-value having exactly one *y*-value, whereas a scatter plot may have multiple *y*-values for one *x*-value.

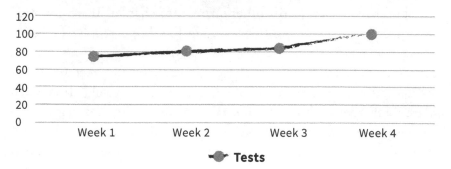

Figure 4.5. Line Graph

EXAMPLE

Create a line graph based on the following survey values, where the first column represents an individual's age and the other represents that individual's reported happiness level on a 20-point scale (0 being the least happy that person has been and 20 being the happiest). Then interpret the resulting graph to determine whether the following statement is true or false: *On average, middle-aged people are less happy than young or older people are.*

Age	Happiness
12	16
13	15
20	18
15	12
40	5
17	17
18	18
19	15
42	7
70	17
45	10
60	12
63	15
22	14
27	15

Age	Happiness
33	10
44	8
55	10
80	10
15	13
40	8
17	15
18	17
19	20
22	16
27	15
36	9
33	10
44	6

Answer:

To construct a line graph, the data must be ordered into consolidated categories by averaging the data of people who have the same age so that the data is one-to-one. For example, there are 2 twenty-two-year-olds who are reporting. Their average happiness level is 15. When all the data has been consolidated and ordered from least to greatest, the table and graph below can be presented.

Age	Happiness
12	16
13	15
15	12.5
17	16
18	17.5
19	17.5
20	18
22	15
27	15
33	10
36	10.5
40	6.5
42	7
44	7
45	10
55	10

Age	Happiness
60	12
63	15
70	17
80	10

Average Happiness Rating Versus Age

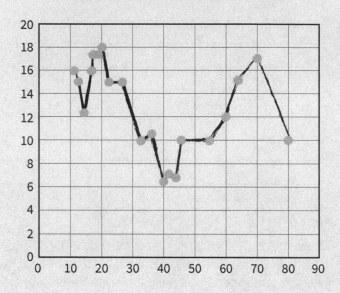

The statement that, on average, middle-aged people are less happy than young or older people appears to be true. According to the graph, people in their thirties, forties, and fifties are less happy than people in their teens, twenties, sixties, and seventies.

Bar Graphs

Bar graphs compare differences between categories or changes over a time. The data is grouped into categories or ranges and represented by rectangles. A bar graph's rectangles can be vertical or horizontal, depending on whether the dependent variable is placed on the *x*- or *y*-axis. Instead of the *xy*-plane, however, one axis is made up of categories (or ranges) instead of a numeric scale. Bar graphs are useful

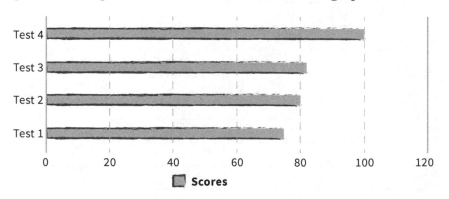

Figure 4.6. Bar Graph

because the differences between categories are easy to see: the height or length of each bar shows the value for each category.

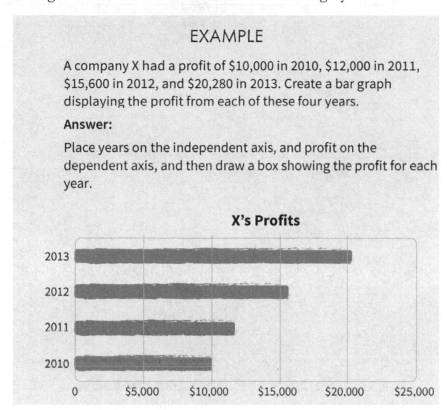
Stem-and-Leaf Plots

Stem-and-leaf plots are ways of organizing large amounts of data by grouping it into classes. All data points are broken into two parts: a stem and a leaf. For instance, the number 512 might be broken into a stem of 5 and a leaf of 12. All data in the 500 range would appear in the same row (this group of data is a class). Usually a simple key is provided to explain how the data is being represented. For instance, $5|12 = 512$ would show that the stems are representing hundreds. The advantage of this display is that it shows general density and shape of the data in a compact display, yet all original data points are preserved and available. It is also easy to find medians and quartiles from this display.

Stem	Leaf
0	5
1	6, 7
2	8, 3, 6
3	4, 5, 9, 5, 5, 8, 5
4	7, 7, 7, 8
5	5, 4
6	0

Figure 4.7. Stem and Leaf Plot

The table gives the weights of wrestlers (in pounds) for a certain competition. What is the mean, median, and IQR of the data?

2	05, 22, 53, 40
3	07, 22, 29, 45, 89, 96, 98
4	10, 25, 34
6	21

Key: 2|05 = 205 pounds

Answer:

$\mu = \dfrac{\Sigma x}{N}$ $= \dfrac{5281}{15}$ **= 353.1 lbs.**	Find the mean using the equation for the population mean.
Q1 = 253 Q2 = 345 Q3 = 410 IQR = 410 − 253 = 157 **The median is 345 lbs.** **The IQR is 157 lbs.**	Find the median and IQR by counting the leaves and identifying Q1, Q2, and Q3.

Frequency Tables and Histograms

The frequency of a particular data point is the number of times that data point occurs. Constructing a frequency table requires that the data or data classes be arranged in ascending order in one column and the frequency in another column.

A histogram is a graphical representation of a frequency table used to compare frequencies. A histogram is constructed in quadrant I of the *xy*-plane, with data in each equal-width class presented as a bar and the height of each bar representing the frequency of that class. Unlike bar graphs, histograms cannot have gaps between bars. A histogram is used to determine the distribution of data among the classes.

Histograms can be symmetrical, skewed left or right, or multimodal (data spread around). Note that SKEWED LEFT means the peak of the data is on the *right*, with a tail to the left, while SKEWED RIGHT means the peak is on the *left*, with a tail to the right. This seems counterintuitive to many; the "left" or "right" always refers to the tail of the data. This is because a long tail to the right, for example, means there are high outlier values that are skewing the data to the right.

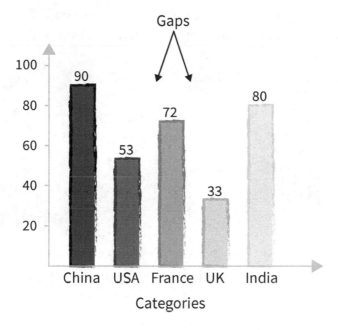

Bar Chart

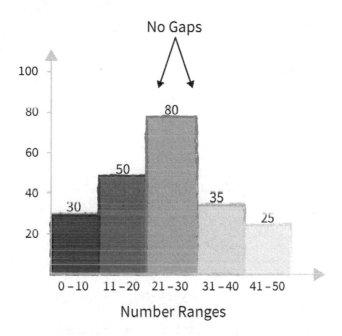

Histogram

Figure 4.8. Bar Chart vs. Histogram

A TWO-WAY FREQUENCY TABLE compares CATEGORICAL DATA (data in more than one category) of two related variables (bivariate data). Two-way frequency tables are also called CONTINGENCY TABLES and are often used to analyze survey results. One category is displayed along the top of the table and the other category down along the side. Rows and columns are added and the sums appear at the end of the row or column. The sum of all the row data must equal the sum of all the column data.

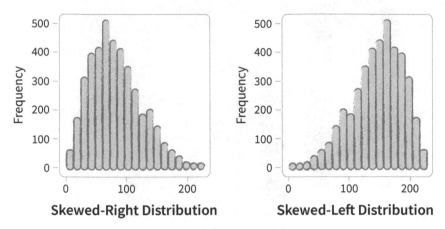

Figure 4.9. Histrograms

From a two-way frequency table, the JOINT RELATIVE FREQUENCY of a particular category can be calculated by taking the number in the row and column of the categories in question and dividing by the total number surveyed. This gives the percent of the total in that particular category. Sometimes the CONDITIONAL RELATIVE FREQUENCY is of interest. In this case, calculate the relative frequency confined to a single row or column.

Students by Grade and Gender

	9TH GRADE	10TH GRADE	11TH GRADE	12TH GRADE	TOTAL
Male	57	63	75	61	256
Female	54	42	71	60	227
Total	111	105	146	121	483

Figure 4.10. Two-Way Frequency Table

EXAMPLES

1) A café owner tracked the number of customers he had over a twelve-hour period in the following frequency table. Display the data in a histogram and determine what kind of distribution there is in the data.

TIME	NUMBER OF CUSTOMERS
6 a.m. – 8 a.m.	5
8 a.m. – 9 a.m.	6
9 a.m. – 10 a.m.	5
10 a.m. – 12 p.m.	23

Time	Number of Customers
12 p.m. – 2 p.m.	24
2 p.m. – 4 p.m.	9
4 p.m. – 6 p.m.	4

Answer:

Since time is the independent variable, it is on the *x*-axis and the number of customers is on the *y*-axis. For the histogram to correctly display data continuously, categories on the *x*-axis must be equal 2-hour segments. The 8 a.m. – 9 a.m. and 9 a.m. – 10 a.m. categories must be combined for a total of 11 customers in that time period. Although not perfectly symmetrical, the amount of customers peaks in the middle and is therefore considered symmetrical.

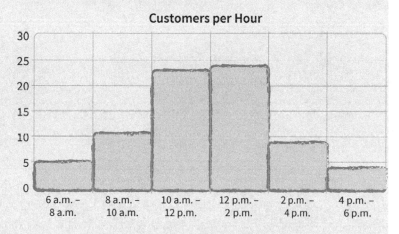

Customers per Hour

2) Cineflix movie theater polled its moviegoers on a weeknight to determine their favorite type of movie. The results are in the two-way frequency table below.

Moviegoers	Comedy	Action	Horror	Totals
Male	15	24	21	60
Female	8	18	17	43
Totals	23	42	38	103

Determine whether each of the following statements is true or false.

A. Action films are the most popular type of movie

B. About 1 in 5 moviegoers prefers comedy films

C. Men choose the horror genre more frequently than women do

Answer:

A. **True**. More people (42) chose action movies than comedy (23) or horror (38).

B. **True.** Find the ratio of total number of people who prefer comedy to total number of people. $\frac{23}{103} = 0.22$; 1 in 5 is 20% so 22% is about the same.

C. **False.** The percentage of men who choose horror is less than the percentage of women who do.

part = number of men who prefer horror =21

whole = number of men surveyed = 60

$percent = \frac{part}{whole}$

$= \frac{21}{60} = 0.35 = 35\%$

part = number of women who prefer horror =17

whole = number of women surveyed = 43

$percent = \frac{part}{whole}$

$= \frac{17}{43} = 0.40 = 40\%$

five

PROBABILITY

Set Theory

A **SET** is any collection of items. In mathematics, a set is represented by a capital letter and described inside curly brackets. For example, if S is the set of all integers less than 10, then $S = \{x|x$ is an integer and $x < 10\}$. The vertical bar | is read *such that*. The set that contains no elements is called the **EMPTY SET** or the **NULL SET** and is denoted by empty brackets { } or the symbol $\emptyset$.

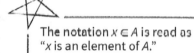

The notation $x \in A$ is read as "x is an element of A."

Usually there is a larger set that any specific problem is based in, called the **UNIVERSAL SET** or **U**. For example, in the set S described above, the universal set might be the set of all real numbers. The **COM-PLEMENT** of set A, denoted by $\overline{A}$ or A', is the set of all items in the universal set, but NOT in A. It can be helpful when working with sets to represent them with a **VENN DIAGRAM**.

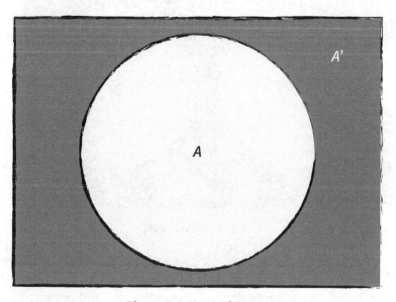

Figure 5.1. Venn Diagram

Oftentimes, the task will be working with multiple sets: A, B, C, etc. A UNION between two sets means that the data in both sets is combined into a single, larger set. The union of two sets, denoted $A \cup B$ contains all the data that is in either set A or set B or both (called an INCLUSIVE OR). If $A = \{1, 4, 7\}$ and $B = \{2, 4, 5, 8\}$, then $A \cup B = \{1, 2, 4, 5, 7, 8\}$ (notice 4 is included only once). The INTERSECTION of two sets, denoted $A \cap B$ includes only elements that are in both A and B. Thus, $A \cap B = \{4\}$ for the sets given above.

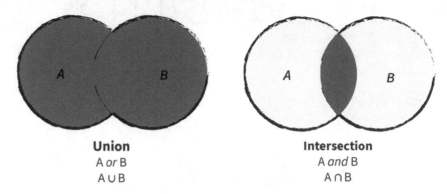

Union
A *or* B
A∪B

Intersection
A *and* B
A∩B

Figure 5.2. Unions and Intersections

If there is no common data in the sets in question, then the intersection is the null set. Two sets that have no elements in common (and thus have a null in the intersection set) are said to be DISJOINT. The DIFFERENCE $B - A$ or RELATIVE COMPLEMENT between two sets is the set of all the values that are in B, but not in A. For the sets defined above, $B - A = \{2, 5, 8\}$ and $A - B = \{1, 7\}$. The relative complement is sometimes denoted as $B \backslash A$.

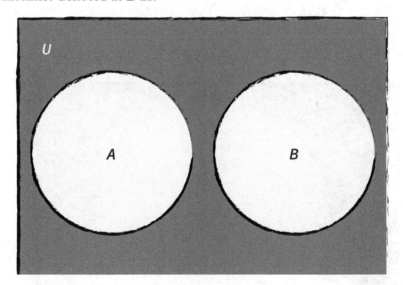

Figure 5.3. Disjoint Sets

Mathematical tasks often involve working with multiple sets. Just like numbers, sets and set operations have identities and properties.

Set Identities

$A \cup \varnothing = A$	$A \cup U = U$	$A \cup \overline{A} = U$
$A \cap \varnothing = A$	$A \cap U = A$	$A \cap \overline{A} = \varnothing$

Set Properties

Commutative Property	$A \cup B = B \cup A$	$A \cap B = B \cap A$
Associative Property	$A \cup (B \cup C) = (A \cup B) \cup C$	$A \cap (B \cap C) = (A \cap B) \cap C$
Distributive Property	$A \cup (B \cap C) = (A \cup B) \cap (A \cup C)$	$A \cap (B \cup C) = (A \cap B) \cup (A \cap C)$

De Morgan's Laws

$$\overline{(A \cup B)} = \overline{A} \cap \overline{B} \qquad \overline{(A \cap B)} = \overline{A} \cup \overline{B}$$

The number of elements in a set A is denoted $n(A)$. For the set A above, $n(A) = 3$, since there are three elements in that set. The number of elements in the union of two sets is $n(A \cup B) = n(A) + n(B) - n(A \cap B)$. Note that the number of elements in the intersection of the two sets must be subtracted because they are being counted twice, since they are both in set A and in set B. The number of elements in the complement of A is the number of elements in the universal set minus the number in set A: $n(\overline{A}) = n(U) - n(A)$.

It is helpful to note here how similar set theory is to the logic operators of the previous section: negation corresponds to complements, the "and" ($\wedge$) operator to intersection ($\cap$), and the "or" ($\vee$) operator to unions ($\cup$); notice even the symbols are similar.

EXAMPLES

1) Construct a Venn diagram depicting the intersection, if any, of $Y = \{x \mid x \text{ is an integer and } 0 < x < 9\}$ and $Z = \{-4, 0, 4, 8, 12, 16\}$.

   Answer:

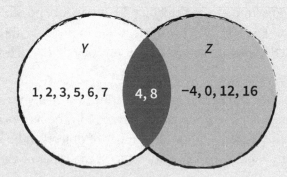

Probability

Probability describes how likely something is to happen. In probability, an **EVENT** is the single result of a trial, and an **OUTCOME** is a possible event that results from a trial. The collection of all possible outcomes for a particular trial is called the **SAMPLE SPACE**. For example, when rolling a die, the sample space is the numbers 1 – 6. Rolling a single number, such as 4, would be a single event.

Counting Principles

Counting principles are methods used to find the number of possible outcomes for a given situation. The **FUNDAMENTAL COUNTING PRINCIPLE** states that, for a series of independent events, the number of outcomes can be found by multiplying the number of possible outcomes for each event. For example, if a die is rolled (6 possible outcomes) and a coin is tossed (2 possible outcomes), there are 6 × 2 = 12 total possible outcomes.

Combinations and permutations describe how many ways a number of objects taken from a group can be arranged. The number of objects in the group is written n, and the number of objects to be arranged is represented by r (or k). In a **COMBINATION**, the order of the selections does not matter because every available slot to be filled is the same. Examples of combinations include:

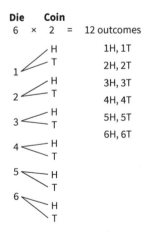

Figure 5.4. Fundamental Counting Principle

- picking 3 people from a group of 12 to form a committee (220 possible committees)
- picking 3 pizza toppings from 10 options (120 possible pizzas)

In a **PERMUTATION**, the order of the selection matters, meaning each available slot is different. Examples of permutations include:

- handing out gold, silver, and bronze medals in a race with 100 participants (970,200 possible combinations)
- selecting a president, vice-president, secretary, and treasurer from among a committee of 12 people (11,880 possible combinations)

The formulas for the both calculations are similar. The only difference—the $r!$ in the denominator of a combination—accounts for redundant outcomes. Note that both permutations and combinations can be written in several different shortened notations.

$$\text{Permutation: } P(n, r) = {}_nP_r = \frac{n!}{(n-r)!}$$

$$\text{Combination: } C(n, r) = {}_nC_r = \binom{n}{r} = \frac{n!}{(n-r)!r!}$$

EXAMPLES

1) A personal assistant is struggling to pick a shirt, tie, and cufflink set that go together. If his client has 70 shirts, 2 ties, and 5 cufflinks, how many possible combinations does he have to consider?

   Answer:

   Multiply the number of outcomes for each individual event:

   $(70)(2)(5) = $ **700 outfits**

2) If there are 20 applicants for 3 open positions, in how many different ways can a team of 3 be hired?

   Answer:

   The order of the items doesn't matter, so use the formula for combinations:

   $$C(n, r) = \frac{n!}{(n-r)!r!}$$

   $$C(20, 3) = \frac{20!}{(20-3)!3!}$$

   $$= \frac{20!}{(17!3!)}$$

   $$= \frac{(20)(19)(18)}{3!} = \textbf{1140 possible teams}$$

3) Calculate the number of unique permutations that can be made with five of the letters in the word *pickle*.

   Answer:

   To find the number of unique permutations of 5 letters in pickle, use the permutation formula:

$$P(n,r) = \frac{n!}{(n-r)!}$$

$$P(6,5) = \frac{6!}{(6-5)!}$$

$$= \frac{720}{1} = \mathbf{720}$$

4) Find the number of permutations that can be made out of all the letters in the word *cheese*.

Answer:

The letter *e* repeats 3 times in the word *cheese*, meaning some permutations of the 6 letters will be indistinguishable from others. The number of permutations must be divided by the number of ways the three *e*'s can be arranged to account for these redundant outcomes:

$$total\ number\ of\ permutations = \frac{number\ of\ ways\ of\ arranging\ 6\ letters}{number\ of\ ways\ of\ arranging\ 3\ letters}$$

$$= \frac{6!}{3!} = 6 \times 5 \times 4 = \mathbf{120}$$

Probability of a Single Event

The probability of a single event occurring is the number of outcomes in which that event occurs (called **FAVORABLE EVENTS**) divided by the number of items in the sample space (total possible outcomes):

$$P\,(an\ event) = \frac{number\ of\ favorable\ outcomes}{total\ number\ of\ possible\ outcomes}$$

The probability of any event occurring will always be a fraction or decimal between 0 and 1. It may also be expressed as a percent. An event with 0 probability will never occur and an event with a probability of 1 is certain to occur. The probability of an event not occurring is referred to as that event's **COMPLEMENT**. The sum of an event's probability and the probability of that event's complement will always be 1.

EXAMPLES

1) What is the probability that an even number results when a six-sided die is rolled? What is the probability the die lands on 5?

Answer:

$$P(rolling\ even) = \frac{number\ of\ favorable\ outcomes}{total\ number\ of\ possible\ outcomes} = \frac{3}{6} = \frac{1}{2}$$

$$P(rolling\ 5) = \frac{number\ of\ favorable\ outcomes}{total\ number\ of\ possible\ outcomes} = \mathbf{\frac{1}{6}}$$

2) Only 20 tickets were issued in a raffle. If someone were to buy 6 tickets, what is the probability that person would not win the raffle?

Answer:

$$P(not\ winning) = \frac{number\ of\ favorable\ outcomes}{total\ number\ of\ possible\ outcomes} = \frac{14}{20} = \frac{7}{10}$$

or

$$P(not\ winning) = 1 - P(winning) = 1 - \frac{6}{20} = \frac{14}{20} = \mathbf{\frac{7}{10}}$$

3) A bag contains 26 tiles representing the 26 letters of the English alphabet. If 3 tiles are drawn from the bag without replacement, what is the probability that all 3 will be consonants?

Answer:

$$P = \frac{number\ of\ favorable\ outcomes}{total\ number\ of\ possible\ outcomes}$$

$$= \frac{number\ of\ 3\text{-}consonant\ combinations}{number\ of\ 3\text{-}tile\ combinations}$$

$$= \frac{{}_{21}C_3}{{}_{26}C_3}$$

$$= \frac{1330}{2600}$$

$$= 0.511 = \mathbf{51\%}$$

Probability of Multiple Events

If events are **INDEPENDENT**, the probability of one occurring does not affect the probability of the other event occurring. Rolling a die and getting one number does not change the probability of getting any particular number on the next roll. The number of faces has not changed, so these are independent events.

If events are **DEPENDENT**, the probability of one occurring changes the probability of the other event occurring. Drawing a card from a deck without replacing it will affect the probability of the next card drawn because the number of available cards has changed.

To find the probability that two or more independent events will occur (*A* and *B*), simply multiply the probabilities of each individual event together. To find the probability that one, the other, or both will occur (*A* or *B*), it's necessary to add their probabilities and then subtract their overlap (which prevents the same values from being counted twice).

CONDITIONAL PROBABILITY is the probability of an event occurring given that another event has occurred. The notation $P(B|A)$ represents the probability that event *B* occurs, given that event *A* has already occurred (it is read "probability of *B*, given *A*").

When drawing objects, the phrase *with replacement* describes independent events, and *without replacement* describes dependent events.

Table 5.1. Probability Formulas

INDEPENDENT EVENTS		**DEPENDENT EVENTS**
Intersection *and*	Union *or*	Conditional
$P(A \cap B) = P(A) \times P(B)$	$P(A \cup B) = P(A) + P(B) - P(A \cap B)$	$P(B|A) = \frac{P(A \cap B)}{P(A)}$

Two events that are MUTUALLY EXCLUSIVE CANNOT happen at the same time. This is similar to disjoint sets in set theory. The probability that two mutually exclusive events will occur is zero. MUTUALLY INCLUSIVE events share common outcomes.

EXAMPLES

1) A card is drawn from a standard 52 card deck. What is the probability that it is either a queen or a heart?

   Answer:

   This is a union (*or*) problem.

   $P(A)$ = the probability of drawing a queen = $\frac{1}{13}$

   $P(B)$ = the probability of drawing a heart = $\frac{1}{4}$

   $P(A \cap B)$ = the probability of drawing a heart and a queen = $\frac{1}{52}$

   $P(A \cup B) = P(A) + P(B) - P(A \cap B)$

   $= \frac{1}{13} + \frac{1}{4} - \frac{1}{52}$

   $= \mathbf{0.31}$

2) A group of ten individuals is drawing straws from a group of 28 long straws and 2 short straws. If the straws are not replaced, what is the probability, as a percentage, that neither of the first two individuals will draw a short straw?

   Answer:

   This scenario includes two events, A and B.

   The probability of the first person drawing a long straw is an independent event:

   $P(A) = \frac{28}{30}$

   The probability the second person draws a long straw changes because one long straw has already been drawn. In other words, it is the probability of event B given that event A has already happened:

   $P(B|A) = \frac{27}{29}$

   The conditional probability formula can be used to determine the probability of both people drawing long straws:

   $P(A \cap B) = P(A)P(B|A)$

   $= \left(\frac{28}{30}\right)\left(\frac{27}{29}\right)$

   $= 0.87$

   There is an **87% chance** that neither of the first two individuals will draw short straws.

PART II: READING

six

READING

The Main Idea

The **MAIN IDEA** of a text describes the author's main topic and general concept; it also generalizes the author's point of view about a subject. It is contained within and throughout the text. The reader can easily find the main idea by considering how the main topic is addressed throughout a passage. In the reading test, the expectation is not only to identify the main idea but also to differentiate it from a text's theme and to summarize the main idea clearly and concisely.

The main idea is closely connected to topic sentences and how they are supported in a text. Questions may deal with finding topic sentences, summarizing a text's ideas, or locating supporting details. The sections and practice examples that follow detail the distinctions between these aspects of text.

Identifying the Main Idea

To identify the main idea, first identify the topic. The difference between these two things is simple: the **TOPIC** is the overall subject matter of a passage; the **MAIN IDEA** is what the author wants to say about that topic. The main idea covers the author's direct perspective about a topic, as distinct from the **THEME**, which is a generally true idea that the reader might derive from a text. Most of the time, fiction has a theme, whereas nonfiction has a main idea. This is the case because in a nonfiction text, the author speaks more directly to the audience about a topic—his or her perspective is more visible. For example, the following passage conveys the topic as well as what the author wants to communicate about that topic.

The author's perspective on the subject of the text and how he or she has framed the argument or story hints at the main idea. For example, if the author framed the story with a description, image, or short anecdote, this suggests a particular idea or point of view.

> The "shark mania" of recent years can be largely pinned on the sensationalistic media surrounding the animals: from the release of *Jaws* in 1975 to the week of ultra-

hyped shark feeding frenzies and "worst shark attacks" countdowns known as Shark Week, popular culture both demonizes and fetishizes sharks until the public cannot get enough. Swimmers and beachgoers may look nervously for the telltale fin skimming the surface, but the reality is that shark bites are extremely rare and they are almost never unprovoked. Sharks attack people at very predictable times and for very predictable reasons. Rough surf, poor visibility, or a swimmer sending visual and physical signals that mimic a shark's normal prey are just a few examples.

Of course, some places are just more dangerous to swim. Shark attack "hot spots," such as the coasts of Florida, South Africa, and New Zealand try a variety of solutions to protect tourists and surfers. Some beaches employ "shark nets," meant to keep sharks away from the beach, though these are controversial because they frequently trap other forms of marine life as well. Other beaches use spotters in helicopters and boats to alert beach officials when there are sharks in the area. In addition, there is an array of products that claim to offer personal protection from sharks, ranging from wetsuits in different colors to devices that broadcast electrical signals in an attempt to confuse the sharks' sensory organs. At the end of the day, though, beaches like these remain dangerous, and swimmers must assume the risk every time they paddle out from shore.

Readers should identify the topic of a text and pay attention to how the details about it relate to one another. A passage may discuss, for example, topic similarities, characteristics, causes, and/or effects.

The author of this passage has a clear topic: sharks and the relationship between humans and sharks. In order to identify the main idea of the passage, the reader must ask what the author wants to say about this topic, what the reader is meant to think or understand. The author makes sure to provide information about several different aspects of the relationship between sharks and humans, and points out that humans must respect sharks as dangerous marine animals, without sensationalizing the risk of attack. This conclusion results from looking at the various pieces of information the author includes as well as the similarities between them. The passage describes sensationalistic media, then talks about how officials and governments try to protect beaches, and ends with the observation that people must take personal responsibility. These details clarify what the author's main idea is. Summarizing that main idea by focusing on the connection between the different details helps the reader draw a conclusion.

EXAMPLES

The art of the twentieth and twenty-first centuries demonstrates several aspects of modern societal advancement. A primary example is the advent and ascendancy of technology: New technologies have developed new avenues for art making, and the globalization brought about by the Internet has both diversified the art world and brought it together simultaneously. Even as artists are able to engage in a global conversation about the categories and characteristics of art, creating a more uniform understanding, they can now express themselves in a diversity of ways for a diversity of audiences. The result has been a rapid change in how art is made and consumed.

1) This passage is primarily concerned with

   A. the importance of art in the twenty-first century.

   B. the use of art to communicate overarching ideals to diverse communities.

   C. the importance of technology to art criticism.

   D. the change in understanding and creation of art in the modern period.

   Answers:

   A. is incorrect. The focus of the passage is what the art of the twentieth and twenty-first centuries demonstrates.

   B. is incorrect. Although the passage mentions a diversity of audiences, it discusses the artists expressing themselves, not attempting to communicate overarching ideals.

   C. is incorrect. The passage discusses how new technologies have "developed new avenues for art making," but nothing about criticism.

   D. is correct. The art of the modern period reflects the new technologies and globalization possible through the Internet.

2) Which of the following best describes the main idea of the passage?

   A. Modern advances in technology have diversified art making and connected artists to distant places and ideas.

   B. Diversity in modern art is making it harder for art viewers to understand and talk about that art.

   C. The use of technology to discuss art allows us to create standards for what art should be.

   D. Art making before the invention of technology such as the Internet was disorganized and poorly understood.

Topic and Summary Sentences

Identifying the main idea requires understanding the structure of a piece of writing. In a short passage of one or two paragraphs, the topic and summary sentences quickly relate what the paragraphs are about and what conclusions the author wants the reader to draw. These sentences function as bookends to a paragraph or passage, telling readers what to think and keeping the passage tied tightly together.

Generally, the **TOPIC SENTENCE** is the first, or very near the first, sentence in a paragraph. It is a general statement that introduces the topic, clearly and specifically directing the reader to access any previous experience with that topic.

The **SUMMARY SENTENCE**, on the other hand, frequently—but not always!—comes at the end of a paragraph or passage, because it wraps up all the ideas presented. This sentence provides an understanding of what the author wants to say about the topic and what conclusions to draw about it. While a topic sentence acts as an introduction to a topic, allowing the reader to activate his or her own ideas and experiences, the summary statement asks the reader to accept the author's ideas about that topic. Because of this, a summary sentence helps the reader quickly identify a piece's main idea.

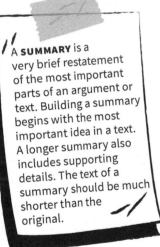

A **SUMMARY** is a very brief restatement of the most important parts of an argument or text. Building a summary begins with the most important idea in a text. A longer summary also includes supporting details. The text of a summary should be much shorter than the original.

EXAMPLES

Altogether, Egypt is a land of tranquil monotony. The eye commonly travels either over a waste of waters, or over a green plain unbroken by elevations. The hills which inclose (*sic*) the Nile valley have level tops, and sides that are bare of trees, or shrubs, or flowers, or even mosses. The sky is generally cloudless. No fog or mist enwraps the distance in mystery; no rainstorm sweeps across the scene; no rainbow spans the empyrean; no shadows chase each other over the landscape. There is an entire absence of picturesque scenery.

A single broad river, unbroken within the limits of Egypt even by a rapid, two flat strips of green plain at its side, two low lines of straight-topped hills beyond them, and a boundless open space where the river divides itself into half a dozen sluggish branches before reaching the sea, constitute Egypt, which is by nature a southern Holland—"weary, stale, flat and unprofitable."

—from *Ancient Egypt* by George Rawlinson

1) Which of the following best explains the general idea and focus indicated by the topic sentence?

   A. Egypt is a boring place without much to do.

   B. The land of Egypt is undisturbed; the reader will read on to find out what makes it so dull.

   C. Egypt is a peaceful place; its people live with a sense of predictability.

   D. The land of Egypt is quiet; the reader wants to know what is missing.

Answers:

A. is incorrect. The word *monotony* does suggest the idea of being bored; however, the focus is the land of Egypt, not what people have to do. In addition, tranquility is part of the general idea.

B. is correct. This option indicates both the main idea and what the reader will focus on while reading.

C. is incorrect. This option leaves out what the focus will be.

D. is incorrect. This option leaves out the general idea of monotony.

2) Which of the following best states what the author wants the reader to understand after reading the summary sentence?

   A. There is not much to get excited about while visiting Egypt.

   B. Egypt is a poverty-stricken wasteland.

   C. The land of Egypt is worn out from overuse.

   D. The land of Egypt lacks anything fresh or inspiring.

Answers:

A. is incorrect. The summary describes the place, not a visit to the place.

B. is incorrect. The word *unprofitable* suggests that the land of Egypt is unrewarding, not poverty stricken.

C. is incorrect. The reason the land is stale and weary may not be due to overuse. This summary describes; it does not explain the reasons the land is worn.

D. is correct. The words *weary*, *stale*, and *unprofitable* suggest a lack of freshness or anything that stimulates enthusiasm.

Supporting Details

Between a topic sentence and a summary sentence, the rest of a paragraph is built with SUPPORTING DETAILS. Supporting details come in many forms; the purpose of the passage dictates the type of details that will support the main idea. A persuasive passage may use facts and data or detail specific reasons for the author's opinion. An informative passage will primarily use facts about the topic to support the main idea. Even a narrative passage will have supporting details—specific things the author says to develop the story and characters.

The most important aspect of supporting details is exactly what the term states: They support the main idea. Examining the various supporting details and how they work with one another will solidify how the author views a topic and what the main idea of the passage is. Supporting details are key to understanding a passage.

Identifying Supporting Details

How can the reader identify the most important pieces of information in a passage? Supporting details build an argument and contain the concepts upon which the main idea rests. While supporting details will help the reader determine the main idea, it is actually easier to find the most important supporting details by first understanding the main idea; the pieces that make up the main argument then become clear.

SIGNAL WORDS—transitions and conjunctions—explain to the reader how one sentence or idea is connected to another. These words and phrases can be anywhere in a sentence, and it is important to understand what each signal word means. Signal words can add information, provide counterarguments, create organization in a passage, or draw conclusions. Some common signal words include *in particular*, *in addition*, *besides*, *contrastingly*, *therefore*, and *because*.

EXAMPLES

The war is inevitable—and let it come! I repeat it, sir, let it come! It is in vain, sir, to extenuate the matter. Gentlemen may cry, "Peace! Peace!"—but there is no peace. The war is actually begun! The next gale that sweeps from the north will bring to our ears the clash of resounding arms! Our brethren are already in the field! Why stand we here idle? What is it that gentlemen wish? What would they have? Is life so dear, or peace so sweet, as to be purchased at the price of chains and slavery? Forbid it, Almighty God! I know not what course others may take; but as for me, give me liberty or give me death!

—from "Give Me Liberty or Give Me Death" speech by Patrick Henry

---

1) In the fourth sentence of the text, the word *but* signals

A. an example.

B. a consequence.

C. an exception.

D. a counterargument.

Answers:

A. is incorrect. The author includes an example that the war has begun when he says "Our brethren are already in the field!" The word *but* does not signal this example.

B. is incorrect. The phrase "but there is no peace" is a fact, not a consequence.

C. is incorrect. In order to be an exception, the word *but* would have to be preceded by a general point or observation. In this case, *but* is preceded by a demand for peace.

D. is correct. The argument or claim that the country should be at peace precedes the word *but*. *But* counters the demand for peace with the argument that there is no peace; the war has begun.

2) What argument does the author use to support his main point?

A. Life in slavery is not the goal of the country.

B. To die bravely is worthwhile.

C. Life without freedom is intolerable.

D. The cost of going to war is too great.

Answers:

A. is incorrect. The main point is that the country has to go to war with England to be free. The author does not support his point with a discussion of the goals of the country.

B. is incorrect. This does not relate to the main point of going to war.

C. is correct. The author indicates that life is not so dear, or peace so sweet, "as to be purchased at the price of chains and slavery."

D. is incorrect. This is inaccurate. The author insists that the cost of not fighting for freedom is too great.

Evaluating Supporting Details

Besides using supporting details to help understand a main idea, the reader must evaluate them for relevance and inconsistency. An author selects details to help organize a passage and support its main idea. Sometimes, the author's bias results in details left out that don't directly support the main idea or that support an opposite idea. The reader has to be able to notice not only what the author says but also what the author leaves out.

To understand how a supporting detail relates to the main idea, the purpose of the passage should be discerned: what the author is trying to communicate and what the author wants from the reader. Every passage has a specific goal, and each paragraph in a passage is meant to support that goal. For each supporting detail, the position in the text, the signal words, and the specific content work together to alert the reader to the relationship between the supporting ideas and the main idea.

Close reading involves noticing the striking features of a text. For example, does a point made in the text appeal to the reader's sense of justice? Does a description seem rather exaggerated or overstated? Do certain words—such as *agonizing*—seem emotive? Are rhetorical questions being used to lead the reader to a certain conclusion?

Though the author generally includes details that support the text's main idea, the reader must decide how those details relate to one another as well as find any gaps in the support of the author's argument. This is particularly important in a persuasive piece of writing, when an author may allow bias to show through. Discovering the author's bias and how the supporting details reveal that bias is also key to understanding a text.

EXAMPLES

In England in the 'fifties came the Crimean War, with the deep stirring of national feeling which accompanied it, and the passion of gratitude and admiration which was poured forth on Miss Florence Nightingale for her work on behalf of our wounded soldiers. It was universally felt that there was work for women, even in war—the work of cleansing, setting in order, breaking down red tape, and soothing the vast sum of human suffering which every war is bound to cause. Miss Nightingale's work in war was work that never had been done until women came forward to do it, and her message to her countrywomen was educate yourselves, prepare, make ready; never imagine that your task can be done by instinct, without training and preparation. Painstaking study, she insisted, was just as necessary as a preparation for women's work as for men's work; and she bestowed the whole of the monetary gift offered her by the gratitude of the nation to form training-schools for nurses at St. Thomas's and King's College Hospitals.

—from *Women's Suffrage: A Short History of a Great Movement* by Millicent Garrett Fawcett

1) Which of the following best states the bias of the passage?

    A.   Society underestimates the capacity of women.

    B.   Generally, women are not prepared to make substantial contributions to society.

    C.   If women want power, they need to prove themselves.

    D.   One strong woman cannot represent all women.

Answers:

A. is correct. The author is suggesting that the work Florence Nightingale did had not been done before women came forward. Up till that point, what a woman could do had not been recognized.

B. is incorrect. This fact may have been true at the time this text was written, but only because educational opportunities were not available to women, and women were not encouraged to develop their abilities. Including this fact reveals the bias that women should be granted opportunities to train and to contribute.

C. is incorrect. This option does not apply; Florence Nightingale did more than prove herself.

D. is incorrect. The fact that Florence Nightingale donated the money awarded her to the training of women indicates that other women were preparing themselves to contribute.

2) Which of the following best summarizes what the author left out of the passage?

    A.   Women can fight in wars.

    B.   Other women should be recognized.

    C.   Women need to stop wasting time giving speeches at conventions and start proving themselves.

    D.   Without the contributions of women, society suffers.

Answers:

A. is incorrect. "It was universally felt that there was work for women, even in war" suggests that women had much to offer and didn't need to be sheltered; however, "there was work" does not mean the author thought women should engage in combat.

B. is incorrect. Since the passage is specifically about Florence Nightingale, nothing in it suggests the author included information about what other women did.

C. is incorrect. Information about women's suffrage conventions is unrelated to the topic of the paragraph.

D. is correct. The author emphasizes that "Miss Nightingale's work in war was work that never had been done until women came forward to do it."

Facts and Opinions

Authors use both facts and opinions as supporting details. While it is usually a simple task to identify the two, authors may mix facts with opinions or state an opinion as if it were a fact. The difference between the two is simple: A **fact** is a piece of information that can be verified as true or false, and it retains the quality of truthfulness or falsity no matter who verifies it. An **opinion** reflects a belief held by the author and may or may not be something each reader agrees with.

To distinguish between fact and opinion, the reader should rely on what can be proven. Subjectivity is determined by asking if an observation varies according to the situation or the person observing.

EXAMPLES

I remember thinking how comfortable it was, this division of labor which made it unnecessary for me to study fogs, winds, tides, and navigation, in order to visit my friend who lived across an arm of the sea. It was good that men should be specialists, I mused. The peculiar knowledge of the pilot and captain sufficed for many thousands of people who knew no more of the sea and navigation than I knew. On the other hand, instead of having to devote my energy to the learning of a multitude of things, I concentrated it upon a few particular things, such as, for instance, the analysis of Poe's place in American literature—an essay of mine, by the way, in the current *Atlantic*. Coming aboard, as I passed through the cabin, I had noticed with greedy eyes a stout gentleman reading the *Atlantic*, which was open at my very essay. And there it was again, the division of labor, the special knowledge of the pilot and captain which permitted the stout gentleman to read my special knowledge on Poe while they carried him safely from Sausalito to San Francisco.

—from *The Sea-Wolf* by Jack London

1) Which of the following best summarizes an opinion stated by the narrator?

   A. Poe has a place in American literature.

   B. People have the time to read magazines like the *Atlantic* because there are other people to take care of other tasks.

   C. The narrator has no knowledge of the sea and navigation.

   D. Division of labor is a beneficial practice.

Answers:

A. is incorrect. This is a fact. The *significance* of Poe's place in American literature is an opinion.

B. is incorrect. This is a fact. The reader is expected to agree with the point that if someone else had not been managing the boat, the people who wanted to get across the water would have had to do the work of getting themselves across.

C. is incorrect. This is a fact. The narrator admits to "this division of labor which made it unnecessary for me to study fogs, winds, tides, and navigation."

D. is correct. The narrator provides several facts proving that he and the other passengers benefit from the specialized knowledge and labor of others.

2) Which of the following is an opinion expressed by the narrator that is not supported by facts within the passage?

A. People should live life focusing on and learning about only a few things.

B. Having general knowledge is good.

C. He has time to focus on writing about literature.

D. People depend on other people.

Answers:

A. is correct. When the narrator says "instead of having to devote my energy to the learning of a multitude of things, I concentrated it upon a few particular things," he conveys his view that he does not have to learn much. There are no facts to support the view that he has to learn only a few particular things in life.

B. is incorrect. The narrator does not express this opinion. He is speaking about specialized knowledge.

C. is incorrect. This is a fact that the narrator shares about his life.

D. is incorrect. The passage does offer facts to support this; both the narrator and the passenger reading depend on the pilot to navigate the boat safely.

Text Structure

The structure of a text determines how the reader understands the argument and how the various details interact to form the argument. There are many ways to arrange text, and various types of arrangements have distinct characteristics.

The organizing structure of a passage is defined by the order in which the author presents information and the transitions used to connect those pieces. Problem-and-solution and cause-and-effect structures use transitions that show causal relationships: *because, as a result, consequently, therefore.* These two types of structures may also use transitions that show contradiction. A problem-and-solution structure may provide alternative solutions; a cause-and-effect structure may explain alternative causes: *however, alternatively, although.*

Authors often use repetition to reinforce an idea, including repeated words, phrases, or images.

Specific text structures include not only problem and solution and cause and effect but also compare and contrast, descriptive, order of importance, and chronological. When analyzing a text, the reader should consider how text structure influences the author's meaning. Most important, the reader needs to be aware of how an author emphasizes an idea by the way he or she presents information. For instance, including a contrasting idea makes a central idea stand out, and including a series of concrete examples creates a force of facts to support an argument.

EXAMPLES

It was the green heart of the canyon, where the walls swerved back from the rigid plan and relieved their harshness of line by making a little sheltered nook and filling it to the brim with sweetness and roundness and softness. Here all things rested. Even the narrow stream ceased its turbulent down-rush long enough to form a quiet pool....On one side, beginning at the very lip of the pool, was a tiny meadow, a cool, resilient surface of green that extended to the base of the frowning wall. Beyond the pool a gentle slope of earth ran up and up to meet the opposing wall. Fine grass covered the slope—grass that was spangled with flowers, with here and there patches of color, orange and purple and golden. Below, the canyon was shut in. There was no view. The walls leaned together abruptly and the canyon ended in a chaos of rocks, moss-covered and hidden by a green screen of vines and creepers and boughs of trees. Up the canyon rose far hills and peaks, the big foothills, pine-covered and remote. And far beyond, like clouds upon the border of the slay, towered minarets of white, where the Sierra's eternal snows flashed austerely the blazes of the sun.

—from "All Gold Canyon" by Jack London

1) The organizational structure of the passage is

   A. order of importance.

   B. cause and effect.

   C. problem and solution.

   D. descriptive.

Answers:

A. is incorrect. A series of reasons is not presented from most to least or least to most important. The passage describes a restful nook in the canyon.

B. is incorrect. The passage does not explain the origin of this nook or its effect on anything, although the reader understands from the details what makes the nook so restful.

C. is incorrect. The description of the nook presents no problem, although time in the nook could be seen as a solution for many problems.

Drawing Conclusions

Reading text begins with making sense of the explicit meanings of information or a narrative. Understanding occurs as the reader draws conclusions and makes logical inferences. To draw a conclusion, the reader considers the details or facts. He or she then comes to a conclusion—the next logical point in the thought sequence. For example, in a Hemingway story, an old man sits alone in a café. A young waiter says that the café is closing, but the old man continues to drink. The waiter starts closing up, and the old man signals for a refill. Based on these details, the reader might conclude that the old man has not understood the young waiter's desire for him to leave.

An inference is distinguished from a conclusion drawn. An INFERENCE is an assumption the reader makes based on details in the text as well as his or her own knowledge. It is more of an educated guess that extends the literal meaning. Inferences begin with the given details; however, the reader uses the facts to determine additional facts.

What the reader already knows informs what is being suggested by the details of decisions or situations in the text. Returning to the example of the Hemingway story, the reader might infer that the old man is lonely, enjoys being in the café, and is reluctant to leave.

When reading fictional text, inferring character motivations is essential. The actions of the characters move the plot forward; a series of events is understood by making sense of why the characters did what they did. Hemingway includes contrasting details as the young waiter and an older waiter discuss the old man.

The older waiter sympathizes with the old man; both men have no one at home and experience a sense of emptiness in life, which motivates them to seek the café.

Another aspect of understanding text is connecting it to other texts. Readers may connect the Hemingway story about the old man in the café to other Hemingway stories about individuals struggling to deal with loss and loneliness in a dignified way. They can extend their initial connections to people they know or their personal experiences. When readers read a persuasive text, they often connect the arguments made to counterarguments and opposing evidence of which they are aware. They use these connections to infer meaning.

When considering a character's motivations, the reader should ask what the character wants to achieve, what the character will get by accomplishing this, and what the character seems to value the most.

Conclusions are drawn by thinking about how the author wants the reader to feel. A group of carefully selected facts can cause the reader to feel a certain way.

EXAMPLES

I believe it is difficult for those who publish their own memoirs to escape the imputation of vanity; nor is this the only disadvantage under which they labor: it is also their misfortune, that what is uncommon is rarely, if ever, believed, and what is obvious we are apt to turn from with disgust, and to charge the writer with impertinence. People generally think those memoirs only worthy to be read or remembered which abound in great or striking events, those, in short, which in a high degree excite either admiration or pity: all others they consign to contempt and oblivion. It is therefore, I confess, not a little hazardous in a private and obscure individual, and a stranger too, thus to solicit the indulgent attention of the public; especially when I own I offer here the history of neither a saint, a hero, nor a tyrant. I believe there are few events in my life, which have not happened to many: it is true the incidents of it are numerous; and, did I consider myself an European, I might say my sufferings were great: but when I compare my lot with that of most of my countrymen, I regard myself as a *particular favorite of Heaven*, and acknowledge the mercies of Providence in every occurrence of my life. If then the following narrative does not appear sufficiently interesting to engage general attention, let my motive be some excuse for its publication. I am not so foolishly vain as to expect from it either immortality or literary reputation. If it affords any satisfaction to my numerous friends, at whose request it has been written, or in the smallest degree promotes the interests of humanity, the ends for which it was undertaken will be fully attained, and every wish of my heart gratified. Let it therefore be remembered, that, in wishing to avoid censure, I do not aspire to praise.

—from *The Interesting Narrative of the Life of Olaudah Equiano, or Gustavus Vassa, The African* by Olaudah Equiano

1) Which of the following best explains the primary motivation of the narrator?

   A. He wants his audience to know that he is not telling his story out of vanity.

   B. He is hoping people will praise his courage.

   C. He wants to give credit to God for protecting him.

   D. He is not seeking personal notoriety; he is hoping people will be influenced by his story and the human condition will improve.

   Answers:

   A. is incorrect. That motive is how the passage begins, but it is not his primary motive.

   B. is incorrect. He says he does not aspire to praise, and he does not suggest that he was courageous.

   C. is incorrect. He does state that the "mercies of Providence" were always with him; however, that acknowledgement is not his primary motive.

   D. Is correct. In the passage "If It…In the smallest degree promotes the interests of humanity, the ends for which it was undertaken will be fully attained, and every wish of my heart gratified," the narrator's use of the word *humanity* could mean he wants to improve the human condition or he wants to increase human benevolence, or brotherly love.

2) Given the details of what the narrator says he is *not*, as well as what he claims his story is *not*, it can be inferred that his experience was

   A. a story that could lead to his success.

   B. an amazing story of survival and struggle that will be unfamiliar to many readers.

   C. an adventure that will thrill the audience.

   D. a narrow escape from suffering.

   Answers:

   A. is incorrect. The narrator says that what is obvious in his story is what people "are apt to turn from with disgust, and to charge the writer with impertinence." The narrator is telling a story that his audience couldn't disagree with and might consider rude.

Understanding the Author

Many questions on the Praxis Reading test will ask for an interpretation of an author's intentions and ideas. This requires an examination of the author's perspective and purpose as well as the way the author uses language to communicate these things.

In every passage, an author chooses words, structures, and content with specific purpose and intent. With this in mind, the reader can begin to comprehend why an author opts for particular words and structures and how these ultimately relate to the content.

The Author's Purpose

The author of a passage sets out with a specific goal in mind: to communicate a particular idea to an audience. The **AUTHOR'S PURPOSE** is determined by asking why the author wants the reader to understand the passage's main idea. There are four basic purposes to which an author can write: narrative, expository, technical, and persuasive. Within each of these general purposes, the author may direct the audience to take a clear action or respond in a certain way.

The purpose for which an author writes a passage is also connected to the structure of that text. In a **NARRATIVE**, the author seeks to tell a story, often to illustrate a theme or idea the reader needs to consider. In a narrative, the author uses characteristics of storytelling, such as chronological order, characters, and a defined setting, and these characteristics communicate the author's theme or main idea.

In an **EXPOSITORY** passage, on the other hand, the author simply seeks to explain an idea or topic to the reader. The main idea will probably be a factual statement or a direct assertion of a broadly held opinion. Expository writing can come in many forms, but one essential feature is a fair and balanced representation of a topic. The author may explore one detailed aspect or a broad range of characteristics, but he or she mainly seeks to prompt a decision from the reader.

Similarly, in **TECHNICAL** writing, the author's purpose is to explain specific processes, techniques, or equipment in order for the reader to use that process or equipment to obtain a desired result. Writing like

Reading persuasive text requires an awareness of what the author believes about the topic.

this employs chronological or spatial structures, specialized vocabulary, and imperative or directive language.

In PERSUASIVE writing, though the reader is free to make decisions about the message and content, the author actively seeks to convince him or her to accept an opinion or belief. Much like expository writing, persuasive writing is presented in many organizational forms, but the author will use specific techniques, or RHETORICAL STRATEGIES, to build an argument. Readers can identify these strategies in order to clearly understand what an author wants them to believe, how the author's perspective and purpose may lead to bias, and whether the passage includes any logical fallacies.

Common rhetorical strategies include the appeals to ethos, logos, and pathos. An author uses these to build trust with the reader, explain the logical points of his or her argument, and convince the reader that his or her opinion is the best option.

An ETHOS—ETHICAL—APPEAL uses balanced, fair language and seeks to build a trusting relationship between the author and the reader. An author might explain his or her credentials, include the reader in an argument, or offer concessions to an opposing argument.

A LOGOS—LOGICAL—APPEAL builds on that trust by providing facts and support for the author's opinion, explaining the argument with clear connections and reasoning. At this point, the reader should beware of logical fallacies that connect unconnected ideas and build arguments on incorrect premises. With a logical appeal, an author strives to convince the reader to accept an opinion or belief by demonstrating that not only is it the most logical option but it also satisfies his or her emotional reaction to a topic.

A PATHOS—EMOTIONAL—APPEAL does not depend on reasonable connections between ideas; rather, it seeks to remind the reader, through imagery, strong language, and personal connections, that the author's argument aligns with his or her best interests.

Many persuasive passages seek to use all three rhetorical strategies to best appeal to the reader.

Clues will help the reader determine many things about a passage, from the author's purpose to the passage's main idea, but understanding an author's purpose is essential to fully understanding the text.

> Readers should consider how different audiences will react to a text. For example, how a slave owner's reactions to the narrative of Olaudah Equiano (on page 19) will differ from a slave trader's.

EXAMPLES

Evident truth. Made so plain by our good Father in Heaven, that all *feel* and *understand* it, even down to brutes and creeping insects. The ant, who has toiled and dragged a crumb to his nest, will furiously defend the fruit of his labor, against whatever robber assails him. So plain, that the most dumb and stupid slave that ever toiled for a master, does constantly *know* that he is wronged.

So plain that no one, high or low, ever does mistake it, except in a plainly *selfish* way; for although volume upon volume is written to prove slavery a very good thing, we never hear of the man who wishes to take the good of it, *by being a slave himself*.

Most governments have been based, practically, on the denial of the equal rights of men, as I have, in part, stated them; *ours* began, by *affirming* those rights. *They* said, some men are too *ignorant*, and *vicious*, to share in government. Possibly so, said we; and, by your system, you would always keep them ignorant and vicious. We proposed to give *all* a chance; and we expected the weak to grow stronger, the ignorant, wiser; and all better, and happier together.

We made the experiment; and the fruit is before us. Look at it. Think of it. Look at it, in its aggregate grandeur, of extent of country, and numbers of population, of ship, and steamboat.

—from Abraham Lincoln's speech fragment on slavery

1) The author's purpose is to

    A. explain ideas.

    B. narrate a story.

    C. describe a situation.

    D. persuade to accept an idea.

Answers:

A. is incorrect. The injustice of slavery in America is made clear, but only to convince the audience that slavery cannot exist in America.

B. is incorrect. The author briefly mentions the narrative of America in terms of affirming the equal rights of all people, but he does not tell a story or relate the events that led to slavery.

C. is incorrect. The author does not describe the conditions of slaves or the many ways their human rights are denied.

D. is correct. The author provides logical reasons and evidence that slavery is wrong, that it violates the American belief in equal rights.

2) To achieve his purpose, the author primarily uses

    A. concrete analogies.

    B. logical reasoning.

    C. emotional appeals.

    D. images.

Answers:

A. is incorrect. The author mentions the ant's willingness to defend what is his but does not make an explicit and corresponding conclusion about the slave; instead, he says, "So plain, that the most dumb and stupid slave that ever toiled for a master, does constantly *know* that he is wronged." The implied parallel is between the ant's conviction about being wronged and the slave knowing he is wronged.

B. is correct. The author uses logic when he points out that people who claim slavery is good never wish "to take the good of it, *by being a slave*." The author also points out that the principle of our country is to give everyone, including the "ignorant," opportunity; then he challenges his listeners to look at the fruit of this principle, saying, "Look at it, in its aggregate grandeur, of extent of country, and numbers of population, of ship, and steamboat."

C. is incorrect. The author relies on logic and evidence, and makes no emotional appeals about the suffering of slaves.

D. is incorrect. The author does offer evidence of his point with an image of the grandeur of America, but his primary appeal is logic.

The Audience

The structure, purpose, main idea, and language of a text all converge on one target: the intended audience. An author makes decisions about every aspect of a piece of writing based on that audience, and readers can evaluate the writing through the lens of that audience. By considering the probable reactions of an intended audience, readers can determine many things: whether or not they are part of that intended audience; the author's purpose for using specific techniques or devices; the biases of the author and how they appear in the writing; and how the author uses rhetorical strategies. While readers evaluate each of these things separately, identifying and considering the intended audience adds depth to the understanding of a text and helps highlight details with more clarity.

Several aspects identify the text's intended audience. First, when the main idea of the passage is known, the reader considers who most likely cares about that idea, benefits from it, or needs to know about it. Many authors begin with the main idea and then determine the audience in part based on these concerns.

Then the reader considers language. The author tailors language to appeal to the intended audience, so the reader can narrow down a broad understanding of that audience. The figurative language John Steinbeck uses in his novel *The Grapes of Wrath* reveals the suffering of the migrant Americans who traveled to California to find work during the Great Depression of the 1930s. Steinbeck spoke concretely to the Americans who were discriminating against the migrants. Instead of finding work in the "land of milk and honey," migrants faced unbearable poverty and injustice. The metaphor that gives the novel its title is "and in the eyes of the people there is the failure; and in the eyes of the hungry there is a growing wrath. In the souls of the people the grapes of wrath are filling

When reading a persuasive text, students should maintain awareness of what the author believes about the topic.

A logical argument includes a claim, a reason that supports the claim, and an assumption that the reader makes based on accepted beliefs. All parts of the argument need to make sense to the reader, so authors often consider the beliefs of their audience as they construct their arguments.

and growing heavy, growing heavy for the vintage." Steinbeck, used the image of ripening grapes, familiar to those surrounded by vineyards, to condemn this harsh treatment, provide an education of the human heart, and inspire compassion in his audience. Readers who weren't directly involved in the exodus of people from Oklahoma to the West, could have little difficulty grasping the meaning of Steinbeck's language in the description: "66 is the path of a people in flight, refugees from dust and shrinking land, from the thunder of tractors and invasion, from the twisting winds that howl up out of Texas, from floods that bring no richness to the land and steal what little richness is there."

EXAMPLES

In the following text, consideration should be made for how an English political leader of 1729 might have reacted.

It is a melancholy object to those, who walk through this great town, or travel in the country, when they see the streets, the roads and cabin-doors crowded with beggars of the female sex, followed by three, four, or six children, all in rags, and importuning every passenger for an alms. These mothers instead of being able to work for their honest livelihood, are forced to employ all their time in strolling to beg sustenance for their helpless infants who, as they grow up, either turn thieves for want of work, or leave their dear native country, to fight for the Pretender in Spain, or sell themselves to the Barbados.

I shall now therefore humbly propose my own thoughts, which I hope will not be liable to the least objection.

I have been assured by a very knowing American of my acquaintance in London, that a young healthy child well nursed, is, at a year old, a most delicious nourishing and wholesome food, whether stewed, roasted, baked, or boiled; and I make no doubt that it will equally serve in a fricassee.

I do therefore humbly offer it to public consideration, that of the hundred and twenty thousand children, already computed, twenty thousand may be reserved for breed, whereof only one fourth part to be males; which is more than we allow to sheep, black cattle, or swine, and my reason is, that these children are seldom the fruits of marriage, a circumstance not much regarded by our savages, therefore, one male will be sufficient to serve four females. That the remaining hundred thousand may, at a year old, be offered in sale to the persons of quality and fortune, through the kingdom, always advising the mother to let them suck plentifully in the last month, so as to render them plump, and fat for a good table. A child will make two dishes at an entertainment for friends, and when the family dines alone, the fore or hind quarter will make a reasonable dish, and seasoned with a little pepper or salt, will be very good boiled on the fourth day, especially in winter.

—from *A Modest Proposal for Preventing the Children of Poor People in Ireland From Being a Burden on Their*

Parents or Country, and for Making Them Beneficial to the Public by Jonathan Swift

1) Which of the following best states the central idea of the passage?

    A. Irish mothers are not able to support their children.

    B. The Irish people lived like savages.

    C. The people of England are quality people of fortune.

    D. The kingdom of England has exploited the weaker country of Ireland to the point that the Irish people cannot support their families.

Answers:

A. is incorrect. This is a fact alluded to in the passage, not a central idea.

B. is incorrect. Although the author does refer to the Irish as savages, the reader recognizes that the author is being outrageously satirical.

C. is incorrect. The author does say "That the remaining hundred thousand may, at a year old, be offered in sale to the persons of quality and fortune, through the kingdom," referring to the English. However, this is not the central idea; the opposite is, given that this is satire.

D. is correct. The author is hoping to use satire to shame England.

2) The author's use of phrases like "humbly propose," "liable to the least objection," "wholesome food" suggests which of the following purposes?

    A. to inform people about the attitudes of the English

    B. to use satire to reveal the inhumane treatment of the Irish by the English

    C. to persuade people to survive by any means

    D. to express his admiration of the Irish people

Answers:

A. is incorrect. The author's subject is the poverty of the Irish, and his audience is the English who are responsible for the suffering of the Irish.

B. is correct. The intended meaning of a satire sharply contradicts the literal meaning. Swift's proposal is not humble; it is meant to humble the arrogant. He expects the audience to be horrified. The children would make the worst imaginable food.

C. is incorrect. The author is not serious. His intent is to shock his English audience.

D. is incorrect. The author is expressing sympathy for the Irish.

Tone and Mood

Two important aspects of the communication between author and audience occur subtly. The TONE of a passage describes the author's attitude toward the topic, distinct from the MOOD, which is the pervasive feeling or atmosphere in a passage that provokes specific emotions in the reader. The distinction between these two aspects lies once again in the audience: the mood influences the reader's emotional state in response to the piece, while the tone establishes a relationship between the audience and the author. Does the author intend to instruct the audience? Is the author more experienced than the audience, or does he or she wish to convey a friendly or equal relationship? In each of these cases, the author uses a different tone to reflect the desired level of communication.

Primarily DICTION, or word choice, determines mood and tone in a passage. Many readers make the mistake of thinking about the ideas an author puts forth and using those alone to determine particularly tone; a much better practice is to separate specific words from the text and look for patterns in connotation and emotion. By considering categories of words used by the author, the reader can discover both the overall emotional atmosphere of a text and the attitude of the author toward the subject.

Every word has not only a literal meaning but also a CONNOTATIVE MEANING, relying on the common emotions, associations, and experiences an audience might associate with that word. The following words are all synonyms: *dog, puppy, cur, mutt, canine, pet*. Two of these words—*dog* and *canine*—are neutral words, without strong associations or emotions. Two others—*pet* and *puppy*—have positive associations. The last two—*cur* and *mutt*—have negative associations. A passage that uses one pair of these words versus another pair activates the positive or negative reactions of the audience.

> To determine the author's tone, students should examine what overall feeling they are experiencing.

> To decide the connotation of a word, the reader examines whether the word conveys a positive or negative association in the mind. Adjectives are often used to influence the feelings of the reader, such as in the phrase "an ambitious attempt to achieve."

EXAMPLES

Day had broken cold and grey, exceedingly cold and grey, when the man turned aside from the main Yukon trail and climbed the high earth-bank, where a dim and little-travelled trail led eastward through the fat spruce timberland. It was a steep bank, and he paused for breath at the top, excusing the act to himself by looking at his watch. It was nine o'clock. There was no sun nor hint of sun, though there was not a cloud in the sky. It was a clear day, and yet there seemed an intangible *pall* over the face of things, a subtle gloom that made the day dark, and that was due to the absence of sun. This fact did not worry the man. He was used to the lack of sun. It had been days since he had seen the sun, and he knew that a few more days must pass before that cheerful orb, due south, would just peep above the sky-line and dip immediately from view.

—from "To Build a Fire" by Jack London

1) Which of the following best describes the mood of the passage?

   A. exciting and adventurous

   B. fierce and determined

   C. bleak and forbidding

   D. grim yet hopeful

Answers:

A. is incorrect. The man is on some adventure as he turns off the main trail, but the context is one of gloom and darkness, not excitement.

B. is incorrect. The cold, dark day is fierce, and the man may be determined; however, the overall mood of the entire passage is one of grim danger.

C. is correct. The man is oblivious to the gloom and darkness of the day, which was "exceedingly cold and grey."

D. is incorrect. The atmosphere is grim, and there is no indication the man is hopeful about anything. He is aware only of his breath and steps forward.

2) The connotation of the words intangible *pall* is

   A. a death-like covering.

   B. a vague sense of familiarity.

   C. an intimation of communal strength.

   D. an understanding of the struggle ahead.

Answers:

A. is correct. Within the context of the sentence "It was a clear day, and yet there seemed an intangible *pall* over the face of things, a subtle gloom that made the day dark," the words *gloom* and *dark* are suggestive of death; the words *over the face* suggest a covering.

B. is incorrect. The word *intangible* can mean a vague sense, but there is nothing especially familiar about a clear day that is dark, with no sunlight.

C. is incorrect. The word *intangible* suggests intimation; however, from the beginning, the author shows the man alone, and reports, "the man turned aside from the main Yukon trail."

D. is incorrect. A struggle may be indicated by the darkness and gloom, but the man has no understanding of this possibility. The text refers to the darkness, saying, "This fact did not worry the man. He was used to the lack of sun."

Comparing Passages

Some of the questions in the Praxis Reading exam require test takers to compare texts that have similar themes or topics. Questions involve identifying the similarities and differences in main ideas, styles, supporting details, and text structures. Test takers will find it helpful to preview the questions and to note pertinent similarities and differences in texts while reading.

The following example passages discuss Walt Whitman's text *Leaves of Grass*. The first is from the preface of *Leaves of Grass* and is written by Whitman himself. The second is from a critical essay by Ed Folsom and Kenneth M. Price about *Leaves of Grass*.

Readers should keep in mind the following questions:
- What central idea about Whitman's response to slavery is being expressed in the passages?
- How does Folsom and Price's explanation of Whitman's response to the issue of slavery in America differ from Whitman's own statement of his intention?

EXAMPLES

One

No great literature, nor any like style of behavior or oratory or social intercourse or household arrangements or public institutions, can long elude the jealous and passionate instinct of American standards. Whether or not the sign appears from the mouths of the people, it throbs a live interrogation in every freeman's and freewoman's heart after that which passes by.

Are its disposals without ignominious distinctions? Is it for the ever-growing communes of brothers and lovers, large, well united, proud beyond the old models, generous beyond all models?

I know that what answers for me, an American, must answer for any individual or nation that serves for a part of my materials. Does this answer? Or is it without reference to universal needs?

Does this acknowledge liberty with audible and absolute acknowledgment, and set slavery at naught, for life and death? Will it help breed one good-shaped man, and a woman to be his perfect and independent mate?

—from preface to *Leaves of Grass* by Walt Whitman

Two

A pivotal and empowering change came over Whitman at this time of poetic transformation. His politics—and especially his racial attitudes—underwent a profound alteration. As we have noted, Whitman the journalist spoke to the interests of the day and from a particular class perspective when he advanced the interests of white workingmen while seeming, at times, unconcerned about the plight of blacks. Perhaps the New Orleans experience had prompted a change in attitude, a change that was intensified by an increasing number of friendships with radical thinkers and writers who led Whitman to rethink his attitudes toward the issue of race. Whatever the cause, in Whitman's future-oriented poetry blacks become central to his new literary project and central to his understanding of democracy....His first notebook lines in the manner of *Leaves of Grass* focus directly on the fundamental issue dividing the United States. His notebook breaks into free verse for the first time in lines that seek to bind opposed categories, to link black and white, to join master and slave:

> *I am the poet of the body*
> *And I am the poet of the soul*
> *I go with the slaves of the earth equally with the masters*
> *And I will stand between the masters and the slaves,*
> *Entering into both so that both shall understand me alike.*

The audacity of that final line remains striking. While most people were lining up on one side or another, Whitman placed himself in that space—...*between* master and slave. His extreme political despair led him to replace what he now named the "scum" of corrupt American politics in the 1850s with his own persona—a shaman, a culture-healer, an all-encompassing "I."

—from "Walt Whitman: Racial Politics and the Origins of *Leaves of Grass*" by Ed Folsom and Kenneth M. Price, http://www.whitmanarchive. org/biography/walt_whitman/index.html #racial

1) What main idea do both sources make about Walt Whitman's perspective?

   A. Slavery is anti-American.

   B. Democracy is a force of brotherhood.

   C. Walt Whitman is the voice of American individuality.

   D. American politics is corrupt.

Answers:

A. is correct. The main idea of both passages reveals that Whitman's perspective about the issue of slavery is that slavery is anti-American because it is undemocratic. Whitman saw the liberty of America as a unifying force, a force of brotherhood that could not permit slavery to continue.

B. is incorrect. Whitman does view democracy this way; however, he is speaking specifically about slavery being undemocratic.

C. is incorrect. This option is true but far too broad an interpretation of the passages. A main idea is more specific statement.

D. is incorrect. This option is mentioned in only one passage.

2) What is the main difference between the passages?

   A. In the first passage, the writer is concerned about slavery, but in the second passage the writers reveal the American confusion about slavery.

   B. The first passage is a biography of Whitman; the second passage discusses Whitman's poetry.

   C. The second passage reveals Whitman's consistent opposition to slavery; the first passage details Whitman's pain in relation to slavery.

   D. In the first passage, Whitman states his perspective on slavery, but the second passage is about Whitman's change of perspective on slavery.

Answers:

A. is incorrect. In the first passage, Whitman explains his viewpoint. In the second passage, the authors critique Whitman's changing views on slavery. Initially, as a journalist, Whitman was sympathetic to the white working class, not the blacks. The authors go on to explain that, in time, Whitman's poetic response to the issue of slavery in America displayed his sympathy for the slave that originated in his soul and his ability to form a union with what he observed. He could see the spiritual significance of different aspects of life and nature, including slavery.

B. is incorrect. The first passage is written by Whitman; he is expressing his own perspective.

C. is incorrect. The second passage clearly states that Whitman's view of slavery changed. The first passage is not about pain.

D. is correct. Whitman's perspective is abstract. The second passage helps to make Whitman's thinking clear.

Meaning of Words and Phrases

Context Clues

As previously discussed, specific words used in a text assist the reader in understanding the author, but what about unfamiliar words and phrases? How can the reader determine the meaning and associations of unknown words in a passage? While it may be difficult to fully understand connotation, tone, and mood if a passage contains many unfamiliar words, known words in a passage aid in interpreting the meaning and sometimes even the connotation of these words.

Different parts of a passage can be helpful in this: the sentence the word appears in; the relationship of that sentence to other sentences;

specific words around the unfamiliar word; other words in the passage that demonstrate a relationship or reference to the unfamiliar word; and the overall understanding of the passage, including main idea, mood, and tone.

Often, to grasp a sense of unfamiliar words, readers are able to use context clues or hints in the text. Context clues are especially useful when determining the appropriate meaning of a multiple-meaning word.

One type of context clue is a **DEFINITION**, or **DESCRIPTION**, **CLUE**. Sometimes, authors use a difficult word, then include *that is* or *which is* to signal that they are providing a definition. An author also may provide a synonym or restate the idea in more familiar words:

> *Teachers often prefer teaching students with intrinsic motivation; these students have an internal desire to learn.*

The meaning of *intrinsic* is restated as an *internal desire*.

Similarly, authors may include an **EXAMPLE CLUE**, providing an example phrase that clarifies the meaning of the word:

> *Teachers may view extrinsic rewards as efficacious; however, an individual student may not be interested in what the teacher offers. For example, a student who is diabetic may not feel any incentive to work when offered a sweet treat.*

Efficacious is explained with an example that demonstrates how an extrinsic reward may not be effective.

Another commonly used context clue is the **CONTRAST**, or **ANTONYM**, **CLUE**. In this case, authors indicate that the unfamiliar word is the opposite of a familiar word:

> *In contrast to intrinsic motivation, extrinsic motivation is contingent on teachers offering rewards that are appealing.*

The phrase "in contrast" tells the reader that *extrinsic* is the opposite of *intrinsic*.

EXAMPLES

1) One challenge of teaching is finding ways to incentivize, or to motivate, learning.

   Which of the following is the meaning of *incentivize* as used in the sentence?

   A. encourage

   B. determine

   C. challenge

   D. improve

   Answers:

   A. is correct. The word *incentivize* is defined immediately with the synonym *motivate*, or *encourage*.

B. is incorrect. *Determine* is not a synonym for *motivate*. In addition, the phrase "to determine learning" does not make sense in the sentence.

C. is incorrect. *Challenge* is not a synonym for motivate.

D. is incorrect. *Improve* is closely related to motivation, but it is not the best synonym provided.

2) If an extrinsic reward is extremely desirable, a student may become so apprehensive he or she cannot focus. The student may experience such intense pressure to perform that the reward undermines its intent.

Which of the following is the meaning of **apprehensive** as used in the sentence?

A. uncertain

B. distracted

C. anxious

D. forgetful

Answers:

A. is incorrect. Nothing in the sentence suggests the student is uncertain.

B. is incorrect. *Distracted* is related to the clue "focus" but does not address the clue "pressure to perform."

C. is correct. The reader can infer that the pressure to perform is making the student anxious.

D. is incorrect. Nothing in the sentence suggests the student is forgetful.

Word Structure

In addition to the context of a sentence or passage, an unfamiliar word itself can give the reader clues about its meaning. Each word consists of discrete pieces that determine meaning; the most familiar of these pieces are word roots, prefixes, and suffixes.

WORD ROOTS are the bases from which many words take their form and meaning. The most common word roots are Greek and Latin, and a broad knowledge of these roots can greatly improve a reader's ability to determine the meaning of words in context. The root of a word does not always point to the word's exact meaning, but combined with an understanding of the word's place in a sentence and the context of a passage, it will often be enough to answer a question about meaning or relationships.

Table 5.1. Common Word Roots

Root	Meaning	Examples
alter	other	alternate, alter ego
ambi	both	ambidextrous
ami, amic	love	amiable
amphi	both ends, all sides	amphibian
anthrop	man, human, humanity	misanthrope, anthropologist
apert	open	aperture
aqua	water	aqueduct, aquarium
aud	to hear	audience
auto	self	autobiography
bell	war	belligerent, bellicose
bene	good	benevolent
bio	life	biology
ced	yield, go	secede, intercede
cent	one hundred	century
chron	time	chronological
circum	around	circumference
contra, counter	against	contradict
crac, crat	rule, ruler	autocrat, bureaucrat
crypt	hidden	cryptogram, cryptic
curr, curs, cours	to run	precursory
dict	to say	dictator, dictation
dyna	power	dynamic
dys	bad, hard, unlucky	dysfunctional
equ	equal, even	equanimity
fac	to make, to do	factory
form	shape	reform, conform
fort	strength	fortitude
fract	to break	fracture
grad, gress	step	progression
gram	thing written	epigram
graph	writing	graphic
hetero	different	heterogeneous
homo	same	homogenous
hypo	below, beneath	hypothermia
iso	identical	isolate
ject	throw	projection

Table 5.1. Common Word Roots (continued)

Root	Meaning	Examples
logy	study of	biology
luc	light	elucidate
mal	bad	malevolent
meta, met	behind, between	metacognition (behind the thinking)
meter, metr	measure	thermometer
micro	small	microbe
mis, miso	hate	misanthrope
mit	to send	transmit
mono	one	monologue
morph	form, shape	morphology
mort	death	mortal
multi	many	multiple
phil	love	philanthropist
port	carry	transportation
pseudo	false	pseudonym
psycho	soul, spirit	psychic
rupt	to break	disruption
scope	viewing instrument	microscope
scrib, scribe	to write	inscription
sect, sec	to cut	section
sequ, secu	follow	consecutive
soph	wisdom, knowledge	philosophy
spect	to look	spectator
struct	to build	restructure
tele	far off	telephone
terr	earth	terrestrial
therm	heat	thermal
vent, vene	to come	convene
vert	turn	vertigo
voc	voice, call	vocalize, evocative

In addition to understanding the base of a word, it is vital to recognize common affixes that change the meaning of words and demonstrate their relationships to other words. **Prefixes** are added to the beginning of words and frequently change their meaning, sometimes to an opposite meaning.

Table 5.2. Common Prefixes

Prefix	Meaning	Examples
a, an	without, not	anachronism, anhydrous
ab, abs, a	apart, away from	abscission, abnormal
ad	toward	adhere
agere	act	agent
amphi, ambi	round, both sides	ambivalent
ante	before	antedate, anterior
anti	against	antipathy
archos	leader, first, chief	oligarchy
bene	well, favorable	benevolent, beneficent
bi	two	binary, bivalve
caco	bad	cacophony
circum	around	circumnavigate
corpus	body	corporeal
credo	belief	credible
demos	people	demographic
di	two, double	dimorphism, diatomic
dia	across, through	dialectic
dis	not, apart	disenfranchise
dynasthai	be able	dynamo, dynasty
ego	I, self	egomaniac, egocentric
epi	upon, over	epigram, epiphyte
ex	out	extraneous, extemporaneous
geo	earth	geocentric, geomancy
ideo	idea	ideology, ideation
in	in	induction, indigenous
in, im	not	ignoble, immoral
inter	between	interstellar
lexis	word	lexicography
liber	free, book	liberal
locus	place	locality
macro	large	macrophage
micro	small	micron
mono	one, single	monocle, monovalent
mortis	death	moribund
olig	few	oligarchy

Table 5.2. Common Prefixes (continued)

Prefix	Meaning	Examples
peri	around	peripatetic, perineum
poly	many	polygamy
pre	before	prescient
solus	alone	solitary
subter	under, secret	subterfuge
un	not	unsafe
utilis	useful	utilitarian

SUFFIXES, on the other hand, are added to the end of words, and they generally point out a word's relationship to other words in a sentence. Suffixes might change a part of speech or indicate if a word is plural or related to a plural.

Table 5.3. Common Suffixes

Suffix	Meaning	Examples
able, ible	able, capable	visible
age	act of, state of, result of	wreckage
al	relating to	gradual
algia	pain	myalgia
an, ian	native of, relating to	riparian
ance, ancy	action, process, state	defiance
ary, ery, ory	relating to, quality, place	aviary
cian	processing a specific skill or art	physician
cule, ling	very small	sapling, animalcule
cy	action, function	normalcy
dom	quality, realm	wisdom
ee	one who receives the action	nominee
en	made of, to make	silken
ence, ency	action, state of, quality	urgency
er, or	one who, that which	professor
escent	in the process of	adolescent, senescence
esis, osis	action, process, condition	genesis, neurosis
et, ette	small one, group	baronet, lorgnette
fic	making, causing	specific

Suffix	Meaning	Examples
ful	full of	frightful
hood	order, condition, quality	adulthood
ice	condition, state, quality	malice
id, ide	connected with, belonging to	bromide
ile	relating to, suited for, capable of	puerile, juvenile
ine	nature of	feminine
ion, sion, tion	act, result, state of	contagion
ish	origin, nature, resembling	impish
ism	system, manner, condition, characteristic	capitalism
ist	one who, that which	artist, flautist
ite	nature of, quality of, mineral product	graphite
ity, ty	state of, quality	captivity
ive	causing, making	exhaustive
ize, ise	make	idolize, bowdlerize
ment	act of, state or, result	containment
nomy	law	autonomy, taxonomy
oid	resembling	asteroid, anthropoid
some	like, apt, tending to	gruesome
strat	cover	strata
tude	state of, condition of	aptitude
um	forms single nouns	spectrum
ure	state of, act, process, rank	rupture, rapture
ward	in the direction of	backward
y	inclined to, tend to	faulty

EXAMPLES

Width and intensity are leading characteristics of his writings—width both of subject-matter and of comprehension, intensity of self-absorption into what the poet contemplates and expresses. He scans and presents an enormous panorama, unrolled before him as from a mountain-top; and yet, whatever most large or most minute or casual thing his eye glances upon, that he enters into with a depth of affection which identifies him with it for a time, be the object what it may. There is a singular interchange also of actuality and of ideal substratum and suggestion. While he sees men, with even abnormal exactness and sympathy, as men, he sees them also "as trees walking," and admits us to perceive that the whole show is in a measure spectral and unsubstantial, and the mask of a larger and profounder reality beneath it, of which it is giving perpetual intimations and auguries.

—from "Prefatory Notice," in the first edition of Walt Whitman's *Leaves of Grass,* by W. M. Rossetti

1) Which of the following is the best definition of the word *substratum*?

   A. meaningful crest

   B. distracting idea

   C. reduction

   D. underlying foundation

Answers:

A. is incorrect. Within the context of the sentence "There is a singular interchange also of actuality and of ideal substratum and suggestion," to say an "ideal meaningful crest" would be inaccurate because the *sub* prefix suggests *under*, a foundation.

B. is incorrect. Within the context, an "ideal distracting idea" sounds contradictory.

C. is incorrect. The word *reduction* suggests less than, not under.

D. is correct. Combining the prefix *sub* (*under*) and the root *strata* (*cover*) with the singular suffix *um*, the word *substratum* means underlying layer or substance. An "ideal underlying foundation" makes sense.

2) The prefix *un* in a word like *unsubstantial* indicates the meaning of the word is

   A. not whatever the root word is.

   B. suggestive of an undercurrent of whatever the root word is.

   C. a lower value of the root word.

   D. in opposition to whatever the root word is.

Answers:

A. is correct. The prefix *un* means not, and the root word *substantial* means real. *Unsubstantial* means not of physical reality.

B. is incorrect. The prefix *un* does not suggest under.

C. is incorrect. The prefix *un* does not suggest less than; it is the opposite of the root word.

D. is incorrect. "In opposition to" suggests working against something, not being the opposite of.

Figurative Language

A figure of speech is an expression that is understood to have a non-literal meaning. Instead of meaning what is actually said, figurative language suggests meaning by pointing to something else. When Shakespeare says "All the world's a stage, / And all men and women merely players," he is speaking of the world as if it were a stage. Since the world is not literally a stage, the reader has to ask how the world is a stage and what Shakespeare is implying about the world.

Figurative language extends the meaning of words by giving readers a new way to view a subject. Thinking of the world as a stage on which people are performing is a new way of thinking about life. After reading Shakespeare's metaphor, people may reflect on how often they play a role, act a part. Their minds may go in many directions; they may wonder when their behavior is genuine, whether they're too worried about others evaluating their performance, and so on. Figurative language—such as metaphors and similes—generates thought after thought; with just a few words, it engages the reader's imagination and adds emphasis to different aspects of the text's subject.

A METAPHOR describes a *topic* that may be unfamiliar to the reader as though it were something else—a *vehicle*—that is probably familiar to the reader. The familiar vehicle is used to help the reader understand a new or unfamiliar topic. As the reader reflects on the similarities between the topic and the vehicle, he or she forms a new idea about the topic. For example, if a person refers to an issue as "the elephant in the room," the topic is the issue, and "the elephant in the room" is a vehicle communicating how overwhelming the issue is or that the issue is undeniable.

Similarly, in PERSONIFICATION an object is anthropomorphized in some way or receives a human attribute. In the sentence "The earth swallowed him whole," *earth* is personified because it is described as carrying out a human action. Personification may also represent an abstract quality. For instance, a timid individual may be the "personification of cowardice."

A SIMILE directly points to similarities between two things. The author uses a familiar vehicle to express an idea about the topic. For example, in his poem "The Rime of the Ancient Mariner," Samuel Taylor Coleridge describes his ship as "Idle as a painted ship upon a painted ocean." Readers have most likely seen a painting of a ship; Coleridge has used this knowledge to convey that the ship was completely motionless. Like a simile, an ANALOGY is a correspondence between two things; it shows a partial similarity.

Aristotle claimed that "the greatest thing by far is to have a command of metaphor. This alone cannot be imparted by another; it is the mark of genius, for to make good metaphors implies an eye for resemblances." The resemblance between two unlike things enables understanding of the ideas suggested by metaphoric language.

EXAMPLES

In shape Egypt is like a lily with a crooked stem. A broad blossom terminates it at its upper end; a button of a bud projects from the stalk a little below the blossom, on the left-hand side. The broad blossom is the Delta, extending from Aboosir to Tineh, a direct distance of a hundred and eighty miles, which the projection of the coast—the graceful swell of the petals—enlarges to two hundred and thirty. The bud is the Fayoum, a natural depression in the hills that shut in the Nile valley on the west, which has been rendered cultivable for many thousands of years….The long stalk of the lily is the Nile valley itself, which is a ravine scooped in the rocky soil for seven hundred miles from the First Cataract to the apex of the Delta, sometimes not more than a mile broad, never more than eight or ten miles. No other country in the world is so strangely shaped, so long compared to its width, so straggling, so hard to govern from a single center.

—from *Ancient Egypt* by George Rawlinson

1) What kind of figurative language does the author of *Ancient Egypt* use?

    A. a metaphor

    B. a simile

    C. a comparison

    D. an analogy

Answers:

A. is incorrect. A metaphor involves speaking of one thing as if it is something else, not just like something else.

B. is correct. To describe Egypt, the author uses a simile. "Egypt is like a lily with a crooked stem." The blossom is the Delta region of Egypt, the bud is the hills on the west, and the long stalk is the Nile valley.

C. is incorrect. Similes show only how one thing is similar to another. A comparison usually shows both similarities and differences.

D. is incorrect. An analogy is a correspondence between two things; it shows a partial similarity.

2) What does the figurative language used in *Ancient Egypt* help the reader understand?

    A. how outsiders perceive Egypt

    B. the dominance of the Nile River

    C. how difficult it is to live in Egypt

    D. how strange the shape of the country is

Answers:

A. is incorrect. The problem with this option is the word *outsiders*. Anyone looking at a map can see the similarity between the shape of Egypt and a lily.

B. is incorrect. The Nile River does run through Egypt, but this does not account for the hills or Delta region.

C. is incorrect. Egypt being shaped like a lily does not suggest difficulty in living there. Something like a lack of rainfall could create difficulty.

D. is correct. By showing the similarities between a lily and the shape of the country, the author puts a memorable image in the mind of the reader and provides a clear understanding of his point: that there is no center from which to govern the country.

PART III: WRITING

sevenseven

LANGUAGE SKILLS

Parts of Speech

The **PARTS OF SPEECH** are the building blocks of sentences, paragraphs, and entire texts. Grammarians have typically defined eight parts of speech—nouns, pronouns, verbs, adverbs, adjectives, conjunctions, prepositions, and interjections—all of which play unique roles in the context of a sentence. Thus, a fundamental understanding of the parts of speech is necessary in order to form an understanding of basic sentence construction.

> Although some words fall easily into one category or another, many words can function as different parts of speech based on their usage within a sentence.

Nouns and Pronouns

NOUNS are the words we use to give names to people, places, things, and ideas. Most often, nouns fill the position of subject or object within a sentence. The category of nouns has several subcategories: common nouns (*chair, car, house*), proper nouns (*Julie, David*), abstract nouns (*love, intelligence, sadness*), concrete nouns (*window, bread, person*), compound nouns (*brother-in-law, rollercoaster*), non-countable nouns (*money, water*), countable nouns (*dollars, cubes*), and verbal nouns (*writing, diving*). There is much crossover between these subcategories (for example, *chair* is common, concrete, and countable).

Sometimes, a word that is typically used as a noun will be used to modify another noun. The word then would be labeled as an adjective because of its usage within the sentence. In the following example, *cabin* is a noun in the first sentence and an adjective in the second:

> The family visited the <u>cabin</u> by the lake.

> Our <u>cabin</u> stove overheated during vacation.

PRONOUNS replace nouns in a sentence or paragraph, allowing a writer to achieve a smooth flow throughout a text by avoiding unnecessary repetition. The unique aspect of the pronoun as a part of speech is that the list of pronouns is finite: while there are innumerable nouns in the English language, the list of pronouns is rather limited in contrast. The noun that a pronoun replaces is called its ANTECEDENT.

Pronouns fall into several distinct categories. PERSONAL PRONOUNS act as subjects or objects in a sentence:

She received a letter; I gave the letter to her.

POSSESSIVE PRONOUNS indicate possession:

My coat is red; our car is blue.

REFLEXIVE (intensive) PRONOUNS intensify a noun or reflect back upon a noun:

I myself made the dessert. I made the dessert myself.

Personal, possessive, and reflexive pronouns must all agree with the noun that they replace both in gender (male, female, or neutral), number (singular or plural), and person. PERSON refers to the point of view of the sentence. First person is the point of view of the speaker (I, me), second person is the person being addressed (you), and third person refers to a person outside the sentence (he, she, they).

Table 6.1. Personal, Possessive, and Reflexive Pronouns

CASE	FIRST PERSON		SECOND PERSON		THIRD PERSON	
	singular	plural	singular	plural	singular	plural
Subject	I	we	you	you (all)	he, she, it,	they
Object	me	us	you	you (all)	him, her, it	them
Possessive	my	our	your	your	his, her, its	their
Reflexive	myself	our-selves	yourself	your-selves	himself, herself, itself	them-selves

RELATIVE PRONOUNS begin dependent clauses. Like other pronouns, they may appear in subject or object case, depending on the clause. Take, for example, the sentence below:

Charlie, who made the clocks, works in the basement.

Here, the relative pronoun *who* is substituting for Charlie; that word indicates that Charlie makes the clocks, and so *who* is in the subject case because it is performing the action (*makes the clocks*).

In cases where a person is the object of a relative clause, the writer would use the relative pronoun *whom*. For example, read the sentence below:

My father, whom I care for, is sick.

Even though *my father* is the subject of the sentence, in the relative clause the relative pronoun *whom* is the object of the preposition *for*. Therefore that pronoun appears in the object case.

When a relative clause refers to a non-human, *that* or *which* is used. (*I live in Texas, which is a large state.*) The relative pronoun *whose* indicates possession. (*I don't know whose car that is.*)

Table 6.2. Relative Pronouns

Pronoun Type	Subject	Object
Person	who	whom
Thing		which, that
Possessive		whose

INTERROGATIVE PRONOUNS begin questions (*Who worked last evening?*). They request information about people, places, things, ideas, location, time, means, and purposes.

Table 6.3. Interrogative Pronouns

Interrogative Pronoun	Asks About	Example
who	person	<u>Who</u> lives there?
whom	person	To <u>whom</u> shall I send the letter?
what	thing	<u>What</u> is your favorite color?
where	place	<u>Where</u> do you go to school?
when	time	<u>When</u> will we meet for dinner?
which	selection	<u>Which</u> movie would you like to see?
why	reason	<u>Why</u> are you going to be late?
how	manner	<u>How</u> did the ancient Egyptians build the pyramids?

DEMONSTRATIVE PRONOUNS point out or draw attention to something or someone. They can also indicate proximity or distance.

Table 6.4. Demonstrative Pronouns

Number	Subject/ Proximity	Example	Object/ Distance	Example
Singular	this (subject)	<u>This</u> is my apartment—please come in!	that (object)	I gave <u>that</u> to him yesterday.
	this (proximity)	<u>This</u> is the computer you will use right here, not the one in the other office.	that (distance)	<u>That</u> is the Statue of Liberty across the harbor.

Table 6.4. Demonstrative Pronouns (continued)

Number	Subject/ Proximity	Example	Object/ Distance	Example
Plural	these (subject)	<u>These</u> are flawless diamonds.	those (object)	Give <u>those</u> to me later.
	these (proximity)	<u>These</u> right here are the books we want, not the ones over there.	those (distance)	<u>Those</u> mountains across the plains are called the Rockies.

Indefinite pronouns simply replace nouns to avoid unnecessary repetition:

<u>Several</u> came to the party to see <u>both</u>.

Indefinite pronouns can be either singular or plural (and some can act as both depending on the context). If the indefinite pronoun is the subject of the sentence, it is important to know whether that pronoun is singular or plural so that the verb can agree with the pronoun in number.

Table 6.5. Common Indefinite Pronouns

Singular		Plural	Singular or Plural
each either neither one everyone no one someone anyone	everybody nobody somebody anybody everything nothing something anything another	both few several many	some any none all most more *These pronouns take their singularity or plurality from the object of the prepositions that follow: Some of the pies were eaten. Some of the pie was eaten.*

Verbs

VERBS express action (*run*, *jump*, *play*) or state of being (*is*, *seems*). The former are called action verbs, and the latter are linking verbs. Linking verbs join the subject of the sentence to the subject complement, which follows the verb and provides more information about the subject. See the sentence below:

The dog is cute.

The dog is the subject, *is* is the linking verb, and *cute* is the subject complement.

Verbs can stand alone or they can be accompanied by HELPING VERBS, which are used to indicate tense. Verb tense indicates the time of the action. The action may have occurred in the past, present, or future. The action may also have been simple (occurring once) or continuous (ongoing). The perfect and perfect continuous tenses describe when actions occur in relation to other actions.

Table 6.6. Verb Tenses

TENSE	PAST	PRESENT	FUTURE
Simple	I answered the question.	I answer your questions in class.	I will answer your question.
Continuous	I was answering your question when you interrupted me.	I am answering your question; please listen.	I will be answering your question after the lecture.
Perfect	I had answered all questions before class ended.	I have answered the questions already.	I will have answered every question before the class is over.
Perfect Continuous	I had been answering questions when the students started leaving.	I have been answering questions for 30 minutes and am getting tired.	I will have been answering students' questions for 20 years by the time I retire.
Helping Verbs: is/am/are/was/were, be/being/been, has/had/have, do/does/did, should, would, could, will			

Changing the spelling of the verb and/or adding helping verbs is known as CONJUGATION. In addition to being conjugated for tense, verbs are conjugated to indicate *person* (first, second, and third person) and *number* (whether they are singular or plural). The conjugation of the verb must agree with the subject of the sentence. A verb that has not be conjugated is called an infinitive and begins with *to* (*to swim, to be*).

Table 6.7. Verb Conjugation (Present Tense)

PERSON	SINGULAR	PLURAL
First Person	I answer	we answer
Second Person	you answer	you (all) answer
Third Person	he/she/it answers	they answer

Verbs may be regular, meaning they follow normal conjugation patterns, or irregular, meaning they do not follow a regular pattern.

Table 6.8. Regular and Irregular Verbs

	SIMPLE PRESENT	PRESENT PARTICIPLE	SIMPLE PAST	PAST PARTICIPLE
Regular	help	helping	helped	(have) helped
	jump	jumping	jumped	(have) jumped
Irregular	am	been	was	(have) been
	swim	swimming	swam	(have) swum
	sit	sitting	sat	(have) sat
	set	setting	set	(have) set
	lie	lying	lay	(have) lain
	lay	laying	laid	(have) laid
	rise	rising	rose	(have) risen
	raise	raising	raised	(have) raised

Verbs can be written in the active or passive voice. In the ACTIVE voice, the subject of the sentence performs the main action of the sentence. In the sentence below, Alexis is performing the action:

Alexis played tennis.

In the passive voice, the subject of the sentence is receiving the action of the main verb. In the sentence below, the subject is *tennis*, which receives the action *played*:

Tennis was played.

Note that, in the passive voice, there is no indication of who performed the action. For this reason, passive voice is used when the subject is unknown or unimportant. For example, in science, it is common to use the passive voice:

The experiment was performed three times.

At most other times, it is considered more appropriate to use the active voice because it is more dynamic and gives more information.

Finally, verbs can be classified by whether they take a DIRECT OBJECT, which is a noun that receives the action of the verb. Transitive verbs require a direct object. In the sentence below, the transitive verb *throw* has a direct object (ball):

The pitcher will throw <u>the ball</u>.

Intransitive verbs do not require a direct object. Verbs like *run*, *jump*, and *go* make sense without any object:

He will run.

She jumped.

A noun that receives the direct object is the indirect object.
The pitcher will throw <u>Antoine</u> the ball.

Many sets of similar verbs include one transitive and one intransitive verb, which can cause confusion. These troublesome verbs include combinations such as *lie* or *lay*, *rise* or *raise*, and *sit* or *set*.

Table 6.9. Intransitive and Transitive Verbs

INTRANSITIVE VERBS	TRANSITIVE VERBS	
lie – to recline	lay – to put	lay <u>something</u>
rise – to go or get up	raise – to lift	raise <u>something</u>
sit – to be seated	set – to put	set <u>something</u>
Hint: These intransitive verbs have *i* as the second letter. *Intransitive* begins with *i.*	Hint: The word *transitive* begins with a *t,* and it *TAKES* an object.	

Adjectives and Adverbs

ADVERBS take on a modifying or describing role and often take the ending *–ly*. These words can describe a number of different parts of speech and even phrases or clauses:

- verbs: *He <u>quickly</u> ran to the house next door.*
- adjectives: *Her <u>very</u> effective speech earned her a new job.*
- other adverbs: *Several puppies arrived <u>rather</u> happily after they had eaten dog treats.*
- entire sentences: *<u>Instead</u>, the owner kept his shop.*

Like adverbs, **ADJECTIVES** modify or describe, but they add to the meaning of nouns and pronouns only:

<u>Five thoughtful</u> students came to work at the farm.

The idea from the committee proved a <u>smart</u> one.

One very important note regarding the adjective is that any word used to describe a noun or pronoun will be classified as an adjective. *Her* could be used as a pronoun or an adjective depending on usage:

<u>Her</u> dog barks until midnight. (adjective modifying *dog*)

We gave several books to <u>her</u>. (pronoun)

Also note that *a, and,* and *the* (called articles) are always adjectives.

Conjunctions

CONJUNCTIONS join words into phrases, clauses, and sentences by use of three mechanisms. There are three main types of conjunctions. **COORDINATING CONJUNCTIONS** join together two independent clauses (i.e., two complete thoughts). These include *and, but, or, for, nor, yet, so* (FANBOYS). Note that some of these can also be used to join items in a series.

I'll order lunch, <u>but</u> you need to go pick it up.

Make sure to get sandwiches, chips, <u>and</u> sodas.

Adverbs typically answer the questions *Where? When? Why? How? How often? To what extent? Under what conditions?*

CORRELATIVE CONJUNCTIONS (whether/or, either/or, neither/nor, both/and, not only/but also) work together to join items:

<u>Both</u> the teacher <u>and</u> the students needed a break after the lecture.

SUBORDINATING CONJUNCTIONS join dependent clauses (thoughts that cannot stand alone as sentences) to the related independent clause. They usually describe some sort of relationship between the two parts of the sentence, such as cause/effect or order. They can appear at the beginning or in the middle of a sentence:

We treat ourselves during football season to several orders <u>because</u> we love pizza.

<u>Because</u> we love pizza, we treat ourselves during football season to several orders.

Table 2.10 Subordinating Conjunctions

SUBORDINATING CONJUNCTIONS	
Time	after, as, as long as, as soon as, before, since, until, when, whenever, while
Manner	as, as if, as though
Cause	because
Condition	although, as long as, even if, even though, if, provided that, though, unless, while
Purpose	in order that, so that, that
Comparison	as, than

When using correlative conjunctions, be sure that the structure of the word, phrase, or clause that follows the first part of the conjunction mirrors the structure of the word, phrase, or clause that follows the second part.

I will neither mow the grass nor pull the weeds today. (correct)

I will neither mow the grass nor undertake the pulling of the weeds today. (incorrect)

Prepositions

PREPOSITIONS set up relationships in time (*after the party*) or space (*under the cushions*) within a sentence. A preposition will always function as part of a prepositional phrase, which includes the preposition along with the object of the preposition. If a word that usually acts as a preposition is standing alone in a sentence, the word is likely functioning as an adverb:

She hid <u>underneath</u>.

Table 6.11 Common Prepositions

PREPOSITIONS	COMPOUND PREPOSITIONS
along, among, around, at, before, behind, below, beneath, beside, besides, between, beyond, by, despite, down, during, except, for, from, in, into, near, of, off, on, onto, out, outside, over, past, since, through, till, to, toward, under, underneath, until, up, upon, with, within, without	according to, as of, as well as, aside from, because of, by means of, in addition to, in front of, in place of, in respect to, in spite of, instead of, on account of, out of, prior to, with regard to

Interjections

INTERJECTIONS have no grammatical attachment to the sentence itself other than to add expressions of emotion. These parts of speech may be punctuated with commas or exclamation points and may fall anywhere within the sentence itself:

Ouch! He stepped on my toe.

She shopped at the stores after Christmas and, hooray, found many items on sale.

I have seen his love for his father in many expressions of concern—Wow!

> Interjections should generally be avoided in formal writing.

EXAMPLES

1) List all of the adjectives used in the following sentence:

   Her camera fell into the turbulent water, so her frantic friend quickly grabbed the damp item.

   A. turbulent, frantic, damp

   B. turbulent, frantic, quickly, damp

   C. her, turbulent, her, frantic, damp

   D. her, the, turbulent, her, frantic, the, damp

   Answers:

   A. is incorrect. This list is incomplete.

   B. is incorrect. This list is incomplete and inaccurate; *quickly* is an adverb.

   C. is incorrect. This list is incomplete.

   D. is correct. *Turbulent*, *frantic*, and *damp* are adjectives; *her* is modifying first *camera* and then *friend*; and *the* is always a limiting adjective—the definite article.

2) List all of the pronouns used in the following sentence:

Several of the administrators who had spoken clearly on the budget increase gave both of the opposing committee members a list of their ideas.

A. several, of, their

B. several, who, both

C. several, who, both, their

D. several, both

Answers:

A. is incorrect. The word *of* is a preposition; the word *their* is being used as a possessive adjective.

B. is correct. *Several* is an indefinite plural pronoun; *who* is a relative pronoun introducing the adjectival clause *who had spoken clearly on the budget increase*; *both* is an indefinite plural pronoun.

C. is incorrect. The word *their* is being used as a possessive adjective.

D. is incorrect. The list is missing the word *who* which is a relative pronoun introducing the adjectival clause *who had spoken clearly on the budget increase*.

3) List all of the conjunctions in the following sentence, and indicate after each conjunction whether the conjunctions are coordinating, correlative, or subordinating:

The political parties do not know if the most popular candidates will survive until the election, but neither the voters nor the candidates will give up their push for popularity.

A. if (subordinating), until (subordinating), but (coordinating), neither/nor (correlative), for (coordinating)

B. if (subordinating), but (coordinating), neither/nor (correlative), for (coordinating)

C. if (subordinating), but (coordinating), neither/nor (correlative)

D. if (subordinating), until (subordinating), but (coordinating), neither/nor (correlative), up (subordinating), for (coordinating)

Answers:

A. is incorrect. *Until* and *for* in this sentence are acting as prepositions.

B. is incorrect. *For* is acting as a preposition.

C. is correct. *If* is acting as a subordinating conjunction; *but* is acting as a coordinating conjunction; and *neither/nor* is a correlative conjunction pair.

D. is incorrect. *Up* is acting as an adverb.

Constructing Sentences

SYNTAX is the study of how words are combined to create sentences. In English, words are used to build phrases and clauses, which, in turn, are combined to create sentences. By varying the order and length of phrases and clauses, writers can create sentences that are diverse and interesting.

Phrases and clauses are made up of either a subject, a predicate, or both. The **SUBJECT** is what the sentence is about. It will be a noun that is usually performing the main action of the sentence, and it may be accompanied by modifiers. The **PREDICATE** describes what the subject is doing or being. It contains the verb(s) and any modifiers or objects that accompany it.

Phrases

A **PHRASE** is a group of words that communicates a partial idea and lacks either a subject or a predicate. Several phrases may be strung together, one after another, to add detail and interest to a sentence.

> The animals crossed <u>the large bridge to eat the fish on the wharf</u>.

Phrases are categorized based on the main word in the phrase. A **PREPOSITIONAL PHRASE** begins with a preposition and ends with an object of the preposition; a **VERB PHRASE** is composed of the main verb along with its helping verbs; and a **NOUN PHRASE** consists of a noun and its modifiers.

> prepositional phrase: The dog is hiding <u>under the porch</u>.

> verb phrase: The chef <u>would have created</u> another soufflé, but the staff protested.

> noun phrase: *The big, red barn* rests beside <u>the vacant chicken house</u>.

An **APPOSITIVE PHRASE** is a particular type of noun phrase that renames the word or group of words that precedes it. Appositive phrases usually follow the noun they describe and are set apart by commas.

> My dad, <u>a clock maker</u>, loved antiques.

VERBAL PHRASES begin with a word that would normally act as a verb but is instead filling another role within the sentence. These phrases can act as nouns, adjectives, or adverbs. **GERUND PHRASES** begin with gerunds, which are verbs that end in *–ing* and act as nouns. The word *gerund* has an *n* in it, a helpful reminder that the gerund acts as a noun. Therefore, the gerund phrase might act as the subject, the direct object, or the object of the preposition just as another noun would.

> gerund phrase: <u>Writing numerous Christmas cards</u> occupies her aunt's time each year.

A PARTICIPIAL PHRASE is a verbal phrase that acts as an adjective. These phrases start with either present participles (which end in –*ing*) or past participles (which usually end in –*ed*). Participial phrases can be extracted from the sentence, and the sentence will still make sense because the participial phrase is playing only a modifying role:

Enjoying the stars that filled the sky, Dave lingered outside for quite a while.

Finally, an INFINITIVE PHRASE is a verbal phrase that may act as a noun, an adjective, or an adverb. Infinitive phrases begin with the word *to*, followed by a simple form of a verb (to eat, to jump, to skip, to laugh, to sing).

To visit Europe had always been her dream.

Clauses

CLAUSES contain both a subject and a predicate. They can be either independent or dependent. An INDEPENDENT (or main) CLAUSE can stand alone as its own sentence:

The dog ate her homework.

Dependent (or subordinate) clauses cannot stand alone as their own sentences. They start with a subordinating conjunction, relative pronoun, or relative adjective, which will make them sound incomplete:

Because the dog ate her homework

Table 2.12. Words That Begin Dependent Clauses

SUBORDINATING CONJUNCTIONS	RELATIVE PRONOUNS AND ADJECTIVES
after, before, once, since, until, when, whenever, while, as, because, in order that, so, so that, that, if, even if, provided that, unless, although, even though, though, whereas, where, wherever, than, whether	who, whoever, whom, whomever, whose, which, that, when, where, why, how

Types of Sentences

Sentences can be classified based on the number and type of clauses they contain. A SIMPLE SENTENCE will have only one independent clause and no dependent clauses. The sentence may contain phrases, complements, and modifiers, but it will comprise only one independent clause, one complete idea.

The cat under the back porch jumped against the glass yesterday.

A COMPOUND SENTENCE has two or more independent clauses and no dependent clauses:

The cat under the back porch jumped against the glass yesterday, and he scared my grandma.

A COMPLEX SENTENCE has only one independent clause and one or more dependent clauses:

The cat under the back porch, who loves tuna, jumped against the glass yesterday.

A COMPOUND-COMPLEX SENTENCE has two or more independent clauses and one or more dependent clause:

The cat under the back porch, who loves tuna, jumped against the glass yesterday; he left a mark on the window.

Table 6.13. Sentence Structure and Clauses

SENTENCE STRUCTURE	INDEPENDENT CLAUSES	DEPENDENT CLAUSES
Simple	1	0
Compound	2 +	0
Complex	1	1 +
Compound-complex	2 +	1 +

Writers can diversify their use of phrases and clauses in order to introduce variety into their writing. Variety in SENTENCE STRUCTURE not only makes writing more interesting but also allows writers to emphasize that which deserves emphasis. In a paragraph of complex sentences, a short, simple sentence can be a powerful way to draw attention to a major point.

EXAMPLES

1) Identify the prepositional phrase in the following sentence:

Wrapping packages for the soldiers, the kind woman tightly rolled the t-shirts to see how much space remained for the homemade cookies.

A. Wrapping packages for the soldiers

B. the kind woman

C. to see how much space

D. for the homemade cookies

Answers:

A. is incorrect. This is a participial phrase that begins with the participle *wrapping*.

B. is incorrect. This is a noun phrase that contains the noun *woman* and modifiers.

C. is incorrect. This is an infinitive phrase that begins with the infinitive *to see*.

D. is correct. This phrase begins with the preposition *for*.

Punctuation

Many of the choices writers must make relate to **PUNCTUATION**. While creative writers have the liberty to play with punctuation to achieve their desired ends, academic and technical writers must adhere to stricter conventions. The main punctuation marks are periods, question marks, exclamation marks, colons, semicolons, commas, quotation marks, and apostrophes.

There are three terminal punctuation marks that can be used to end sentences. The **PERIOD** is the most common and is used to end declarative (statement) and imperative (command) sentences. The **QUESTION MARK** is used to end interrogative sentences, and exclamation marks are used to indicate that the writer or speaker is exhibiting intense emotion or energy.

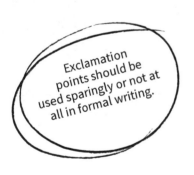

Exclamation points should be used sparingly or not at all in formal writing.

> Sarah and I are attending a concert.
>
> How many people are attending the concert?
>
> What a great show that was!

The **COLON** and the **SEMICOLON**, though often confused, have a unique set of rules surrounding their respective uses. While both punctuation marks are used to join clauses, the construction of the clauses and the relationship between them varies.

The **SEMICOLON** is used to show a general relationship between two independent clauses (IC; IC):

The disgruntled customer tapped angrily on the <u>counter;</u> <u>she</u> had to wait nearly ten minutes to speak to the manager.

Coordinating conjunctions (FANBOYS) cannot be used with semi-colons. However, conjunctive adverbs can be used following a semi-colon:

She may not have to take the course this <u>year; however,</u> she will eventually have to sign up for that specific course.

The COLON, somewhat less limited than the semicolon in its usage, is used to introduce a list, definition, or clarification. While the clause preceding the colon must be an independent clause, the clause that follows does not have to be one:

The buffet offers three choices that include: ham, turkey, or roast. (incorrect)

The buffet offers three choices: ham, turkey, or roast. (correct)

The buffet offers three choices that include the following: ham, turkey, or roast. (correct)

Note that neither the semicolon nor the colon should be used to set off an introductory phrase from the rest of the sentence.

After the trip to the raceway; we realized that we should have brought ear plugs. (incorrect)

After the trip to the raceway: we realized that we should have brought ear plugs. (incorrect)

After the trip to the raceway, we realized that we should have brought ear plugs. (correct)

The COMMA is a complicated piece of punctuation that can serve many different purposes within a sentence. Many times comma placement is an issue of style, not mechanics, meaning there is not necessarily one correct way to write the sentence. There are, however, a few important hard-and-fast comma rules to be followed.

1. Commas should be used to separate two independent clauses along with a coordinating conjunction.

   George ordered the steak, but Bruce preferred the ham.

2. Commas should be used to separate coordinate adjectives (two different adjectives that describe the same noun).

   The shiny, regal horse ran majestically through the wide, open field.

3. Commas should be used to separate items in a series. The comma before the conjunction is called the Oxford or serial comma, and is optional.

   The list of groceries included cream, coffee, donuts, and tea.

Many people are taught that a comma represents a pause for breath. While this trick is useful for helping young readers, it is not a helpful guide for comma usage when writing.

4. Commas should be used to separate introductory words, phrases, and clauses from the rest of the sentence.

   Slowly, Nathan became aware of his surroundings after the concussion.

   Within an hour, the authorities will descend on the home.

   After Alice swam the channel, nothing intimidated her.

5. Commas should be used to set off non-essential information and appositives.

   Estelle, our newly elected chairperson, will be in attendance.

   Ida, my neighbor, watched the children for me last week.

6. Commas should be used to set off titles of famous individuals.

   Charles, Prince of Wales, visited Canada several times in the last ten years.

7. Commas should be used to set off the day and month of a date within a text.

   My birthday makes me feel quite old because I was born on February 16, 1958, in Minnesota.

8. Commas should be used to set up numbers in a text of more than four digits.

   We expect 25,000 visitors to the new museum.

QUOTATION MARKS are used for many purposes. First, quotation marks are used to enclose direct quotations within a sentence. Terminal punctuation that is part of the quotation should go inside the marks, and terminal punctuation that is part of the larger sentence goes outside:

   She asked him menacingly, "Where is my peanut butter?"

   What is the original meaning of the phrase "king of the hill"?

In American English, commas are used to set quotations apart from the following text and are placed inside the marks:

   "Although I find him tolerable," Arianna wrote, "I would never want him as a roommate."

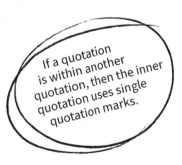
If a quotation is within another quotation, then the inner quotation uses single quotation marks.

Additionally, quotation marks enclose titles of short, or relatively short, literary works such as short stories, chapters, and poems. (The titles of longer works, like novels and anthologies, are italicized.) Writers also use quotation marks to set off words used in special sense or for a non-literary purpose:

   The shady dealings of his Ponzi scheme earned him the ironic name "Honest Abe."

APOSTROPHES, sometimes referred to as single quotation marks, show possession; replace missing letters, numerals, and signs; and form plurals of letters, numerals, and signs in certain instances.

1. To signify possession by a singular noun not ending in *s*, add *'s*.

   boy → boy's

2. To signify possession by a singular noun ending in *s*, add *'s*.

   class → class's

3. To signify possession by an indefinite pronoun not ending in *s*, add *'s*.

   someone → someone's

4. To signify possession by a plural noun not ending in *s*, add *'s*.

   children → children's

5. To signify possession by a plural noun ending in *s*, add only the apostrophe.

   boys → boys'

6. To signify possession by singular, compound words and phrases, add *'s* to the last word in the phrase.

   everybody else → everybody else's

7. To signify joint possession, add *'s* only to the last noun.

   John and Mary's house

8. To signify individual possession, add *'s* to each noun.

   John's and Mary's houses

9. To signify missing letters in a contraction, place the apostrophe where the letters are missing.

   do not → don't

10. To signify missing numerals, place the apostrophe where the numerals are missing.

    1989 → '89

11. There are differing schools of thought regarding the pluralization of numerals and dates, but be consistent within the document with whichever method you choose.

    1990's/1990s; A's/As

Other marks of punctuation include:

- EN DASH (–) to indicate a range of dates
- EM DASH (—) to indicate an abrupt break in a sentence and emphasize the words within the em dashes
- PARENTHESES ( ) to enclose insignificant information
- BRACKETS [ ] to enclose added words to a quotation and to add insignificant information within parentheses
- SLASH (/) to separate lines of poetry within a text or to indicate interchangeable terminology

- ELLIPSES (…) to indicate information removed from a quotation, to indicate a missing line of poetry, or to create a reflective pause

SAMPLE QUESTIONS

1) Identify the marks of punctuation needed in the following sentence:

Freds brother wanted the following items for Christmas a red car a condo and a puppy.

   A.   Fred's / Christmas; / car, /condo,

   B.   Fred's / Christmas: / car, / condo,

   C.   Fred's / Christmas: / red, / car,

   D.   Fred's / items' / Christmas: / car, / condo,

Answers:

A. is incorrect. *Christmas* must have a colon after it and not a semicolon. A semicolon must have an independent clause that precedes and follows.

B. is correct. To be possessive, *Fred's* requires an apostrophe before the s. *Christmas* needs a colon to indicate the upcoming list, and *car* and *condo* should be followed by a comma since they are items in a series.

C. is incorrect. The correct comma placement for items in a series is a, b, and c. *Red* is an adjective modifying *car* and so does not require a comma; it is not an item in the series of nouns.

D. is incorrect. The word *items* is simply plural without showing possession.

2) Which of the following sentences contains a comma usage error?

   A)   On her way home she stopped to pick up groceries, pay her electric bill, and buy some flowers.

   B.   I used to drink coffee every morning but my office took away the coffee machine.

   C.   Elizabeth will order the cake for the party after she orders the hats.

   D.   My cousin, who lives in Indiana, is coming to visit this weekend.

Answers:

A. is incorrect. The commas are used correctly in this series.

B. is correct. This compound sentence requires a comma before the conjunction *but*.

C. is incorrect. This complex sentence does not require a comma.

Avoiding Common Usage Errors

Errors in Agreement

Some of the most common grammatical errors are those involving agreement between subjects and verbs, and between nouns and pronouns. While it is impossible to cover all possible errors, the lists below include the most common agreement rules to look for on the test.

Ignore words between the subject and the verb to help make conjugation clearer: The new library ~~with its many books and rooms~~ fills a long-felt need.

SUBJECT/VERB AGREEMENT

1. Single subjects agree with single verbs; plural subjects agree with plural verbs.

   The girl walks her dog.

   The girls walk their dogs.

2. Compound subjects joined by *and* typically take a plural verb unless considered one item.

   Correctness and precision are required for all good writing.

   Macaroni and cheese makes a great snack for children.

3. Compound subjects joined by *or* or *nor* agree with the nearer or nearest subject.

   Neither I nor my friends are looking forward to our final exams.

   Neither my friends nor I am looking forward to our final exams.

4. For sentences with inverted word order, the verb will agree with the subject that follows it.

   Where are Bob and his friends going? Where is Bob going?

5. All single, indefinite pronouns agree with single verbs.

   Neither of the students is happy about the play.

   Each of the many cars is on the grass.

   Every one of the administrators speaks highly of Trevor.

6. All plural, indefinite pronouns agree with plural verbs.

   Several of the students are happy about the play.

   Both of the cars are on the grass.

   Many of the administrators speak highly of Trevor.

7. Collective nouns agree with singular verbs when the collective acts as one unit. Collective nouns agree with plural verbs when the collective acts as individuals within the group.

   The band plans a party after the final football game.

The <u>band play</u> their instruments even if it rains.

The <u>jury announces</u> its decision after sequestration.

The <u>jury make</u> phone calls during their break time.

8. The linking verbs agree with the subject and the predicate.

My <u>favorite is</u> strawberries and apples.

My <u>favorites are</u> strawberries and apples.

9. Nouns that are plural in form but singular in meaning will agree with singular verbs.

<u>Measles is</u> a painful disease.

<u>Sixty dollars is</u> too much to pay for that book.

10. Singular verbs come after titles, business corporations, and words used as terms.

<u>"Three Little Kittens" is</u> a favorite nursery rhyme for many children.

<u>General Motors is</u> a major employer for the city.

Pronoun/Antecedent Agreement

1. Antecedents joined by *and* typically require a plural pronoun.

The <u>children and their dogs</u> enjoyed <u>their</u> day at the beach.

2. For compound antecedents joined by *or*, the pronoun agrees with the nearer or nearest antecedent.

Either the resident mice <u>or the manager's cat</u> gets <u>itself</u> a meal of good leftovers.

3. When indefinite pronouns function in a sentence, the pronoun must agree with the number of the pronoun.

<u>Neither</u> student finished <u>his or her</u> assignment.

<u>Both</u> of the students finished <u>their</u> assignments.

4. When collective nouns function as antecedents, the pronoun choice will be singular or plural depending on the function of the collective.

The <u>audience</u> was cheering as <u>it</u> rose to <u>its</u> feet in unison.

Our <u>family</u> are spending <u>their</u> vacations in Maine, Hawaii, and Rome.

5. When *each* and *every* precede the antecedent, the pronoun agreement will be singular.

<u>Each and every man, woman, and child</u> brings unique qualities to <u>his or her</u> family.

<u>Every creative writer, technical writer, and research writer</u> is attending <u>his or her</u> assigned lecture.

Errors in Sentence Construction

ERRORS IN PARALLELISM occur when items in a series are not put in the same form. For example, if a list contains two nouns and a verb, the sentence should be rewritten so that all three items are the same part of speech. Parallelism should be maintained in words, phrases, and clauses:

The walls were painted <u>green</u> and <u>gold</u>.

Her home is <u>up the hill</u> and <u>beyond the trees</u>.

<u>If we shop on Friday</u> and <u>if we have enough time</u>, we will then visit the aquarium.

SENTENCE ERRORS fall into three categories: fragments, comma splices (comma fault), and fused sentences (run-on). A FRAGMENT occurs when a group of words does not have both a subject and verb as needed to construct a complete sentence or thought. Many times a writer will mirror conversation and write down only a dependent clause, for example, which will have a subject and verb but will not have a complete thought grammatically.

Why are you not going to the mall? Because I do not like shopping. (incorrect)

Because I do not like shopping, I will not plan to go to the mall. (correct)

A COMMA SPLICE (comma fault) occurs when two independent clauses are joined together with only a comma to "splice" them together. To fix a comma splice, a coordinating conjunction should be added, or the comma can be replaced by a semicolon:

My family eats turkey at Thanksgiving, we eat ham at Christmas. (incorrect)

My family eats turkey at Thanksgiving, and we eat ham at Christmas. (correct)

My family eats turkey at Thanksgiving; we eat ham at Christmas. (correct)

FUSED (run-on) sentences occur when two independent clauses are joined with no punctuation whatsoever. Like comma splices, they can be fixed with a comma and conjunction or with a semicolon:

My sister lives nearby she never comes to visit. (incorrect)

My sister lives nearby, but she never comes to visit. (correct)

My sister lives nearby; she never comes to visit. (correct)

Commonly Confused Words

A, AN: *a* is used before words beginning with consonants or consonant sounds; *an* is used before words beginning with vowels or vowel sounds.

AFFECT, EFFECT: *affect* is most often a verb; *effect* is usually a noun (*The experience affected me significantly* OR *The experience had a significant effect on me.*)

AMONG, AMONGST, BETWEEN: *among* is used for a group of more than two people; *amongst* is archaic and not commonly used in modern writing; *between* is reserved to distinguish two people, places, things, or groups.

AMOUNT, NUMBER: *amount* is used for non-countable sums; *number* is used with countable nouns (*She had a large amount of money in her purse, nearly fifty dollars.*)

CITE, SITE: *cite* is a verb used in documentation to credit an author of a quotation, paraphrase, or summary; *site* is a location.

ELICIT, ILLICIT: *elicit* means to draw out a response from an audience or a listener; *illicit* refers to illegal activity.

EVERY DAY, EVERYDAY: *every day* is an indefinite adjective modifying a noun—*each day* could be used interchangeably with *every day*; *everyday* is a one-word adjective to imply frequent occurrence (*Our visit to the Minnesota State Fair is an everyday activity during August.*)

FEWER, LESS: *fewer* is used with a countable noun; *less* is used with a non-countable noun (*Fewer parents are experiencing stress since the new teacher was hired; parents are experiencing less stress since the new teacher was hired.*)

FIRSTLY, SECONDLY: These words are archaic; today, *first* and *second* are more commonly used.

GOOD, WELL: *good* is always the adjective; *well* is always the adverb except in cases of health (*She felt well after the surgery.*)

IMPLIED, INFERRED: *implied* is something a speaker does; *inferred* is something the listener does after assessing the speaker's message (*The speaker implied something mysterious, but I inferred the wrong thing.*)

IRREGARDLESS, REGARDLESS: *irregardless* is non-standard usage and should be avoided; *regardless* is the proper usage of the transitional statement.

ITS, IT'S: *its* is a possessive case pronoun; *it's* is a contraction for *it is*.

MORAL, MORALE: *moral* is a summative lesson from a story or life event; *morale* is the emotional attitude of a person or group of people.

PRINCIPAL, PRINCIPLE: *principal* is the leader of a school in the noun usage; *principal* means *main* in the adjectival usage; *principle* is a noun meaning *idea* or *tenet* (*The principal of the school spoke on the principal meaning of the main principles of the school.*)

QUOTE, QUOTATION: *quote* is a verb and should be used as a verb; *quotation* is the noun and should be used as a noun.

REASON WHY: *reason why* is a redundant expression—use one or the other (*The reason we left is a secret. Why we left is a secret.*)

SHOULD OF, SHOULD HAVE: *should of* is improper usage, likely resulting from misunderstood speech—*of* is not a helping verb and can therefore cannot complete the verb phrase; *should have* is the proper usage. (*He should have driven.*)

THAN, THEN: *than* sets up a comparison of some kind; *then* indicates a reference to a point in time (*When I said that I liked the hat better than the gloves, my sister laughed; then she bought both for me.*)

THEIR, THERE, THEY'RE: *their is* the possessive case of the pronoun *they. There* is the demonstrative pronoun indicating location, or place. *They're* is a contraction of the words *they are*, the third-person plural subject pronoun and third-person plural, present-tense conjugation of the verb *to be.* These words are very commonly confused in written English.

TO LIE (TO RECLINE), TO LAY (TO PLACE): *to lie* is the intransitive verb meaning *to recline*, so the verb does not take an object; *to lay* is the transitive verb meaning *to place something.* (*I lie out in the sun; I lay my towel on the beach.*)

TO TRY AND: *to try and* is sometimes used erroneously in place of *to try to.* (*She should try to succeed daily.*)

UNIQUE: *unique* is an ultimate superlative. The word *unique* should not be modified technically. (*The experience was ~~very~~ unique.*)

WHO, WHOM: *who* is the subject relative pronoun. (*My son, who is a good student, studies hard.*) Here, the son is carrying out the action of studying, so the pronoun is a subject pronoun (*who*). *Whom* is the object relative pronoun. (*My son, whom the other students admire, studies hard.*) Here, *son* is the object of the other students' admiration, so the pronoun standing in for him, *whom*, is an object pronoun.

YOUR, YOU'RE: *your* is the possessive case of the pronoun *you*. *You're* is a contraction of the words *you are*, the second-person subject pronoun and the second-person singular, present-tense conjugation of the verb *to be*. These words are commonly confused in written English.

EXAMPLES

1) Which sentence does NOT contain an error?

   A. My sister and my best friend lives in Chicago.

   B. My parents or my brother is going to pick me up from the airport.

   C. Neither of the students refuse to take the exam.

   D. The team were playing a great game until the rain started.

Answers:

A. is incorrect. Because the sentence reads *My sister and my best friend*, the subject is plural and needs a plural verb (*live*).

B. is correct. The verb agrees with the closest subject—in this case, the singular *brother*.

C. is incorrect. *Neither* is a singular, indefinite pronoun, so the agreement is singular. *Neither refuses*

D. is incorrect. In the context of a game, the *team* is functioning as a singular, so it should take a singular verb. *The team was*

---

2) Which sentence does NOT contain an error?

   A. The grandchildren and their cousins enjoyed their day at the beach.

   B. Most of the grass has lost their deep color.

   C. The jury was cheering as their commitment came to a close.

   D. Every boy and girl must learn to behave themselves in school.

Answers:

A. is correct. *Grandchildren and cousins/their*

B. is incorrect. *Most of the grass has lost <u>its</u> deep color.*

C. is incorrect. *The jury was cheering as <u>its</u> commitment came to a close.*

D. is incorrect. *Every boy and girl must learn to behave himself or herself in school.*

10) Which of the following sentence errors is labeled correctly?

   A. Since she went to the store. (fused)

   B. The football game ended in a tie, the underdog caught up in the fourth quarter. (fragment)

   C. The football game ended in a tie the underdog caught up in the fourth quarter. (fused)

   D. When the players dropped their gloves, a fight broke out on the ice hockey rink floor. (comma splice)

Answers:

A. is incorrect. The group of words in A is not a complete thought and would, therefore, be classified as a fragment.

B. is incorrect. The sentence in B joins two complete thoughts with only a comma and would therefore be classified as a comma splice.

C. is correct. These two independent clauses in C are fused because there is no punctuation where the two clauses meet.

D. is incorrect. The sentence in D is punctuated properly and constructed correctly. The introductory, adverbial clause is punctuated with a comma; then an independent clause follows.

eight

WRITING

Regardless of the format or topic, a high-scoring essay can be written by following several simple rules. First, identify the type of essay to be written: if the essay doesn't correctly address the prompt, it will always receive a low score. Second, determine what the main point and organizational structure of the essay will be. It is much easier to write using a clear outline than to haphazardly organize along the way. Third, make sure that the essay uses sound evidence while maintaining a style that's appropriate to the test. A good essay doesn't have to be complicated; it just needs to have a clear, well-reasoned position. Finally, all of this must be accomplished within a limited time frame. Fortunately, the essay graders will understand that a first draft written under test conditions does not need to be as polished as a final essay in a classroom assignment.

Types of Essays

It is important to note that essays do not follow a single format. Rather, the format is determined by the intended purpose of each essay. For example, an essay may attempt to inform or persuade the reader, or perhaps describe or narrate a scene. It is important to use the appropriate type of essay for a given task.

Persuasive

A PERSUASIVE ESSAY is meant to convince the reader of the author's point of view on a particular issue. Typically, such an essay will also include a call to action. Thus, a persuasive essay should cause the reader to feel and act in a particular way.

A persuasive essay can be written on any topic on which people can have a difference of opinion. For example, an essay may argue that social media is harmful to teenagers or that a noise ordinance should be adopted in a community. These both seek to sway the reader's opinion to that of the author's. In contrast, essays describing the social media habits of teenagers or telling the story of a neighborhood's attempt to pass local noise ordinances are not persuasive because they do not present a specific opinion.

In writing a persuasive essay, it is vital to take a clear stance on an issue. The reader should be left with no doubt as to which side of an issue the writer supports. In addition, a persuasive essay must include facts and logical reasoning to show that the ideas put forth by the author are superior to other ideas on the topic. This type of essay should be written with a specific audience in mind to tailor the arguments and language to the intended readers.

When writing persuasive essays in an exam setting, keep in mind that the actual stance taken in the essay is not important. The graders don't care about the specific opinion expressed in the essay; they only care that the opinion is well written and supported by logically relevant evidence.

PERSUASIVE ESSAY EXAMPLE

PROMPT: Technology has launched us into a new era and, with it, a new way of living with and relating to one another. It has opened doors and allowed us to accomplish things that would have been impossible in the past: we are able to keep up closely with a large number of people in an easy and comfortable way. As it continues to develop, social media technology will, time and again, offer us new and better ways of staying in touch with one another and, because of it, will make our lives and our relationships fuller and more meaningful.

Discuss the extent to which you agree or disagree with this opinion. Support your position with specific reasoning and examples from your experience, observations, and reading.

One would be foolish to argue that technology has not had a real and pervasive impact on our daily lives. Many of us rely daily on cell phones, tablets, and computers that allow us to reach family, friends, and business associates with little to no trouble. However, this ease of access does not necessarily mean our relationships are improving: the impersonal and anonymous nature of social media and other communication technologies make it even more difficult for us to make meaningful, lasting connections with the people around us.

Social media is, by nature, impersonal. Though we are able to build personal profiles that reflect whom we want the world to see, these profiles do little to improve our connection and communication with others. In fact, it is these very tools that are distancing us from our fellow humans. Birthday notifications, for example, remind social media users every day of the "friends" who are celebrating that day. While this tool seems, in theory, to be a great way to keep up with others, it actually desensitizes us. In truth, when I receive birthday notifications via social media, I end up either ignoring them altogether or sending an impersonal "Happy Birthday" just to be able to say I did. In fact, I never send birthday notes via social media to friends and family whose birthdays I actually care about because I do so in a more personal way—via a phone call or in person. Furthermore, I don't need an app to remember those birthdays. Though it may seem more useful or convenient to be able to stay in touch through social media, the relationships that rely on it are, in my experience, rarely very meaningful. By allowing us to stay in touch with larger numbers of people, social media also makes our connections shallower.

In addition to being impersonal, social media and other communication technologies can also be anonymous, creating a world of users that are disconnected from the things they post and read and, ultimately, from each other. Cyber bullying has been a significant concern of the twenty-first century, with numerous incidents leading to depressing outcomes, like teenage suicide. Through the lens of social media, bullies are able to disregard the humanity of the person on the other end and say things that they might never say in real life. A similar effect is clear during important political events: people post, with aggressive fervor, in favor of their own beliefs and respond, with equally aggressive insults, to anyone they disagree with. While this may, on the surface, seem to encourage open dialogue, social media and other communication technologies fail to have any effect on the quality of the conversation itself. Rather than learning to interact with one another respectfully, a tactic that may actually lead to increased understanding and greater acceptance of others, social media users learn that what they say has little to no consequence in real life.

The sense of community created by social media is deceptive. The ease with which people can "connect" often makes those connections meaningless. The friend who "Likes" a photo you post isn't putting any real energy into that friendship—he just clicked once and moved on. Similarly, people can use the anonymity of the internet to just as easily create enemies. One angry comment (that would never be said face-to-face) can launch a hundred nasty replies. These types of relationships don't make our lives fuller or more meaningful. They make our lives empty and shallow.

Writing a Thesis Statement

The thesis, or THESIS STATEMENT, is central to the structure and meaning of an essay: it presents the writer's argument or position on an issue. In other words, it tells readers specifically what the author is going to say in the essay. A strong, direct thesis statement is key to the organization of any essay. It introduces both the central idea of the essay and the main points that will be used to support that idea. Thus, the thesis will mirror the organization of the essay as a whole: each paragraph can elaborate on each supporting point.

In writing a thesis statement, it is important to respond to the prompt provided. The author must identify keywords in the prompt and think about what the prompt is asking. For example, the prompt may be asking for a clear stance to be taken a particular issue, or it may require a detailed explanation of a topic. Once a clear understanding of the task is reached, the author must develop a central idea along with supporting points from relevant sources, including any provided documents and personal knowledge or experience. The central idea and supporting points can then be concisely packaged into a one or two sentence statement. Generally, a thesis statement is no more than two sentences.

Find an op-ed article in the newspaper. Read it carefully and try to identify the thesis and supporting points.

THESIS STATEMENT EXAMPLES

PROMPT: Many high schools have begun to adopt 1:1 technology programs, meaning that each school provides every student with a computing device, such as a laptop or tablet. Educators who support these initiatives say that the technology allows for more dynamic collaboration and that students need to learn technology skills to compete in the job market. On the other hand, opponents cite increased distraction and the dangers of cyber-bullying or unsupervised internet use as reasons not to provide students with such devices.

In your essay, take a position on this question. You may write about either one of the two points of view given, or you may present a different point of view on this question. Use specific reasons and examples to support your position.

Possible thesis statements:

1) Providing technology to every student is good for education because it allows students to learn important skills such as typing, web design, and video editing, and it also gives students more opportunities to work cooperatively with their classmates and teachers.

2) I disagree with the idea that schools should provide technology to students because most students will simply be distracted by the free access to games and websites when they should be studying or doing homework.

3) By providing each student with a laptop or tablet, schools can help students apply technology to work more effectively with other students, communicate with teachers and classmates, and conduct research for class projects.

Structuring the Essay

There are a lot of different ways to organize an essay. In the limited timeframe of an exam, however, it is best to stick to a basic five-paragraph essay that includes an introduction, body, and conclusion. This structure can be used to discuss nearly any topic and will be easy for graders to follow.

Introductions

The purpose of an **INTRODUCTION** is to set the stage for the essay. This is accomplished by capturing the reader's interest, introducing and providing context for the topic, and stating the central idea and main points of the essay. Usually the introductory paragraph ends with a thesis statement, which clearly sets forth the position or point the essay will argue.

INTRODUCTION EXAMPLE

Technology has changed massively in recent years, but today's generation barely notices—high school students are already experienced with the internet, computers, apps, cameras, cell phones, and more. It's inevitable that these technologies will be begin to make their way into classrooms. Opponents of 1:1 technology programs might argue that students will be distracted or misuse the technology, but that is exactly why schools must teach them to use it. Students need to know how to navigate technology safely and effectively, and schools have a responsibility to ensure they learn these skills. By providing each student with a laptop or tablet, schools can help students learn how to apply technology to work more effectively with other students, communicate with teachers and classmates, and conduct research for class projects.

Explanation: This introduction *introduces* the topic in the first sentence. It then provides context by discussing why technology in the classroom is an important—and controversial—topic. The paragraph closes with a thesis statement that takes a firm stance and introduces the supporting ideas that the essay will be organized around.

The Body Paragraphs

The body of the essay should consist of two to four paragraphs, each of which is focused on a single supporting idea. The body of an essay can be organized in a number of ways:

- Body paragraphs can explain each supporting detail given in the thesis statement.
- Body paragraphs can describe a problem then discuss the pros and cons of a solution in separate paragraphs.
- Body paragraphs can tell a story, with the story broken into two to four logical parts.
- Body paragraphs can compare and contrast the merits of two arguments, possibly drawing a conclusion about which is better at the end.

Each paragraph should be structurally consistent, beginning with a topic sentence to introduce the main idea, followed by supporting ideas and examples. No extra ideas unrelated to the paragraph's focus should appear. Transition words and phrases can be used to connect body paragraphs and to improve the flow and readability of the essay.

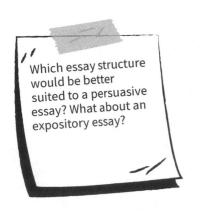

Which essay structure would be better suited to a persuasive essay? What about an expository essay?

BODY PARAGRAPH EXAMPLE

Technology can be a powerful tool for collaboration. When all of the students in a classroom have access to reliable laptops or tablets, they are able to more effectively share information and work together on projects. Students can communicate quickly via email, share files through a cloud service, and use a shared calendar for scheduling. They also have the opportunity to teach each other new skills since each student may bring to the group unique knowledge about particular apps or programs. When the availability of technology is limited or inconsistent, these opportunities are lost.

Explanation: This body paragraph discusses a supporting detail given the thesis (*schools can help students apply technology to work more effectively with other students*). It introduces the topic, then provides concrete examples of how technology makes it easier to work with other students. The final sentence reemphasizes the paragraph's main idea.

Conclusions

To end an essay smoothly, the author must compose a conclusion that reminds the reader of the importance of the topic and then restates the essay's thesis and supporting details. The writer should revisit the ideas in the introduction and thesis statement, but these ideas should not be simply repeated word-for-word. Rather, a well-written conclusion will reinforce the argument using wording that differs from the thesis statement but conveys the same idea. The conclusion should leave the reader with a strong impression of the essay's main idea and provide the essay with a sense of closure.

CONCLUSION EXAMPLE

As technology continues to change and become more incorporated into everyday life, students will need to adapt to it. Schools already teach young people a myriad of academic and life skills, so it makes sense that they would teach students how to use technology appropriately, too. When technology is incorporated into schoolwork, students will learn to collaborate, communicate, and research more effectively. Providing students with their own devices is one part of this important task, and schools that do so should be supported.

Explanation: This conclusion reminds the reader why the topic is important and then restates the thesis and supporting ideas. It ends with a strong, clear statement of the writer's stance on the issue.

Supporting Evidence

An essay's arguments are made up of claims, which in turn are backed by supporting evidence. This evidence can be drawn from a number of sources. Some essay prompts will include texts from which to draw supporting evidence. Other essays will require the writer to use his or her own background knowledge of the issue. For some essay prompts, it may be appropriate to use personal anecdotes and experiences. Regardless of the source of the evidence, it is important that it be conveyed in a clear, specific, and accurate manner.

Providing Specific Examples

In body paragraphs, general statements should be followed with specific examples that will help to convince the reader that the argument has merit. These specific examples do not bring new ideas to the paragraph; rather, they explain or defend the general ideas that have already been stated. A poorly written essay will be full of general claims supported by little to no evidence or specific examples. Conversely, successful essays will use multiple specific examples to back up general claims.

EXAMPLES OF GENERAL AND SPECIFIC STATEMENTS

The following are some examples of general statements, followed by examples of specific statements that provide more detailed support of an idea.

General: Students may get distracted online or access harmful websites.

Incorporating Sources

Providing evidence from outside sources is an excellent way to provide support for the claims in an essay. Some essay prompts will include texts that may be cited in the essay, or writers may want to cite sources from memory. In either case, this supporting evidence should be incorporated smoothly into the essay. Context should be provided for the quote, and the quote should always be followed by a discussion of its importance or relevance to the essay.

When using outside sources, it is vital to credit the author or source within the text. Usually a full citation isn't needed—it can simply be sufficient to note the author's name in the text. And, as always, the writer must make sure to place direct quotations in quotation marks.

> In an essay, a quote never speaks for itself; the writer must always explain where it came from and why it is important.

Writing Well

Although the content of an essay is of primary importance, the writing itself will also factor into the essay's final score. Writing well means that the language and tone are appropriate for the purpose and audience of the essay, the flow of ideas and the relationships among them are logical and clear, and the sentences are varied enough to keep the reader interested.

Transitions

Transitions are words, phrases, and ideas that help connect ideas throughout a text both between sentences and between paragraphs. Transitions can be used to imply a range of relationships, including cause and effect, sequence, contradictions, and continuance of an idea. Consistent and creative use of transitions will help the essay flow logically from one idea to the next and will make the essay easy for the reader to follow.

Transitions between paragraphs can also be polished by starting paragraphs with references to ideas mentioned in previous paragraphs or by ending them with a transition to the next topic. Such guideposts will guide the reader from one paragraph to the next.

Common transitions include *then, next, in other words, as well, in addition to, another, because, first, finally, in conclusion, however, in fact, therefore,* and *on the other hand.*

EXAMPLES OF TRANSITIONS

Teens often think they are hidden behind their computer screens. <u>However,</u> providing personal information online can lead to danger in the real world.

<u>In addition to</u> helping students work better with each other, technology can also help students communicate more effectively with teachers.

They <u>also</u> have the opportunity to teach each other new skills.

Syntax

A variety of well-written sentences will help maintain the reader's interest in the essay. To create this theme, a writer can use sentences that differ in length and that begin with varying words, rather than repeating the same word at the start of each new sentence. It is also important for the writer to use a mix of different sentence structures, including simple, complex, compound, and compound-complex sentences.

Word Choice and Tone

The words a writer chooses influence the reader's assessment of the essay. When writing essays, it is always necessary to choose words that are appropriate to the task.

For instance, a formal essay on an academic topic may benefit from complex sentences and an expansive vocabulary. However, a first-person essay on a personal topic may use a more causal vocabulary and organization. In general, when writing for exam graders, it is best to use clear, direct vocabulary and avoid using vague, general words such as good, bad, very, or a lot. Showing variety in word choice can also help improve an essay's score. However, it is better to use more familiar vocabulary than to try to impress the exam grader with unfamiliar words or words that do not fit the context of the essay.

Technology is everywhere in modern life. We've all walked into a coffee shop full of laptops or have seen people walking with their phones in front of their faces. I know I've often looked up from my tablet to realize I've missed a whole conversation. With technology everywhere, it seems obvious that we would start using it in classrooms. Opponents of 1:1 technology programs say that technology will be too distracting or will be abused by students, but it seems like that's an even more important reason for students to learn how to use it. Schools are where students learn all kinds of life skills, and technology is just another skill to learn. By giving students laptops or tablets, schools can help students work better with each other, work better with teachers, and learn to do better research.

Explanation: The two paragraphs above discuss the same topic. The first has a word choice and tone for an academic essay; the second is written in a more relaxed, personal style.

Managing Time

When working on an essay under time constraints, it is important to manage time wisely. Simply launching into the introduction will likely result in a hurried, unorganized essay and a low score. Instead, the writer should take a few minutes to plan. As a first step, the writer should thoroughly read the prompt and any accompanying texts, and then determine the type of essay that is required. Next, the writer must decide on a thesis and what kind of supporting evidence to use. Once the thesis is clear, it is a good idea for the writer to create a brief outline of the essay. This whole process should only take a few minutes, leaving the bulk of the time for writing. However, it is always a good idea to leave a few minutes at the end to proofread and revise as necessary.

Underline key words in the prompt so you can refer to them while writing the essay. This can help keep you and your essay focused.

Example Essays

PROMPT: The rise in popularity of e-cigarettes has reduced the overall smoking rate according to the Centers for Disease Control and Prevention. Many hail the new technology for helping smokers quit traditional tobacco cigarettes. However, others raise concerns about the appeal of e-cigarettes to young people and advocate FDA regulation of e-cigarettes to prevent negative side effects of their use on a new generation of smokers.

In your essay, take a position on this question. You may write about either one of the two points of view given, or you may present a different point of view on this question. Use specific reasons and examples to support your position.

EXAMPLE ESSAY ONE

For decades, youth smoking was a major concern for both parents and public health advocates. With education campaigns informing youth of the dangers of smoking and legal action taken against tobacco producers for their advertising tactics, the number of youth smoking traditional cigarettes has never been lower. But new technology is threatening to overturn that progress as electronic (e-cigarettes) have skyrocketed in popularity among both adults and youth. E-cigarettes should be regulated by the FDA to prevent youth from smoking since the long-term effects of e-cig use are unknown, youth are still becoming addicted to nicotine, and e-cigs could be a gateway to traditional smoking.

Smoking has long been a way for young people to feel cool or sophisticated. Popular culture, including film and television, glamorized smoking and led generations of Americans to pick up the habit. Although traditional smoking is no longer considered cool, the use of e-cigarettes, or vaping, threatens to take the same position in popular culture. Companies which produce traditional cigarettes have long been banned from advertising their products on television, but because e-cigarettes are not regulated by the FDA, there are no restrictions on their advertisement. This allows e-cig companies to reach youth through a wide range of media. Furthermore, the gadget-like design of e-cigs and the variety of candy-like flavors make them especially appealing to youth—a tactic that seems designed to hook a new generation on smoking.

This is particularly concerning as the long-term effects of vaping are not yet known for either adults or youth. The technology is too new to have been studied adequately. The FDA must study a drug for years before it can become available to the general public. Yet a device that delivers a highly-addictive substance remains unregulated. It is true that e-cigarettes are healthier for smokers than traditional cigarettes, but we cannot yet know the impact on youth who would have otherwise not smoked but for the easy access to these drug-delivery devices.

In addition, we do know that nicotine is a highly-addictive drug and that once this habit is established, it is very difficult to quit. If nothing else, this is a wasteful way for young people to spend their money. But even more concerning is the danger that nicotine use could alter the brain chemistry of young people and potentially make them prone to other addictions. Even if vaping does not become a gateway to hard drug use, it does make the leap to traditional smoking much more likely, and we know how harmful cigarettes have been.

The FDA has a responsibility to protect the public's health, and it is clear that regulation is needed to stop the momentum of the e-cigarette industry from getting youth addicted to their products. Although long-term health effects of vaping are unknown at this time, we must be cautious and err on the side of safety. At the very least, youth can be spared from an expensive, addictive habit; at best, an entire generation can live longer, healthier lives.

Explanation: This response provides good context for the discussion of the topic and takes a clear stance on the issue raised in the prompt. Strong examples and sound reasoning support the thesis. The essay is cohesive, and strong transitions connect ideas. Vocabulary and tone are appropriate, and the conclusion leaves the reader with a sense of the importance of the issue. Overall, this response would receive a high score.

EXAMPLE ESSAY TWO

Everyone knows smoking is bad for you. So, it's good that lots of people are quitting, and I think e-cigarettes, or vapes as they are also called, are helping people quit. Even though I don't use them, I know some people who use vapes, and they seem pretty healthy. It may be true that e-cigarettes have harmful side-effects, but it will be too far into the future before we know. The FDA should be studying this so that we do know if vapes are safe to use, especially for kids. No one wants kids to get hooked on drugs or to be unhealthy.

If they do start smoking, it is better for the kids to use e-cigarettes. They are less harmful because they don't use real tobacco or produce the terrible smelling smoke that normal cigarettes do. Some of my friends vape, and I don't even mind being in the same room. They actually smell pretty sweet. I don't think it's good to vape too much, but once in a while is fine, and I hope people make good choices about smoking.

Explanation: This response does not sufficiently address the prompt. The writer seems to disagree with the position of FDA regulation of e-cigarettes but does not develop this into a clear thesis. The writer's position is further confused by stating that the FDA should be studying the matter. The response is short and lacks adequate supporting detail. Although some personal examples are used, they are weak and a divergence from the main point. Although free of most errors, the language is simplistic, personal pronouns are overused, and the tone is not appropriate for academic writing. Overall, this response would receive a low score.

PART IV: PRACTICE

nine

PRACTICE TEST

Mathematics

Directions: For each of the questions below, choose the
best answer from the four choices given.

1. If $j = 4$, what is the value of
$2(j-4)^4 - j + \frac{1}{2}j$?

   A) 0

   B) −2

   C) 2

   D) 4

2. Simplify: $\sqrt[3]{64} + \sqrt[3]{729}$

   A) 13

   B) 17

   C) 31

   D) 35

3. If the surface area of a cylinder with
radius of 4 feet is 48π square feet,
what is its volume?

   A) 1π ft.^{3}

   B) 16π ft.^{3}

   C) 32π ft.^{3}

   D) 64π ft.^{3}

4. The average speed of cars on a
highway (s) is inversely proportional
to the number of cars on the road (n).
If a car drives at 65 mph when there
are 250 cars on the road, how fast will
a car drive when there are 325 cars on
the road?

   A) 50 mph

   B) 55 mph

   C) 60 mph

   D) 85 mph

5. Which of the following is a solution of
the given equation?

   $4(m + 4)^2 - 4m^2 + 20 = 276$

   A) 3

   B) 6

   C) 12

   D) 24

6. New York had the fewest months with less than 3 inches of rain in every year except:

Number of Months with 3 or Fewer Than 3 Inches of Rain

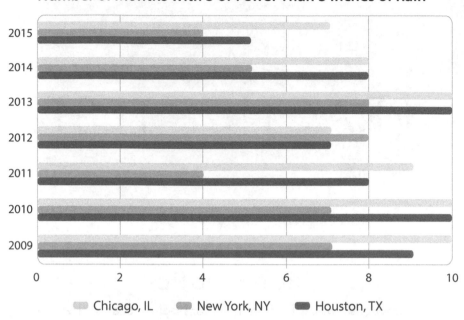

A) 2012

B) 2013

C) 2014

D) 2015

7. Which of the following is a solution to the inequality $2x + y \le -10$?

A) $(0, 0)$

B) $(10, 2)$

C) $(10, 10)$

D) $(-10, -10)$

8. If $\dfrac{4x-5}{3} = \dfrac{\frac{1}{2}(2x-6)}{5}$, what is the value of x?

A) $-\dfrac{2}{7}$

B) $-\dfrac{4}{17}$

C) $\dfrac{16}{17}$

D) $\dfrac{8}{7}$

9. Which of the following is the y-intercept of the given equation?

$7y - 42x + 7 = 0$

A) $(0, \frac{1}{6})$

B) $(6, 0)$

C) $(0, -1)$

D) $(-1, 0)$

10. In a class of 20 students, how many conversations must be had so that every student talks to every other student in the class?

A) 190

B) 380

C) 760

D) 6840

11. What is the value of z in the following system?

$z - 2x = 14$

$2z - 6x = 18$

A) -7

B) 3

C) 5

D) 24

12. Simplify: $\left(\dfrac{4x^{-3}y^4z}{8x^{-5}y^3z^{-2}}\right)^2$

A) $\dfrac{x^4yz^3}{2}$

B) $\dfrac{x^4y^2z^6}{2}$

C) $\dfrac{x^4y^2z^6}{4}$

D) $\dfrac{x^4yz^3}{4}$

13. The line $f(x)$ is shown on the graph below. If $g(x) = f(x - 2) + 3$, which of the following points lies on $g(x)$?

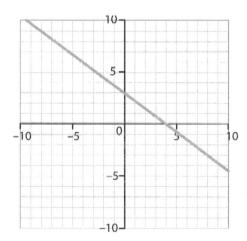

A) $(1, 2)$

B) $(2, 3)$

C) $(6, 3)$

D) $(7, 2)$

14. The line of best fit is calculated for a data set that tracks the number of miles that passenger cars traveled annually in the US from 1960 to 2010. In the model, $x = 0$ represents the year 1960, and y is the number of miles traveled in billions. If the line of best fit is $y = 0.0293x + 0.563$, approximately how many additional miles were traveled for every 5 years that passed?

A) 0.0293 billion

B) 0.1465 billion

C) 0.563 billion

D) 0.710 billion

15. If $\triangle ABD \sim \triangle DEF$ and the similarity ratio is 3:4, what is the measure of DE if $AB = 12$?

A) 9

B) 16

C) 96

D) 12

16. The mean of 13 numbers is 30. The mean of 8 of these numbers is 42. What is the mean of the other 5 numbers?

A) 5.5

B) 10.8

C) 16.4

D) 21.2

17. Fifteen DVDs are to be arranged on a shelf. 4 of the DVDs are horror films, 6 are comedies, and 5 are science fiction. In how many ways can the DVDs be arranged if DVDs of the same genre must be placed together?

A) 2,073,600

B) 6,220,800

C) 12,441,600

D) 131,216,200

18. Which inequality is represented by the following graph?

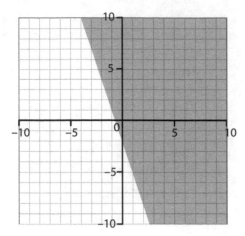

A) $y \geq -3x - 2$

B) $y \geq 3x - 2$

C) $y > -3x - 2$

D) $y \leq -3x - 2$

19. If the length of a rectangle is increased by 40% and its width is decreased by 40%, what is the effect on the rectangle's area?

A) The area is the same.

B) It increases by 16%.

C) It increases by 20%.

D) It decreases by 16%.

20. A cube is inscribed in a sphere such that each vertex on the cube touches the sphere. If the volume of the sphere is 972π cm³, what is the approximate volume of the cube in cubic centimeters?

A) 9

B) 10.4

C) 1125

D) 1729

Reading

Read the passage and then choose the best answer to the question. Answer the question on the basis of what is stated or implied in the passage.

It's that time again—the annual Friendswood Village Summer Fair is here! Last year we had a record number of visitors, and we're expecting an even bigger turnout this year. The fair will be bringing back all our traditional food and games, including the famous raffle. This year, we'll have a carousel, petting zoo, and climbing wall (for teenagers and adults only, please). We're also excited to welcome Petey's BBQ and Happy Tummy's Frozen Treats, who are both new to the fair this year. Tickets are available online and at local retailers.

1) According to the passage, which of the following will NOT be a new presence at the Fair this year?

    A. the raffle

    B. the petting zoo

    C. the carousel

    D. the climbing wall

In Greek mythology, two gods, Epimetheus and Prometheus, were given the work of creating living things. Epimetheus gave good powers to the different animals. To the lion he gave strength; to the bird, swiftness; to the fox, sagacity; and so on. Eventually, all of the good gifts had been bestowed, and there was nothing left for humans. As a result, Prometheus returned to heaven and brought down fire, which he gave to humans. With fire, human beings could protect themselves by making weapons. Over time, humans developed civilization and superiority.

2) In sentence 4, the word "bestowed" most nearly means

    A. purchased

    B. forgotten

    C. accepted

    D. given

It has now been two decades since the introduction of thermonuclear fusion weapons into the military inventories of the great powers, and more than a decade since the United States, Great Britain, and the Soviet Union ceased to test nuclear weapons in the atmosphere. Today our understanding of the technology of thermonuclear weapons seems highly advanced, but our knowledge of the physical and biological consequences of nuclear war is continuously evolving.

3) Which of the following best describes the topic of the passage?

    A. the impact of thermonuclear weapons on the military

    B. the technology of thermonuclear weapons

    C. atmospheric testing of nuclear weapons

    D. the physical and biological consequences of nuclear war

Alexander Hamilton and James Madison called for the Constitutional Convention to write a constitution as the foundation of a stronger federal government. Madison and other Federalists like John Adams believed in separation of powers, republicanism, and a strong federal government. Despite the separation of powers that would be provided for in the US Constitution, anti-Federalists like Thomas Jefferson called for even more limitations on the power of the federal government.

4) Details in the passage suggest that which of the following would most likely NOT support a strong federal government?

    A. Alexander Hamilton

    B. James Madison

    C. John Adams

    D. Thomas Jefferson

I say moreover that you make a great, a very great mistake, if you think that psychology, being the science of the mind's laws, is something from which you can deduce definite programs and schemes and methods of instruction for immediate schoolroom use. Psychology is a science, and teaching is an art; and sciences never generate arts directly out of themselves. An intermediary inventive mind must make the application, by using its originality.

5) What is the main purpose of this passage?

    A. to explain that psychology is a science.

    B. to emphasize that the science of psychology cannot determine educational programs and methods.

    C. to describe the artistic nature of educational practices, programming, and step-by-step planning.

    D. to compare the values of art to those of science.

In the eleven years that separated the Declaration of the Independence of the United States from the completion of that act in the ordination of our written Constitution, the great minds of America were bent upon the study of the principles of government that were essential to the preservation of the liberties which had been won at great cost and with heroic labors and sacrifices. Their studies were conducted in view of the imperfections that experience had developed in the government of the Confederation, and they were, therefore, practical and thorough.

6) The passage implies that the writers of the Constitution

    A. studied principles of government in relation to the government of the Confederation; their goal was to write a Constitution that would secure liberty in America.

    B worked to make sure that Americans would never lose the freedom that they fought to achieve.

    C. were both thorough and practical as they wrote the Constitution.

    D. studied the government of the Confederation and worked very hard to take into account the imperfections of this government.

For an adult person to be unable to swim points to something like criminal negligence; every man, woman and child should learn. A person who cannot swim may not only become a danger to himself, but to someone, and perhaps to several, of his fellow beings. Children as early as the age of four may acquire the art; none are too young, none too old.

Frank Eugen Dalton, Swimming Scientifically Taught, 1912

7) What is the main purpose of this passage?

    A. to encourage the reader to learn to swim

    B. to explain how people who cannot swim are a danger to others

    C. to inform the reader that it's never too late to learn to swim

    D. to argue that people who cannot swim should be punished

The greatest changes in sensory, motor, and perceptual development happen in the first two years of life. When babies are first born, most of their senses operate in a similar way to those of adults. For example, babies are able to hear before they are born; studies show that babies turn toward the sound of their mothers' voices just minutes after being born, indicating they recognize the mother's voice from their time in the womb.

The exception to this rule is vision. A baby's vision changes significantly in its first year of life; initially it has a range of vision of only 8 – 12 inches and no depth perception. As a result, infants rely primarily on hearing; vision does not become the dominant sense until around the age of 12 months. Babies also prefer faces to other objects. This preference, along with their limited vision range, means that their sight is initially focused on their caregiver.

8) Which of the following is an accurate summary of the passage?

    A. Babies have no depth perception until 12 months, which is why they focus only on their caregivers' faces.

    B. Babies can recognize their mothers' voices when born, so they initially rely primarily on their sense of hearing.

    C. Babies have senses similar to those of adults except for their sense of sight, which doesn't fully develop until 12 months.

    D. Babies' senses go through many changes in the first year of their lives.

9) According to the passage, which of the following senses do babies primarily rely on?

    A. vision

    B. hearing

    C. touch

    D. smell

In its most basic form, geography is the study of space; more specifically, it studies the physical space of the earth and the ways in which it interacts with, shapes, and is shaped by its habitants. Geographers look at the world from a spatial perspective. This means that at the center of all geographic study is the question, where? For geographers, the where of any interaction, event, or development is a crucial element to understanding it.

This question of where can be asked in a variety of fields of study, so there are many sub-disciplines of geography. These can be organized into four main categories: 1) regional studies, which examine the characteristics of a particular place; 2) topical studies, which look at a single physical or human feature that impacts the whole world; 3) physical studies, which focus on the physical features of Earth; and 4) human studies, which examine the relationship between human activity and the environment.

10) According to the passage, a researcher studying the relationship between farming and river systems would be engaged in which of the following geographical sub-disciplines?

    A. regional studies

    B. topical studies

    C. physical studies

    D. human studies

11) Which of the following is a concise summary of the passage?

    A. The most important questions in geography are where an event or development took place.

    B. Geography, which is the study of the physical space on Earth, can be broken down into four sub-disciplines.

    C. Regional studies is the study of a single region or area.

    D. Geography can be broken down into four sub-disciplines: regional studies, topical studies, physical studies, and human studies.

Skin coloration and markings have an important role to play in the world of snakes. Those intricate diamonds, stripes, and swirls help the animals hide from predators, but perhaps most importantly (for us humans, anyway), the markings can also indicate whether the snake is venomous. While it might seem counterintuitive for a venomous snake to stand out in bright red or blue, that fancy costume tells any nearby predator that approaching him would be a bad idea.

If you see a flashy-looking snake in the woods, though, those markings don't necessarily mean it's venomous: some snakes have found a way to ward off predators without the actual venom. The scarlet kingsnake, for example, has very similar markings to the venomous coral snake with whom it frequently shares a habitat. However, the kingsnake is actually nonvenomous; it's merely pretending to be dangerous to eat. A predatory hawk or eagle, usually hunting from high in the sky, can't tell the difference between the two species, and so the kingsnake gets passed over and lives another day.

12) The passage implies which of the following?

    A. The kingsnake is dangerous to humans.

    B. The coral snake and the kingsnake are both hunted by the same predators.

    C. It's safe to handle snakes in the woods because you can easily tell whether they're poisonous.

    D. The kingsnake changes its markings when hawks or eagles are close by.

13) Which statement is NOT a detail from the passage?

    A. Predators will avoid eating kingsnakes because their markings are similar to those on coral snakes.

    B. Kingsnakes and coral snakes live in the same habitats.

    C. The coral snake uses its coloration to hide from predators.

    D. The kingsnake is not venomous.

14) In sentence 2, the word "intricate" most nearly means

    A. complex

    B. colorful

    C. purposeful

    D. changeable

15) According to the passage, what is the difference between kingsnakes and coral snakes?

    A. Both kingsnakes and coral snakes are nonvenomous, but coral snakes have colorful markings.

    B. Both kingsnakes and coral snakes are venomous, but kingsnakes have colorful markings.

    C. Kingsnakes are nonvenomous while coral snakes are venomous.

    D. Coral snakes are nonvenomous while kingsnakes are venomous.

We've been told for years that the recipe for weight loss is fewer calories in than calories out. In other words, eat less and exercise more, and your body will take care of the rest. As many of those who've tried to diet can attest, this edict doesn't always produce results. If you're one of those folks, you might have felt that you just weren't doing it right—that the failure was all your fault.

However, several new studies released this year have suggested that it might not be your fault at all. For example, a study of people who'd lost a high percentage of their body weight (>17%) in a short period of time found that they could not physically maintain their new weight. Scientists measured their resting metabolic rate and found that they'd need to consume only a few hundred calories a day to meet their metabolic needs. Basically, their bodies were in starvation mode and seemed to desperately hang on to each and every calorie. Eating even a single healthy, well-balanced meal a day would cause these subjects to start packing back on the pounds.

Other studies have shown that factors like intestinal bacteria, distribution of body fat, and hormone levels can affect the manner in which our bodies process calories. There's also the fact that it's actually quite difficult to measure the number of calories consumed during a particular meal and the number used while exercising.

16) Which of the following would be the best summary statement to conclude the passage?

    A. It turns out that conventional dieting wisdom doesn't capture the whole picture of how our bodies function.

    B. Still, counting calories and tracking exercise is a good idea if you want to lose weight.

    C. In conclusion, it's important to lose weight responsibly: losing too much weight at once can negatively impact the body.

    D. It's easy to see that diets don't work, so we should focus less on weight loss and more on overall health.

17) Which of the following type of arguments is used in the passage?

    A. emotional argument

    B. appeal to authority

    C. specific evidence

    D. rhetorical questioning

18) Which of the following would weaken the author's argument?

    A. a new diet pill from a pharmaceutical company that promises to help patients lose weight by changing intestinal bacteria

    B. the personal experience of a man who was able to lose a significant amount of weight by taking in fewer calories than he used

    C. a study showing that people in different geographic locations lose different amounts of weight when on the same diet

    D. a study showing that people often misreport their food intake when part of a scientific study on weight loss

Popcorn is often associated with fun and festivities, both in and out of the home. It's eaten in theaters, usually after being salted and smothered in butter, and in homes, fresh from the microwave. But popcorn isn't just for fun—it's also a multimillion-dollar-a-year industry with a long and fascinating history.

While popcorn might seem like a modern invention, its history actually dates back thousands of years, making it one of the oldest snack foods enjoyed around the world. Popcorn is believed by food historians to be one of the earliest uses of cultivated corn. In 1948, Herbert Dick and Earle Smith discovered old popcorn dating back 4000 years in the New Mexico Bat Cave. For the Aztec Indians who called the caves home, popcorn (or momochitl) played an important role in society, both as a food staple and in ceremonies. The Aztecs cooked popcorn by heating sand in a fire; when it was heated, kernels were added and would pop when exposed to the heat of the sand.

The American love affair with popcorn began in 1912, when popcorn was first sold in theaters. The popcorn industry flourished during the Great Depression when it was advertised as a wholesome and economical food. Selling for five to ten cents a bag, it was a luxury that the downtrodden could afford. With the introduction of mobile popcorn machines at the World's Columbian Exposition, popcorn moved from the theater into fairs and parks. Popcorn continued to rule the snack food kingdom until the rise in popularity of home televisions during the 1950s.

The popcorn industry reacted to the decline in sales quickly by introducing pre-popped and unpopped popcorn for home consumption. However, it wasn't until microwave popcorn became commercially available in 1981 that at-home popcorn consumption began to grow exponentially. With the wide availability of microwaves in the United States, popcorn also began popping up in offices and hotel rooms. However, the home still remains the most popular popcorn eating spot: today, 70 percent of the 16 billion quarts of popcorn consumed annually in the United States are eaten at home.

19) The passage implies that

    A. People ate less popcorn in the 1950s than in previous decades because they went to the movies less.

    B. Without mobile popcorn machines, people would not have been able to eat popcorn during the Great Depression.

    C. People enjoyed popcorn during the Great Depression because it was a luxury food.

    D. During the 1800s, people began abandoning theaters to go to fairs and festivals.

20) In paragraph 2, the word "staple" most nearly means

    A. something produced only for special occasions

    B. something produced regularly in large quantities

    C. something produced by cooking

    D. something fastened together securely

21) What is the main purpose of this passage?

    A. to explain how microwaves affected the popcorn industry

    B. to show that popcorn is older than many people realize

    C. to illustrate the history of popcorn from ancient cultures to modern times

    D. to demonstrate the importance of popcorn in various cultures

22) Which factor does the author of the passage credit for the growth of the popcorn industry in the United States?

    A. the use of popcorn in ancient Aztec ceremonies

    B. the growth of the home television industry

    C. the marketing of popcorn during the Great Depression

    D. the nutritional value of popcorn

23) Which of the following is NOT a fact stated in the passage?

    A. Archaeologists have found popcorn dating back 4000 years.

    B. Popcorn was first sold in theaters in 1912.

    C. Consumption of popcorn dropped in 1981 with the growing popularity of home televisions.

    D. 70 percent of the popcorn consumed in the United States is eaten in homes.

24) Which of the following is the best summary of this passage?

    A. Popcorn is a popular snack food that dates back thousands of years. Its popularity in the United States has been tied to the growth of theaters and the availability of microwaves.

    B. Popcorn has been a popular snack food for thousands of years. Archaeologists have found evidence that many ancient cultures used popcorn as a food staple and in ceremonies.

    C. Popcorn was first introduced to America in 1912, and its popularity has grown exponentially since then. Today, over 16 billion quarts of popcorn are consumed in the United States annually.

    D. Popcorn is a versatile snack food that can be eaten with butter or other toppings. It can also be cooked in a number of different ways, including in microwaves.

Writing

Directions for questions 1 – 7.

Read the following early draft of an essay and then choose the best answer to the question or the best completion of the statement.

(1) Becoming president of the United States is a privilege few people will ever get to experience. (2) Since its founding in 1776, <u>many years ago,</u> the country has seen only forty-four presidents in office. (3) Most of them have since left office and have gone on to lead lives of comfort and influence. (4) <u>However,</u> they may never again experience the power or the excitement of their former office, retired presidents continue to enjoy many benefits as a result of their service as president of the United States.

(5) Presidents receive a number of benefits upon retirement, many of which are afforded by the Former Presidents Act of 1958. (6) First and foremost, they receive an <u>annual pension payment. (7) The amount of the pension</u> has been reviewed and changed a number of times, most recently to reflect the salary of a high-level government executive (roughly $200,000 in the 2010s). (8) In addition to their pension, retired presidents and their families are also entitled to ongoing Secret Service protection, which lasts until the death of the president.

(9) In addition to the assurances of safety and stability, retired presidents continue to enjoy some of the influence <u>that accompanies their former office and a few have even gone on</u> to accomplish great work in their post-presidency years. (10) <u>Particularly notable are</u> the careers of William Howard Taft and Jimmy Carter. (11) In 1921, eight years after leaving office, William Howard Taft was appointed Chief Justice of the Supreme Court by President Warren G. Harding, an office he filled until just before his death; to this day, he is the only individual to ever fill both offices. (12) Jimmy Carter went on to become an enthusiastic and impactful campaigner for human rights. (13) He started the Carter Center in 1982 to advance his efforts and, in 2002, was granted the Nobel Peace Prize for his work.

1) Which of the following replacements for the underlined phrase in sentence 2 (reproduced below) most impactfully communicates the amount of time that has passed since 1776?

   Since its founding in 1776, <u>many years ago,</u> the country has seen only forty-four presidents in office.

   A. as it is now
   B. long before any of our grandparents were born,
   C. which no one alive can remember,
   D. almost 250 years ago,

2) In context, which of the following replacements for the underlined portion would best begin sentence 4 (reproduced below)?

   <u>However,</u> they may never again experience the power or the excitement of their former office, retired presidents continue to enjoy many benefits as a result of their service as president of the United States.

   A. Therefore,
   B. Consequently,
   C. Though
   D. Still,

3) Which of the following would NOT be an acceptable way to revise and combine sentences 6 and 7 (reproduced below) at the underlined point?

First and foremost, they receive an <u>annual pension payment. The amount of the pension</u> has been reviewed and changed a number of times, most recently to reflect the salary of a high-level government executive (roughly $200,000 in the 2010s).

A. as it is now

B. annual pension payment, the amount of which

C. annual pension payment; the amount of the pension

D. annual pension payment, the amount of the pension

4) Which of the following would provide the most logical conclusion to the second paragraph?

A. Interestingly, Richard Nixon was the only president ever to relinquish his right to ongoing Secret Service security.

B. However, spouses who remarry after the president has left office become ineligible for Secret Service security.

C. The Secret Service is a special security task force that is responsible for protecting the president, the vice president, and their families.

D. These measures ensure that retired presidents, as thanks for their years of demanding service, continue to live lives of safety and security.

5) Which of the following is the best version of the underlined portion of sentence 9 (reproduced below)?

In addition to the assurances of safety and stability, retired presidents continue to enjoy some of the influence <u>that accompanies their former office and a few have even gone on</u> to accomplish great work in their post-presidency years.

A. as it is now

B. that accompanies their former office; however, a few have even gone on

C. that accompanies their former office; a few have even gone on

D. that accompanies their office—a few have even gone on

6) Which of the following would NOT be an acceptable replacement for the underlined portion of sentence 10 (reproduced below)?

<u>Particularly notable are</u> the careers of William Howard Taft and Jimmy Carter.

A. Exceptionally outstanding are

B. Of particular interest are

C. Especially noteworthy are

D. Of particular interest were

7) Which of the following would be the most effective introductory phrase for sentence 12 (reproduced below)?

Jimmy Carter went on to become an enthusiastic and impactful campaigner for human rights.

  A. Eventually,

  B. After his own presidency,

  C. When he was not in office,

  D. However,

Directions for questions 8 – 15.

Select the best version of the underlined part of the sentence. If you think the original sentence is best, choose the first answer.

8) The famously high death toll at the end of the Civil War was not exclusively due to battle losses; <u>in addition,</u> large numbers of soldiers and civilians fell ill and died as a result of living conditions during the war.

  A. in addition,

  B. therefore,

  C. however,

  D. on the other hand,

9) The public defense attorney was able to maintain her optimism despite <u>her dearth of courtroom wins, lack of free time she had, and growing list of clients she was helping.</u>

  A. her dearth of courtroom wins, lack of free time she had, and growing list of clients she was helping.

  B. her dearth of courtroom wins, lack of free time, and growing list of clients.

  C. her dearth of courtroom wins, the free time she lacked, and the list of clients she was growing.

  D. the losses she had experienced, the free time she lacked, and her growing client list.

10) <u>Being invented in France in the early nineteenth century,</u> the stethoscope underwent a number of reiterations before the modern form of the instrument was introduced in the 1850s.

  A. Being invented in France in the early nineteenth century,

  B. It was invented in France in the early nineteenth century,

  C. Though it was invented in France in the nineteenth century,

  D. Invented in France in the early nineteenth century,

11) In 1983, almost twenty years after his death, T. S. Eliot won two Tony Awards for his contributions to the well-loved musical *Cats*, <u>it was based on a book of his poetry.</u>

  A. it was based on a book of his poetry.

  B. which was based on a book of his poetry.

  C. being based on a book of his poetry.

  D. having been based on a book of his poetry.

12) Because the distance between stars in the galaxy is far greater than the distance between planets, interstellar travel <u>is expected to be an even bigger challenge than</u> interplanetary exploration.

    A. is expected to be an even bigger challenge than

    B. will be expected to be an even bigger challenge than

    C. is expected to be an even bigger challenge then

    D. is expecting to be an even bigger challenge than

13) The <u>painters who are often confused for each other</u> Claude Monet and Édouard Manet actually did have a couple things in common: they were born only six years apart in Paris, France, and both contributed important early Impressionist works to the artistic canon.

    A. painters who are often confused for each other

    B. common confused painters

    C. painters who are confusing because of their similar names

    D. commonly confused painters

14) The field of child development is concerned with <u>the emotional, the psychological, and biological developments</u> of infants and children.

    A. the emotional, the psychological, and biological developments

    B. the emotional, psychological, and biological developments

    C. the emotional developments, the psychological, and the biological developments

    D. emotional, psychological, and the biological developments

15) Though it is often thought of as an extreme sport, spelunking involves much more than adrenaline: enthusiasts dive into unexplored caves <u>to study structures of, take photographs, and create maps of</u> the untouched systems.

    A. to study structures of, take photographs, and create maps of

    B. to study structures of, to take photographs, and create maps of

    C. to study structures of, taking photographs of, and creating maps of

    D. to study structures, take photographs, and create maps of

Directions for questions 16 – 20.

Think about how you would rewrite the following sentence according to the directions given, and then choose the best answer. Keep in mind that your revision should not change the meaning of the original sentence.

GO ON

16) The city of Trieste in northern Italy was the fourth-largest city of the Austro-Hungarian Empire and a cultural crossroads where people of Latin, Slavic, and Germanic backgrounds historically mixed.

Rewrite, beginning with

The fourth-largest city of the Austro-Hungarian Empire, the city of Trieste in northern Italy

…

The next words will be

A) was a cultural crossroads where people

B) and a cultural crossroads where people

C) historically mixed a cultural crossroads

D) where a cultural crossroads of people was

17) Significant groups of Christians and Muslims live in the small African country of Togo, but those with indigenous beliefs make up the largest religious community.

Rewrite, beginning with

Even though significant groups of Christians and Muslims live in the small African country of Togo,

…

The next words will be

A) they make up the largest religious community

B) however those with indigenous beliefs make up the largest

C) the largest religious community makes up indigenous beliefs

D) the largest religious community is made up of those with indigenous

18) Thanks to its flexible hind paws, the squirrel can climb down trees headfirst, a trait unique to the species.

Rewrite, beginning with

Squirrels' unique ability to climb down trees headfirst

…

The next words will be

A) thanks to its flexible hind paws.

B) is thanks to their flexible hind paws.

C) is a trait unique to the species.

D) is thanks to its flexible hind paws.

19) The tusk of the narwhal, previously thought to be a defensive tool for the animal, is now known to be a sensory organ.

Rewrite, beginning with

<u>Narwhal tusks are sensory organs</u>

…

The next words will be

A) but had previously been used for defensive purposes.

B) but had previously been believed to be defensive tools.

C) previously known to be a defensive tool for the animal.

D) previously they had been believed to be defensive tools.

20) To change a tire, be sure you are in a safe location, turn your hazard lights on, and apply the parking brake before beginning work.

Rewrite, beginning with

<u>It is important to find a safe location, turn the hazard lights on,</u>

…

Your new sentence will include

A) after applying the parking brake

B) before applying the parking brake

C) before changing a tire

D) after changing a tire

The Essay

On this essay, you must effectively express and develop your ideas in writing. Read a short passage; an assignment question follows about an important issue. Develop your own point of view on the issue in an essay. Be sure to support your argument with examples and reasoning. Your perspective on the issue will not influence your score.

Passage

O judgment! Thou art fled to brutish beasts, and men have lost their reason.

> From William Shakespeare, *Julius Caesar*

Don't judge a book by its cover.

> From George Eliot, *The Mill on the Floss*

Assignment

Can we be too quick to judge the actions of another person?

ANSWER KEY

Mathematics

1. **B)** Plug 4 in for j and simplify.

$2(j-4)^4 - j + \frac{1}{2}j$

$\mathbf{2(4-4)^4 - 4 + \frac{1}{2}(4) = -2}$

2. **A)** Simplify each root and add.

$\sqrt[3]{64} = 4$

$\sqrt[3]{729} = 9$

$\mathbf{4 + 9 = 13}$

3. **C)** Find the height of the cylinder using the equation for surface area.

$SA = 2\pi rh + 2\pi r^2$

$48\pi = 2\pi(4)h + 2\pi(4)^2$

$h = 2$

Find the volume using the volume equation.

$V = \pi r^2 h$

$\mathbf{V = \pi(4)^2(2) = 32\pi \ ft.^3}$

4. **A)** Use the formula for inversely proportional relationships to find k and then solve for s.

$sn = k$

$(65)(250) = k$

$k = 16{,}250$

$s(325) = 16{,}250$

$s = \mathbf{50}$

5. **B)** Plug each value into the equation.

$4(3+4)^2 - 4(3)^2 + 20 = 180 \neq 276$

$4(6+4)^2 - 4(6)^2 + 20 = \mathbf{276}$

$4(12+4)^2 - 4(12)^2 + 20 = 468 \neq 276$

$\mathbf{4(24+4)^2 - 4(24)^2 + 20 = 852 \neq 276}$

6. **A)** In 2012, New York had more months with less than 3 inches of rain than either Chicago or Houston.

7. **D)** Plug in each set of values and determine if the inequality is true.

$2(0) + 0 < -10$ FALSE

$2(10) + 2 \leq -10$ FALSE

$2(10) + 10 \leq -10$ FALSE

$\mathbf{2(-10) + (-10) \leq -10 \ TRUE}$

8. **C)** Cross multiply and solve for x.

$\frac{4x-5}{3} = \frac{\frac{1}{2}(2x-6)}{5}$

$5(4x-5) = \frac{3}{2}(2x-6)$

$20x - 25 = 3x - 9$

$17x = 16$

$x = \mathbf{\frac{16}{17}}$

9. **C)** Plug 0 in for x and solve for y.

$7y - 42x + 7 = 0$

$7y - 42(0) + 7 = 0$

$y = -1$

The y-intercept is at (0, −1).

10. **A)** Use the combination formula to find the number of ways to choose 2 people out of a group of 20.

$$C(20, 2) = \frac{20!}{2!\,18!} = 190$$

$$\frac{54}{5} = 10.8$$

11. **D)** Solve the system using substitution.

$z - 2x = 14 \rightarrow z = 2x + 14$

$2z - 6x = 18$

$2(2x + 14) - 6x = 18$

$4x + 28 - 6x = 18$

$-2x = -10$

$x = 5$

$z - 2(5) = 14$

$z = 24$

12. **C)** Use the rules of exponents to simplify the expression.

$$\frac{4x^{-3}y^4z^2}{8(x^{-5}y^3z^{-2})} = \left(\frac{x^2yz^{32}}{2}\right) = \frac{x^4y^2z^6}{4}$$

13. **C)** The function $g(x) = f(x - 2) + 3$ is a translation of ⊠2, 3⊠ from $f(x)$. Test each possible point by undoing the transformation and checking if the point lies on $f(x)$.

$(1, 2) \rightarrow (-1, -1)$: This point is not on $f(x)$.

$(2, 3) \rightarrow (0, 0)$: This point is not on $f(x)$.

$(6, 3) \rightarrow (4, 0)$: **This point is on $f(x)$.**

$(7, 2) \rightarrow (5, -1)$: This point is not on $f(x)$.

14. **B)** The slope 0.0293 gives the increase in passenger car miles (in billions) for each year that passes. Muliply this value by 5 to find the increase that occurs over 5 years: 5(0.0293) = **0.1465 billion miles**.

15. **B)** Set up a proportion and solve.

$$\frac{AB}{DE} = \frac{3}{4}$$

$$\frac{12}{DE} = \frac{3}{4}$$

$3(DE) = 48$

$DE = 16$

16. **B)** Find the sum of the 13 numbers whose mean is 30.

$13 \times 30 = 390$

Find the sum of the 8 numbers whose mean is 42.

$8 \times 42 = 336$

Find the sum and mean of the remaining 5 numbers.

$390 - 336 = 54$

17. **C)** Use the fundamental counting principle to determine how many ways the DVDs can be arranged within each category and how many ways the 3 categories can be arranged.

ways to arrange horror = 4! = 24

ways to arrange comedies = 6! = 720

ways to arrange science fiction = 5! = 120

ways to arrange categories = 3! = 6

(24)(720)(120)(6) = 12,441,600

18. Eliminate answer choices that don't match the graph.

A) Correct.

B) The graph has a negative slope while this inequality has a positive slope.

C) The line on the graph is solid, so the inequality should include the "or equal to" symbol.

D) The shading is above the line, meaning the inequality should be "y is greater than."

19. **D)** Use the formula for the area of a rectangle to find the increase in its size.

$A = lw$

$A = (1.4l)(0.6w)$

$A = 0.84lw$

The new area will be 84% of the original area, a decrease of 16%.

20. **C)** Use the formula for the volume of a sphere to find its radius.

$V = \frac{4}{3}\pi r^3$

$972\pi = \frac{4}{3}\pi r^3$

$r = 9$

Use the super Pythagorean theorem to find the side of the cube.

$d^2 = a^2 + b^2 + c^2$

$18^2 = 3s^2$

$s \approx 10.4$

Use the length of the side to find the volume of the cube.

$V = s^3$

$V \approx (10.4)^3$

$V \approx 1,125$

Reading

1)

A. **Correct.** The raffle is the only feature described as an event the organizers will be "bringing back[.]"

B. Incorrect. The author states, "This year, we'll have a carousel, petting zoo, and climbing wall[,]" implying these attractions are all new this year.

C. Incorrect. The author states, "This year, we'll have a carousel, petting zoo, and climbing wall[,]" implying these attractions are all new this year.

D. Incorrect. The author states, "This year, we'll have a carousel, petting zoo, and climbing wall[,]" implying these attractions are all new this year.

2)

A. Incorrect. According to the passage, gifts were assigned by Epimetheus and Prometheus, not purchased.

B. Incorrect. The passage gives no indication that gifts were forgotten.

C. Incorrect. The passage gives no indication that gifts were accepted by the animals, only that they were given by Epimetheus and Prometheus.

D. **Correct.** The word given best describes the idea that the gifts have been handed out: "to the lion [Epimetheus] gave strength; to the bird, swiftness; to the fox, sagacity, and so on."

3)

A. Incorrect. The passage implies that "the physical and biological consequences of nuclear war" have impacts that reach much further than the military.

B. Incorrect. The second part of the second sentence suggests that the consequences of nuclear war—rather than the specific technology of nuclear weapons—are the focus of this student's paper.

C. Incorrect. The author mentions the decision by world powers to cease testing nuclear weapons in the atmosphere; however, this is only one detail and is likely not the focus of the essay as a whole.

D. **Correct.** The passage gives a short history of thermonuclear weapons and then introduces its main topic—the physical and biological consequences of nuclear war.

4)

A. Incorrect. The author states that "Alexander Hamilton...called for the Constitutional Convention to write a constitution as the foundation of a stronger federal government."

B. Incorrect. The author states that "James Madison called for the Constitutional Convention to write a constitution as the foundation of a stronger federal government."

C. Incorrect. The author states that "Federalists like John Adams believed in... a strong federal government."

D. **Correct.** In the passage, Thomas Jefferson is defined as an anti-Federalist, in contrast with Federalists who believed in a strong federal government.

5)

A. Incorrect. Although the passage states that psychology is a science, it does not explain the science. The primary concern is distinguishing the science of psychology from the art of teaching.

B. **Correct.** The text states that educational programs and plans cannot be deduced from the laws of the mind.

C. Incorrect. Although the text indicates that teaching is an art, the practices and plans of educational programs are not described.

D. Incorrect. The focus of the art of teaching and of the science of psychology is identified, but their values are not mentioned.

6)

A. **Correct.** The suggested idea is how thorough and practical the writers were as they studied the principles of government and analyzed their experience with government of the Confederation.

B. Incorrect. This option is too general; it does not mention the specifics of the work of the writers (studying government in view of the government of the Confederation).

C. Incorrect. This option offers no indication of what they were thorough and practical about.

D.   Incorrect. This is only partially accurate. It omits the writers' study of the principles of government and the focus of their work, a Constitution that would protect freedom.

7)

A.   Correct. The author argues that "every man, woman and child should learn" to swim, and then explains to the reader why he or she should be able to swim.

B.   Incorrect. Though the author mentions the danger posed by individuals who cannot swim, he does not explain how they are a danger.

C.   Incorrect. Though the author does inform the reader that "none are too young [to swim]; none are too old[,]" information itself is not his main purpose.

D.   Incorrect. The author does not advocate for punishment for people who cannot swim.

8)

A.   Incorrect. The passage is about babies' senses in general; therefore this answer choice is too specific.

B.   Incorrect. The passage is about babies' senses in general; therefore this answer choice is too specific.

C.   Correct. The passage states that babies' senses are much like those of their adult counterparts with the exception of their vision, which develops later.

D.   Incorrect. The passage indicates that a baby's vision "changes significantly in its first year of life[,]" but suggests that other senses are relatively well-developed at birth.

9)

A.   Incorrect. The passage states that "vision does not become the dominant sense until around the age of 12 months."

B.   Correct. The passage states that "infants rely primarily on hearing."

C.   Incorrect. The sense of touch in not mentioned in the passage.

D.   Incorrect. The sense of smell is not mentioned in the passage.

10)

A.   Incorrect. In regional studies, geographers "examine the characteristics of a particular place[.]"

B.   Incorrect. In topical studies, geographers "look at a single physical or human feature that impacts the world[.]"

C.   Incorrect. In physical studies, geographers "focus on the physical features of Earth[.]"

D.   Correct. The passage describes human studies as the study of "the relationship between human activity and the environment," which would include farmers interacting with river systems.

11)

A.   Incorrect. This is only one fact from the passage and does not represent an adequate summary of the passage as a whole.

B.   Correct. Only this choice summarizes the two main points of the passage: the definition of geography and the breakdown of its sub-disciplines.

C.   Incorrect. This is only one detail from the passage and does not represent an adequate summary of the passage as a whole.

D.   Incorrect. This choice summarizes the second paragraph only and leaves out any summary of the first paragraph.

12)

A.   Incorrect. The author mentions that "the kingsnake is actually nonvenomous" but provides no more information about whether the kingsnake poses a danger to humans.

B.   Correct. The final paragraph of the passage states that the two species "frequently [share] a habitat" and that "[a] predatory hawk or eagle, usually hunting from high in the sky, can't tell the difference between the two species, and so the kingsnake gets passed over and lives another day."

C.   Incorrect. The author does not imply that it is easy to tell the difference between venomous and nonvenomous snakes, only that it is possible.

D.   Incorrect. The final paragraph states that the kingsnake "has very similar marking to the venomous coral snake" and does not indicate that these markings change with circumstances.

13)

A. Incorrect. The second paragraph states that "[a] predatory hawk or eagle, usually hunting from high in the sky, can't tell the difference between the two species, and so the kingsnake gets passed over and lives another day."

B. Incorrect. The second paragraph states that "[t]he scarlet kingsnake, for example, has very similar markings to the venomous coral snake with whom it frequently shares a habitat."

C. **Correct.** The first paragraph states that "[w]hile it might seem counterintuitive for a venomous snake to stand out in bright red or blue, that fancy costume tells any nearby predator that approaching him would be a bad idea." The coral snake's markings do not allow it to hide from predators but rather to "ward [them] off[.]"

D. Incorrect. The second paragraph states that "the kingsnake is actually nonvenomous; it's merely pretending to be dangerous to eat."

14)

A. **Correct.** The passage states that "intricate diamonds, stripes, and swirls help the animals hide from predators[,]" implying that these markings are complex enough to allow the animals to blend in with their surroundings.

B. Incorrect. The passage indicates that colorful markings do not allow the animals to hide but rather to ward off predators, so the word colorful does not apply in the context of the sentence.

C. Incorrect. This answer choice does not fit in the context of the sentence, as the animals do not choose their markings.

D. Incorrect. The author does not suggest that animals' markings are changeable.

15)

A. Incorrect. The passage states that the coral snake is venomous.

B. Incorrect. The passage states that the kingsnake is nonvenomous.

C. **Correct.** The second paragraph states that "[t]he scarlet kingsnake, for example, has very similar markings to the venomous coral snake with whom it frequently shares a habitat. However, the kingsnake is actually nonvenomous[.]"

D. Incorrect. The passage states that the reverse is true: kingsnakes are nonvenomous, and coral snakes are venomous.

16)

A. **Correct.** The bulk of the passage is dedicated to showing that conventional wisdom about "fewer calories in than calories out" isn't true for many people and is more complicated than previously believed.

B. Incorrect. The author indicates that calorie counting is not an effective way to lose weight.

C. Incorrect. Though the author indicates that this may be the case, the negative impacts of losing weight quickly are not the main point of the passage; a more inclusive sentence is needed to conclude the passage successfully.

D. Incorrect. The author does not indicate that diets don't work at all, simply that the scientific understanding of dieting is still limited.

17)

A. Incorrect. The author relies on specific scientific evidence to prove his point, not emotional arguments.

B. Incorrect. The author addresses a general population who may be dieting and does not appeal to an authority figure.

C. **Correct.** The author cites several scientific studies to support the argument.

D. Incorrect. The author does not employ any rhetorical questions in communicating his or her message.

18)

A. Incorrect. A new diet pill would have no effect on the existing studies and would not prove anything about conventional dieting wisdom.

B. Incorrect. A single anecdotal example would not be enough to contradict the results of well-designed studies; if anything, the account would provide another example of how complex the topics of dieting and weight loss are.

C. Incorrect. This answer choice would strengthen the author's argument by highlighting the complexity of the topic of dieting.

D. **Correct.** People misreporting the amount of food they ate would introduce error into studies on weight loss and might make the studies the author cites unreliable.

19)

A. Correct. The author states that "popcorn continued to rule the snack food kingdom until the rise in popularity of home televisions during the 1950s" when the industry saw a "decline in sales" as a result of the changing pastimes of the American people.

B. Incorrect. The author indicates that "the introduction of the mobile popcorn machine" occurred "at the World's Columbian Exposition" after the Great Depression.

C. Incorrect. The author indicates that the primary reason people consumed popcorn during the Great Depression was the it was advertised as a "wholesome and economical food[,]...a luxury the downtrodden could afford." This implies that the cost, not the luxuriousness, of popcorn was its primary appeal.

D. Incorrect. The author indicates that "[t]he American love affair with popcorn began in 1912" and only after this did "popcorn move from the theatre into fairs and parks."

20)

A. Incorrect. The author states that the Aztec people popped popcorn both for special occasions ("in ceremonies") and for regular consumption ("as a food staple").

B. Correct. The author states, "For the Aztec Indians who called the caves home, popcorn (or momochitl) played an important role in society, both as a food staple and in ceremonies." This implies that the Aztec people popped popcorn both for special occasions ("in ceremonies") and for regular consumption ("as a food staple").

C. Incorrect. Though the author does describe the process the Aztec peoples used to cook popcorn, this definition does not fit in the context of the sentence, when the author contrasts the phrase "as a food staple" with the phrase "in ceremonies."

D. Incorrect. This definition does not fit in the context of the sentence.

21)

A. Incorrect. Though the author does discuss the effect of the microwave on the popcorn industry ("it wasn't until microwave popcorn became commercially available in 1981 that at-home popcorn consumption began to grow exponentially"), this is not the primary purpose of the passage.

B. Incorrect. Though this may be true, it is not the primary purpose of the passage; the author traces the history of popcorn from ancient to modern times.

C. Correct. In the opening paragraph the author writes, "But popcorn isn't just for fun—it's also a multimillion-dollar-a-year industry with a long and fascinating history." The author then goes on to illustrate the history of popcorn from the ancient Aztecs, to early twentieth century America, to the present day.

D. Incorrect. Though the author discusses the ancient Aztecs, the rest of the passage is focused on popcorn's history in American culture.

22)

A. Incorrect. The author mentions that popcorn was consumed "both as a food staple and in ceremonies" in Aztec culture but does not tie this to the popcorn industry in the United States.

B. Incorrect. The author indicates that growth in popularity of home televisions actually hurt the popcorn industry: "Popcorn continued to rule the snack food kingdom until the rise in popularity of home televisions during the 1950s" when the industry saw "a decline in sales[.]"

C. Correct. The author writes, "The popcorn industry flourished during the Great Depression when it was advertised as a wholesome and economical food."

D. Incorrect. Though the nutritional value of popcorn is mentioned as a factor in its popularity during the Great Depression, the author does not indicate that this is the reason for its popularity in the United States.

23)

A. Incorrect. The author writes, "In 1948, Herbert Dick and Earle Smith discovered old popcorn dating back 4000 years in the New Mexico Bat Cave."

B. Incorrect. The author writes, "The American love affair with popcorn began in 1912, when popcorn was first sold in theaters."

C. **Correct.** The author writes, "However, it wasn't until microwave popcorn became commercially available in 1981 that at-home popcorn consumption began to grow exponentially. With the wide availability of microwaves in the United States, popcorn also began popping up in offices and hotel rooms."

D. Incorrect. The author writes, "However, the home still remains the most popular popcorn eating spot: today, 70 percent of the 16 billion quarts of popcorn consumed annually in the United States are eaten at home."

24)

A. **Correct.** This statement summarizes the entire passage, including the brief history of popcorn in ancient cultures and the growth in the popularity of popcorn in America.

B. Incorrect. Though the author does mention the history of popcorn in ancient cultures, this is not an adequate summary of the passage as a whole.

C. Incorrect. Though the author discusses the history of popcorn in America, this is not an adequate summary of the passage as a whole.

D. Incorrect. Though the author does mention the versatility and popularity of popcorn as a snack food, this is not an adequate summary of the passage as a whole.

Writing

1)

A.   Incorrect. *Many years ago* is too vague to be impactful and leaves the interpretation entirely to the reader.

B.   Incorrect. This choice, though true, is irrelevant and detracts from the topic of the passage.

C.   Incorrect. This choice, also true, is too vague to be impactful and leaves too much room for interpretation.

D.   **Correct.** This choice provides specific information, making it impactful and memorable.

2)

A.   Incorrect. *Therefore* incorrectly suggests a cause-and-effect relationship between this sentence and the previous one.

B.   Incorrect. *Consequently* incorrectly suggests a cause-and-effect relationship between this sentence and the previous one.

C.   **Correct.** *Though* signifies an important contradiction between the two clauses in this sentence.

D.   Incorrect. *Still* incorrectly suggests an additive relationship between this sentence and the previous one.

3)

A.   Incorrect. This choice correctly forms two complete sentences.

B.   Incorrect. This choice makes the second clause subordinate and appropriately joins the clauses with a comma.

C.   Incorrect. This choice correctly joins two complete sentences with a semicolon.

D.   **Correct.** This choice creates two complete sentences but joins them incorrectly with a comma, creating a comma splice.

4)

A.   Incorrect. This choice provides unnecessary information that detracts from the main idea of the paragraph.

B.   Incorrect. This choice provides unnecessary information that detracts from the main idea of the paragraph.

C.   Incorrect. This choice provides unnecessary information that is too specific to be an effective conclusion.

D.   **Correct.** This choice is appropriately specific and provides a brief summary of the information mentioned in the paragraph.

5)

A.   Incorrect. This choice incorrectly joins two complete sentences without punctuation, creating a run-on sentence.

B.   Incorrect. This choice correctly joins two complete sentences with a semicolon, but the transition word *however* suggests a contradiction where one does not exist.

C.   **Correct.** This choice correctly joins two related complete sentences with a semicolon.

D.   Incorrect. This choice incorrectly joins two complete sentences with a dash.

6)

A.   Incorrect. *Are* is a plural verb that agrees with its subject *careers*; *exceptionally outstanding* suggests careers that were not only unusual but extremely unusual.

B.   Incorrect. *Are* is a plural verb that agrees with its subject *careers*; *of particular interest* suggests careers that are especially applicable to the author's point.

C.   Incorrect. *Are* is a plural verb that agrees with its subject *careers*; *especially noteworthy* suggests careers that were not only unusual but extremely unusual.

D.   **Correct.** *Were* is a plural verb that agrees with the plural subject *careers*; however, *of particular interest* suggests relevance to the author's point, which should be referred to in present tense.

7)

A.   Incorrect. *Eventually* is too vague to be effective, as it does not tell the reader when Jimmy Carter was working.

B.   **Correct.** *After his own presidency* provides an appropriate amount of detail to describe when the action took place—immediately following his retirement.

C.   Incorrect. *When he was not in office* is too vague to be effective, as it suggests anytime other than when Jimmy Carter was president.

D.   Incorrect. *However* suggests a contradiction, but one does not exist in this context.

8)

A.   **Correct.** *In addition* is the appropriate introductory phrase to signify the additive relationship between the two clauses.

B.   Incorrect. *Therefore* incorrectly suggests a cause-and-effect relationship between the two clauses.

C.   Incorrect. *However* incorrectly suggests a contradictory relationship between the two clauses.

D.   Incorrect. *On the other hand* incorrectly suggests a contradictory relationship between the two clauses.

9)

A.   Incorrect. Though all three items begin with noun phrases (*dearth of*, *lack of*, and *list of*), the second and third are followed by unnecessary verb phrases (*she had* and *she was helping*).

B.   **Correct.** In this iteration, all items in the list are nouns (*dearth*, *lack*, and *list*), followed by prepositions (*of*) and objects of the prepositions (*wins*, *time*, and *clients*).

C.   Incorrect. While the first item in the list is a noun phrase (*dearth of courtroom wins*), the second two include unnecessary verb phrases (*she lacked* and *she was growing*)

D.   Incorrect. While the first two items in the list include verb phrases (*she had experienced* and *she lacked*), the third does not.

10)

A.   Incorrect. *Being invented* is wordy; the same idea can be communicated by beginning the sentence with *invented*.

B.   Incorrect. Joining these two independent clauses with a comma would make this sentence a comma splice.

C.   Incorrect. *Though* suggests a contradiction between the clauses; no such contradiction exists between these two clauses.

D.   **Correct.** *Invented*, the past participle of *invent*, appropriately introduces this participial

phrase that provides more information about the subject of the sentence (*stethoscope*).

11)

A.   Incorrect. As written, these two independent clauses, joined by a comma, form a comma splice.

B.   **Correct.** *Which* is used correctly here to introduce an additional, nonrestrictive clause about an element of the sentence (the musical).

C.   Incorrect. *Being based on* leaves some ambiguity as to who or what this additional clause is describing.

D.   Incorrect. *Having been based on* is a perfect participle, a form that is rarely used because of its wordiness.

12)

A.   **Correct.** *Is* is a present-tense verb, used correctly to refer to current mind-sets; *than* is used correctly to show comparison.

B.   Incorrect. *Will be expected* is future tense, suggesting that the mind-set on interstellar travel does not yet exist; *than* is used correctly to show comparison.

C.   Incorrect. *Is* is a present tense verb, used correctly to refer to current mind-sets; *then* is used incorrectly to show comparison when it should refer to time.

D.   Incorrect. *Is expecting to be* suggests that interstellar travel itself has expectations about the future.

13)

A.   Incorrect. This phrasing is unnecessarily wordy.

B.   Incorrect. *Common* and *confused* are both adjectives that, in this case, are both referring to the painters.

C.   Incorrect. This phrasing is unnecessarily wordy.

D.   **Correct.** *Commonly* is an adverb describing *confused*, which is an adjective describing *painters*.

14)

A.   Incorrect. The first two phrases share a structure (article + adjective) while the third does not (adjective + noun).

B.   **Correct.** The three phrases share a structure; they are parallel adjectives.

C.   Incorrect. The first and third phrases share a structure (article + adjective + noun), while the second one does not (article + adjective).

D.   Incorrect. The first two phrases share a structure (adjective only), while the third does not (article + adjective + noun).

15)

A.   Incorrect. The first and third phrases in the list end with a preposition (*of*), while the second one does not.

B.   Incorrect. None of the phrases share a structure; while the first and second begin with infinitives, the third does not; the first and third end with a preposition (*of*), while the second does not.

C.   Incorrect. The third phrase includes a participle (*creating*), while the first and second do not.

D.   **Correct.** The three phrases have a similar (parallel) structure (verb + direct object).

16)

A)   **Correct.** The sentence should be rewritten "The fourth-largest city of the Austro-Hungarian Empire, the city of Trieste in northern Italy was a cultural crossroads where people of Latin, Slavic, and Germanic backgrounds historically mixed." Choice A correctly places the verb (*was*) after the subject (*the city of Trieste in northern Italy*, or, more precisely, *the city*).

B)   Incorrect. This answer choice does not clearly indicate verb placement; Trieste was also indeed a cultural crossroads, but it is not clear where the verb would fall in the sentence if the next words were *and a cultural crossroads…*

C)   Incorrect. Even if it could be inferred that the word *mixed* here was acting as a verb, the sentence still would not make sense. A city cannot mix a crossroads.

D)   Incorrect. Even though this answer choice includes a verb, the verb is part of a relative clause (that begins with *where*); it is not clear where the main verb would be.

17)

A)   Incorrect. While the sentence would grammatically make sense with the addition

of these words, using the pronoun *they* immediately after the introductory phrase *Even though significant groups of Christians and Muslims live in the small African country of Togo* implies that the rest of the sentence is about these two communities, when it is actually about the large size of the third.

B)   Incorrect. The word *however* is misused; a contradiction has already been implied with the words *even though* at the beginning of the sentence.

C)   Incorrect. This answer choice implies that the beliefs are made up, rather than explaining that the community is made up, or composed, of believers. The two meanings of the verb phrase *to make up* are conflated.

D)   **Correct.** Choice D begins a main clause that describes the largest community as that with indigenous beliefs, the true statement of the sentence. The sentence should be rewritten "Even though significant groups of Christians and Muslims live in the small African country of Togo, the largest religious community is made up of those with indigenous beliefs."

18)

A)   Incorrect. The sentence would lack a verb if it were to be completed with Choice A.

B)   **Correct.** The sentence should be rewritten "Squirrels' unique ability to climb down trees headfirst is thanks to their flexible hind paws." The verb *is* immediately follows and introduces the second idea of the sentence: the flexible hind paws of the squirrel.

C)   Incorrect. This choice includes a verb, but it is repetitive. Not only does it repeat the word *unique*, but it also fails to introduce the flexible hind paws, instead doubling down on the special ability of the squirrel to descend trees headfirst.

D)   Incorrect. In this answer choice, the pronoun *its* does not agree with its subject, the plural *squirrels'*.

19)

A)   Incorrect. The tusks were never used for defensive purposes; this answer choice states differently.

B)   **Correct.** The new sentence should read "Narwhal tusks are sensory organs but had previously been believed to be defensive tools."

C) Incorrect. The tusks were assumed, not known, to be defensive; it is now known that this assumption was incorrect. The original sentence makes that clear; answer choice C would change its meaning.

D) Incorrect. Without the proper punctuation (a semicolon), this answer choice creates a run-on sentence.

20)

A) Incorrect. If the verb *apply* is to be used in this sentence, it should be written in its infinitive form (*to apply*) in order to maintain parallel structure in the sentence. In addition, it would be impossible to move the car to a safe place after applying the parking brake.

B) Incorrect. Again, if the verb *apply* is to be used in this sentence, it should be written in its infinitive form (*to apply*) in order to maintain parallel structure in the sentence. Furthermore, the purpose of the preposition *before* is unclear because changing the tire

cannot begin until after all three steps— finding a safe location, turning on the hazard lights, and applying the parking brake—have occurred. Even though finding a safe location and turning on the hazards should happen before applying the parking brake, there is no way to clarify this if the sentence begins with the words already provided.

C) **Correct.** The new sentence should read "It is important to find a safe location, turn the hazard lights on, and apply the parking brake before changing a tire." All three steps—finding a safe location, turning on the hazard lights, and applying the parking brake—must happen before the tire-changing process can begin. The preposition *before* signals all those steps have occurred.

D) Incorrect. Since finding a safe location, turning on the hazard lights, and applying the parking brake must happen before the process of changing a tire, the preposition *after* is incorrect.

The Essay

All people make mistakes, and it is easy to judge them from the outside. However, sometimes people behave in harmful ways as a result of unseen hardships. People should refrain from judgment until they have the full story. Still, an unusual challenge does not absolve someone from all responsibilities. Even those at a disadvantage are accountable for their responsibilities, but they may be forgiven for certain harms as long as they take steps to rectify them.

For instance, my parents do not get along with their neighbor because he has a messy yard, which brings down their property value. He also has a dog which he lets wander on the streets. My parents' dog, on the other hand, must stay in the house and is only allowed to run freely behind the fence in the yard or at a dog park. However, everyone in the area has approximately the same income. Furthermore, the neighbor is seemingly in good physical health and works normal hours. There seems to be no reason that he cannot spend a little time each week on yard work and keep his dogs in his yard like everyone else. However, he does have one unique characteristic: allergies.

The neighbor's health situation presents a dilemma. While he is responsible for cleaning his yard, he struggles with yardwork because his allergies prevent him from spending too much time among shrubs, bushes, and trees. In addition, it is hard for him to keep his dog in his house for long periods of time, as pet dander makes his allergies worse, but the more time the dog spends in the yard, the messier the yard gets. And on top of all that, he lives alone, with no one to help with chores. Meanwhile, both of my parents enjoy outdoor activity, have no allergies, and can tackle yardwork together quite easily. They are able to keep their dog inside without any health concerns and can take turns walking him. Taking these differences into account, it becomes clearer why the neighbor's yard is in disarray and why his dog is often out. These issues may be less about his character than his circumstances.

Still, the neighbor has a responsibility to those around him. First, he should not have a dog if he cannot properly care for it or keep it in his home. Not only is a dog roaming the streets a nuisance to other neighbors, but it is unsafe for the dog, which could be hit by a car or injured in some other way. Next, he should find a way to properly care for his yard. Perhaps he could pursue medical treatment for his allergies, hire workers to assist periodically, or even ask a friend, family member, or neighbor for assistance if his budget is tight. Even if he is struggling to care for his yard, as a homeowner he is responsible for it.

In this case, the neighbor could be forgiven if he took steps to fix the situation, because he is clearly at a disadvantage when it comes to yardwork and pet care due to his allergies, which are not his fault. However, if he does not take responsibility and make amends, his disadvantages do not matter, and he should not be forgiven. At that point, he could be judged as a poor neighbor or as a person of poor character because he has chosen to remain a nuisance in the neighborhood despite other options.

Answer Explanation

This essay received an 8 because it demonstrates outstanding critical thinking, developing a nuanced argument even while answering the question (Even those at a disadvantage are accountable for their responsibilities, but they may be forgiven for certain harms as long as they take steps to rectify them). The writer supports the argument with one anecdotal example, but the level of detail in the scenario is sufficient to illustrate the author's argument that some disadvantages may be hidden and so one should not be quick to judge: There seems to be no reason that he cannot spend a little time each week on yard work... However, he does have one unique characteristic: allergies. The author offers possible solutions to the harms the neighbor brings on the neighborhood, which would allow him to be forgiven ("he could pursue medical treatment…hire workers to assist…or even ask a friend, family member, or neighbor for assistance" in cleaning the yard). The writing and organization is clear and coherent; the thesis is presented in the introduction, and the anecdotal scenario is fully developed. The writer uses varied sentence structure, strong vocabulary, and transition words. There are few, if any, mechanical errors.

Follow the link below to take your second TSI practice test and to access other online study resources:

www.acceptedinc.com/tsi-online-resources

SOURCES

Beerbohm, Max. *Zuleika Dobson*, 1911.

Curtis, William. *Curtis's Botanical Magazine*, 1790.

Dalton Frank Eugen. "Swimming Scientifically Taught," 1912.

Eliot, George. *The Mill on the Floss*, 1860.

James, William. *Talks to Teachers on Psychology*, 1899.

Shakespeare, William. *Julius Caesar*, 1599.

de Tocqueville Alexis. *Democracy in America*, 1835.

United States Arms Control and Disarmament Agency. *Worldwide Effects of Nuclear War: Some Perspectives*, 1996.

CPSIA information can be obtained
at www.ICGtesting.com
Printed in the USA
LVHW050052150619
621320LV00015B/138/P